Use Cases
Patterns and Blueprints

The Software Patterns Series

Series Editor: John M. Vlissides

The Software Patterns Series (SPS) comprises pattern literature of lasting significance to software developers. Software patterns document general solutions to recurring problems in all software-related spheres, from the technology itself, to the organizations that develop and distribute it, to the people who use it. Books in the series distill experience from one or more of these areas into a form that software professionals can apply immediately.

Relevance and *impact* are the tenets of the SPS. Relevance means each book presents patterns that solve real problems. Patterns worthy of the name are intrinsically relevant; they are borne of practitioners' experiences, not theory or speculation. Patterns have impact when they change how people work for the better. A book becomes a part of the series not just because it embraces these tenets, but because it has demonstrated it fulfills them for its audience.

Titles in the series:

Data Access Patterns: Database Interactions in Object-Oriented Applications, Clifton Nock

Design Patterns in C#, Steven John Metsker

Design Patterns Explained, Second Edition: A New Perspective on Object-Oriented Design, Alan Shalloway/
  James R. Trott

Design Patterns Java™ Workbook, Steven John Metsker

The Design Patterns Smalltalk Companion, Sherman Alpert/Kyle Brown/Bobby Woolf

The Manager Pool: Patterns for Radical Leadership, Don Olson/Carol L. Stimmel

.NET Patterns: Architecture, Design, and Process, Christian Thilmany

Pattern Hatching: Design Patterns Applied, John M. Vlissides

Pattern Languages of Program Design, edited by James O. Coplien/Douglas C. Schmidt

Pattern Languages of Program Design 2, edited by John M. Vlissides/James O. Coplien/
  Norman L. Kerth

Pattern Languages of Program Design 3, edited by Robert C. Martin/Dirk Riehle/
  Frank Buschmann

Small Memory Software, James Noble/Charles Weir

Software Configuration Management Patterns: Effective Teamwork, Practical Integration, Stephen
  P. Berczuk/Brad Appleton

Use Cases: Patterns and Blueprints, Gunnar Övergaard/Karin Palmkvist

For more information, check out the series web site at www.awprofessional.com/series/swpatterns

Use Cases
Patterns and Blueprints

Gunnar Övergaard

Karin Palmkvist

✦✦Addison-Wesley

800 E. 96th Street
Indianapolis, IN 46240

The authors and publisher have taken care in the preparation of this book, but make no expressed or implied warranty of any kind and assume no responsibility for errors or omissions. No liability is assumed for incidental or consequential damages in connection with or arising out of the use of the information or programs contained herein.

Publisher: John Wait
Editor in Chief: Don O'Hagan
Acquisitions Editor: John Neidhart
Editorial Assistant: Raquel Kaplan
Marketing Manager: Chris Guzikowski
Marketing Specialist: Beth Wickenhiser
Cover Designer: Alan Clements
Managing Editor: Gina Kanouse
Senior Project Editor: Lori Lyons
Copy Editor: Keith Cline
Indexer: Lisa Stumpf
Compositor: The Scan Group
Manufacturing Buyer: Dan Uhrig

The publisher offers excellent discounts on this book when ordered in quantity for bulk purchases or special sales, which may include electronic versions and/or custom covers and content particular to your business, training goals, marketing focus, and branding interests. For more information, please contact:

U. S. Corporate and Government Sales
(800) 382-3419
corpsales@pearsontechgroup.com

For sales outside the U.S., please contact:

International Sales
international@pearsoned.com

Visit us on the Web: www.awprofessional.com

Library of Congress Cataloging-in-Publication Data:
2004110954

ISBN 0-13-145134-0
Text printed in the United States on recycled paper at RR Donnelley & Sons in Crawfordsville, IN.
First printing, November 2004

CONTENTS

FOREWORD

In 1995, Eric Gamma *et al.* published their groundbreaking book in software: *Design Patterns* (Addison-Wesley), which introduced one of the most important concepts in software industry of today: *design patterns*. At that time, object-orientation design had been used for a couple of decades, and knowledge of what constituted a good object-oriented design had become evident and could be formalized and described in a book. Today, other books have added to the collection of good (and bad) design patterns.

My own work on use cases was first presented in 1986. At the beginning, their purpose was twofold: to be able to discuss system usages with business people, and to explain to designers how classes and components collaborate to provide the required system functionality. Today, use cases have become one of the cornerstones in software development. They are vital not only for capturing requirements, but also when defining the architecture of a system and testing it. In combination with aspect-orientation, they can even be used for programming.

By now, use cases have been around and used long enough to constitute a mature software development discipline, and the time has come to take use-case modeling to the next level. This includes establishing standard solutions to standard modeling problems and a common pattern vocabulary. This book is a tremendously valuable contribution to that end, written by two of the most experienced use-case modelers. No one has treated use-case patterns to any depth as Gunnar and Karin have in this book, which has all the potential to become a standard reference.

This book captures several basic patterns, which everyone will use in their models, as well as more advanced patterns for more specific models and domains. Both a novice use-case modeler and an expert will find patterns and examples of models that are applicable to their models.

Making this book even more useful, Gunnar and Karin have not only defined a large collection of use-case patterns and examples of how specific usages are to be modeled in a use-case model, they have also provided an accurate, complete, and comprehensible description of the constructs used in use-case modeling.

I am very proud to have had Gunnar and Karin on my team since the beginning of use cases. I am impressed by this book.

—Ivar Jacobson, Jaczone AB (member of advisory board),
Ivar Jacobson Consulting Inc (founder)
ivar@jacobson.com

Preface

Collecting Models and Designs

Our aim with this book is to share some of the experience we have gained in working with use cases for more than 30 years altogether. Over the years, we have participated in the development of hundreds of use-case models, both as use-case modelers and as reviewers and mentors. This has of course given us a lot of know-how and understanding of use-case modeling and how a good use-case model should be organized and described.

One obvious finding is that more or less the same modeling problems are encountered over and over again, because many functions reoccur in multiple systems. Studying how these functions were expressed in the use-case models of these systems has led to many interesting reflections. We saw, for example, that some of these models were easier to understand and maintain than others, and we started to analyze why. We also noticed that some models, although they seemed easy to understand, did not quite capture the intended meaning, because they were too simplistic.

During this period, we have had a great many discussions, often involving other participants, why certain ways to use a system should or should not be modeled in a specific way. Over and over again, we have discussed different aspects of various ways to model a specific usage in a use-case model to make it correct, understandable, and maintainable. What were the important parameters, and what did not have a significant impact? As the years went by, we discerned more and more general solutions to common use-case modeling problems in terms of good models of many of these reoccurring functions or ways to use a system. We chose to refer to the use-case model fragments constituting these general solutions as *use-case blueprints*.

Fairly soon, we also realized that some solutions could be generalized even further. Of the specific usages modeled there were some general, underlying design rules that should be fulfilled independently. Applying these design rules, or *use-case patterns*, made the models even more comprehensible, more maintainable, and, in fact, often more correct according to the essential definitions of use-case modeling.

Over the years, a number of people have suggested that we make our gained experience available in writing. This book is the result of an effort to do so, by presenting and describing several of the patterns and blueprints we have identified. The catalog is by no means complete, so your favorite pattern or blueprint might not be included. However, we believe the assembled list is useful for most use-case modelers, novices as well as experienced modelers.

It is unlikely that one could work with use-case models for such a long time without noticing repeatedly occurring good solutions, and it is just as unlikely not to notice reoccurring mistakes in use-case models. We have therefore also included a collection of common use-case modeling mistakes in this book, hoping that they will prove useful to modelers as well as to reviewers of use-case models.

We hope this book may be a starting point for a growing amount of shared knowledge and vocabulary within the use-case modeling community. Hence, if there is some specific pattern or blueprint that you have found useful, but that is not included in this book, or if you have a modeling problem that you think you would like to share with many other people in this field, please let us know. We would also appreciate any feedback you might have on the current catalog and its contents.

It is not possible to write a book about patterns without mentioning Christopher Alexander and his groundbreaking work on identifying and describing patterns when designing constructions (Alexander, Ishikawa, Silverstein 1977). He was working as a building architect, and as such he and his colleagues studied and documented patterns used in what was generally considered high-quality buildings.

Two decades later, *patterns* became a well-established and important concept in software development. In their pioneering book *Design Patterns* (Gamma et al. 1995), E. Gamma et al. presented a collection of patterns for object-oriented design of software systems. Today patterns are used quite extensively in software development, and you can find any number of books on the subject. *Pattern-Oriented Software Architecture, Volume 1: A System of Patterns* (Buschmann et al. 1996) describes different patterns for software architectures. M. Fowler has produced a book titled *Patterns of Enterprise Application Architecture* (Fowler 2002) that discusses patterns used for developing enterprise architectures. *Patterns for Effective Use Cases*, by S. Adolph and P. Bramble (Adolph and Bramble 2002), discusses patterns that appear in the process of developing a use-case model. There are several books about patterns for specific languages and standards, such as *Java: A Catalog of Reusable Design Patterns Illustrated with UML*, by M. Grand (Grand 2002); *EJB Design Patterns: Advanced Patterns, Processes, and Idioms*, by F. Marinescu (Marinescu 2002); and *Core J2EE Patterns: Best Practices and Design Strategies*, by D. Alur et al. (Alur, Malks, and Crupi 2003). Patterns are defined also for specific domains, such as security. The Open Group has produced *Security Design Patterns* (Open Group 2004), in which different patterns for software security are defined. In fact, patterns are not only used for defining good designs; they are used also for defining bad designs that should be avoided, as in *AntiPatterns: Refactoring Software, Architectures, and Projects in Crisis*, by W. Brown et al. (Brown et al. 1998).

This Book

This book provides a collection of use-case patterns and blueprints extracted from a large number of use-case models that we have encountered in our work with use cases for more than three decades altogether. It is not focused on a specific domain or technology, although we do not expect every pattern and blueprint to be relevant to all systems. The book is intended for use-case modelers, such as software engineers, developers, system analysts, and requirements specifiers. Others who might benefit from reading this book include managers, customers, and students, who want to develop, review, approve, and in general learn about use cases and high-quality use-case models.

By using patterns and blueprints presented in this book, a project will reduce the time spent finding out how to express the usages of the system at hand in terms of use cases as well as the time deciding how to structure and describe these use cases. The time spent developing a use-case model will be reduced because the wheel will not have to be invented once again, and the quality of the model will be increased because well-proven solutions are used. In addition, it will be easier to read and understand a use-case model if it is based on well-known techniques and solutions. Furthermore, because each pattern and each blueprint is given a descriptive name, we hope and expect that a common vocabulary among the use-case modelers will be achieved.

Hence, this is not just another book describing use cases. Nor is it a book about capturing requirements in general. The main purpose of the book is to provide a collection of useful use-case patterns and blueprints. However, to be self-contained, the book also includes a thorough description of what a use case is, as well as what other constructs might be used in a use-case model and what they mean. The constructs and the diagrams used in the book are in accordance with the definitions found in UML 2.0 (Object Management Group 2003). We have also described some approaches to documenting the use cases. However, because it is not our intention to provide another textbook about use cases, we have not included certain aspects of use-case modeling in this book. For example, we have not covered several techniques for describing use cases. Furthermore, we have not focused on how to identify use cases in general, how to organize them in packages, or how to structure diagrams presenting a use-case model. In these matters, we refer you to other books covering these subjects. In *Use Case Modeling*, K. Bittner and I. Spence (Bittner and Spence 2002) give a thorough presentation of the use-case concept and how it is to be used. *Applying Use Cases: A Practical Guide*, by G. Schneider and J. Winters (Schneider and Winters 2001), is another book with a good presentation of use cases. *Writing Effective Use Cases*, by A. Cockburn (Cockburn 2000) provides a detailed discussion about how to describe use cases and how to ensure that they are all at the same level of abstraction.

In this book, we have taken a pragmatic approach to use-case modeling. The main goal for a project is, after all, to produce a new version of a system. However, because a use-case model is used as a basis in a number of different situations, such as signing a contract or developing the design of a system, the meaning of the use-case model must be clear. Some of the patterns and blueprints will therefore lead to somewhat more thorough and complex models than what can be seen in some other books and examples. Obviously, we have preferred correctness to simplicity, but even so, all the examples in the book are what we would prefer to find in real-life use-case models.

The patterns in this book bear some resemblance to the patterns described in the *Design Patterns* book (Gamma et al. 1995) in that they describe modeling of common situations. However, the *Design Patterns* book is about object-oriented designs, whereas this book focuses on use cases. Nevertheless, the reuse aspect is the same in both books. Thus, this book illustrates how usages found in many systems are to be modeled by use cases.

By nature, use-case modeling and the resulting use-case models are less formal than design modeling and design models. This difference is apparent also when it comes to use-case patterns compared to design patterns. Although it is necessary to reach a certain level of formality to achieve the goal of a common understanding of a pattern, it is also necessary to make sure that use-case modeling remains a useful tool in any early-stage system development involving non-technically skilled people. The reader already familiar with design patterns might therefore find the patterns in this book loosely defined, while at the same time an experienced use-case modeler might find them formally described.

Organization of the Book

The book consists of five parts.

In Part I, "Introduction," we introduce the reader to the idea of use-case patterns and blueprints. We also provide a small model example to show how these can be applied when developing a use-case model of a system, and what can be gained by using the catalog of patterns and blueprints.

Part II of the book, called "Use Cases," provides a comprehensive description of the use-case construct and all the other constructs specific to a use-case model. This part concludes with a chapter on how use cases are realized in terms of classes, because a basic knowledge of this is essential if the reader is to understand the corresponding part of the pattern and blueprint descriptions. We have included Part II in the book to make it self-contained; both so that the reader will not have to find another book to understand the constructs used in the patterns, but also to provide accurate definitions of the different constructs that we have used.

The main part of the book, the very reason why we wrote it, is Part III, "Use-Case Patterns," and Part IV, "Use-Case Blueprints." Here you will find 27 different use-case patterns and 30 use-case blueprints applicable to use-case models of various kinds of application domains.

We have chosen to group related patterns or blueprints together in chapters to be able to discuss them together and to make it easier for a reader to look for a relevant pattern or blueprint. Each chapter has a name and a short statement describing the intent or modeling problem that the patterns or the blueprints in the chapter address. Then follows an enumeration of the patterns or the blueprints in the chapter together with a description of how each of them is expressed in a use-case model and when it is applicable. The chapter continues with a thorough discussion of the patterns or blueprints and why they form good use-case models, followed by an example, including use-case descriptions of the participating use cases. The chapter ends with a section presenting how the use cases in the pattern or the blueprint can be realized in a logical class model.

We also enumerate a few common use-case modeling mistakes—that is, situations that should not appear in a use-case model—in Part V, "Common Mistakes." Each such common mistake has a name and short description of the incorrect model, followed by an explanation why this is not a good use-case model. The discussion is followed by suggestions on how to improve the model.

On Patterns and Blueprints

Regardless of your previous knowledge and experience with use cases, we expect you to find some of the patterns and blueprints very valuable, whereas others will probably seem less interesting, or even completely irrelevant, to you. However, different readers will most likely find different subsets of them useful depending on their different experiences, problem domains, as well as application and modeling knowledge.

Furthermore, because we do not know all the specific requirements for a specific project or system, you might encounter modeling situations that might be better expressed in a different way from what is proposed in these patterns and blueprints. This is, of course, a general issue with patterns and blueprints and nothing particular to use-case modeling; nonetheless, it is something to keep in mind.

The collection of patterns and blueprints presented in this book is not exhaustive; there exist several others that are useful and valuable. Again, we encourage you to give us feedback on those presented in this book, give us criticism for our choice of examples, tell us about new applications of the patterns and blueprints, and suggest others that you think should be included.

On Examples

The purpose of the use-case descriptions presented in this book is to provide an understanding of the patterns and the blueprints by giving concrete examples of their application. These use-case descriptions are what we would expect to find in an industrial project, although somewhat simplified regarding details and functionality unnecessary for understanding the pattern or blueprint. In addition, the alternative flows are often fewer and shorter than normal, because we do not want the examples to diverge due to exceptions and error handling.

Because we do not think there is one domain that includes all the necessary examples, we have taken the examples from several different domains. However, this does not mean that the pattern or the blueprint exemplified is applicable only to systems belonging to those domains. In fact, we have encountered all patterns and blueprints in this book in several different domains.

Furthermore, we realize that similar systems are different when it comes to details, and we acknowledge that systems of the same type and with the same purpose function differently in different organizations and in different places over the world. We hope the reader will see the examples for what they are—namely, examples of patterns and blueprints—and not parts of exemplary systems.

How to Use This Book

First of all, we firmly suggest that you do not read this book just once. Instead, we hope you will return to it and use it repeatedly as a catalog, for inspiration, as a reference, and as a catalyst in your work.

Our suggestion on how to approach this book depends on your previous experience with use cases.

If You Are an Experienced Use-Case Modeler

Being an experienced use-case modeler, you should start with Part I. This part consists of two chapters that present what we mean by the use-case pattern and the use-case blueprint concepts and give you an example of how they can be applied.

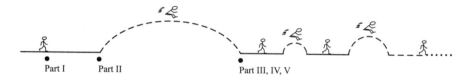

As an experienced use-case modeler, you can probably skip Part II of the book covering the different constructs in a use-case model and go directly to Parts III through V, the catalog of use-case patterns, blueprints, and common mistakes.

We recommend that you read the introduction to each catalog part to get an overview of the structure of the parts before you dive into the different patterns, blueprints, and common mistakes.

We do not expect you to read all details about each pattern, blueprint, and common mistake in the catalog at your first reading. Instead, you should focus on those that you currently find relevant based on your experience and the project at hand. However, we recommend that you read the introduction to all the chapters in Parts III through V to get an overview of what you can find in this book. This means that for each pattern chapter, you should read its *Intent* and *Patterns* sections; for blueprints, the *Problem* and *Blueprints* sections; and for common mistakes, the *Fault* and *Incorrect Model* sections.

If You Are a Novice or Inexperienced with Use Cases in Practice

If you are more or less new to use-case modeling, you need to get an understanding of what use cases are and what they are to be used for before you start studying patterns and blueprints. This implies a different reading path through the book than for the experienced reader.

As an introduction, you might begin by reading Chapter 2, specifically the section that describes a small Internet banking system and the section presenting the complete model of this system. For now, you can skip the rest of the second chapter, which examines the application of some use-case patterns and use-case blueprints to the use-case model of this system.

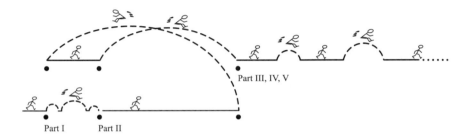

Then you should focus on Part II of the book, describing use-case fundamentals. Chapters 3 through 5 give you all the information you will need on use cases and actors. You should also be familiar with the different kinds of relationships in use-case modeling as well as with how to describe use cases; therefore, you should read Chapters 6 through 14. However, you do not need to study these in detail at this moment. If the relationships are used in the patterns or the blueprints you are about to apply, you can always return to those chapters for reference.

When you understand what use-case modeling is, you can go to Parts III through V of this book to understand the different use-case patterns, blueprints, and common mistakes. Before doing so, however, return to Part I and read Chapter 1 and the whole of Chapter 2 to get an understanding of what use-case patterns and blueprints are and how different patterns and blueprints can be applied when developing a use-case model.

If You Are Not a Designer

In general, if you are not a designer, a software architect, or otherwise interested in the interior structuring of a system, you can skip Chapter 15 in Part II as well as the *Analysis Model* sections in each chapter in Parts III through IV.

Future Use of This Book

After reading through the book, return to it and use it as a dictionary and knowledge base in your future tasks of developing use-case models— both to look up different constructs used in use-case modeling that you feel uncertain about and to look up different patterns and blueprints that might be applied in your model.

History of Use Cases

The *use-case* (Swedish: användningsfall [anvɜndniñs'fal]) construct was invented by Ivar Jacobson, as a result of a need to describe complete sequences of actions in complex telecommunication systems, and not only the components that made up the systems. The term was coined in 1986, but the construct had been presented before (for example, in his Ph.D. thesis (Jacobson 1985), for which he studied concepts for modeling large real-time systems). In his thesis, Ivar Jacobson defined a construct called *course*, which is very similar to the *use-case instance* construct of today. In 1987, the construct received wider attention when he presented a paper about the use-case construct at the OOPSLA '87 conference (Jacobson 1987). The definition of a use case presented in that paper is basically the same as today's definition of the construct.

In 1987, Ivar Jacobson founded a company developing the Objectory software development process. (One of the authors of this book joined him that year and the other joined the company in 1989.) The use-case construct was described in greater detail in Objectory, where it was also slightly modified and enhanced. For example, classes modeling *domain objects* were no longer included in the use-case model. The *extend* relationship existed already, but it was called *builtOn* in those days.

In the next couple of years, the *generalization* relationship was introduced (it was first called *inheritance* and then renamed *uses* because it captured more than traditional inheritance), and the three different kinds of analysis classes and their different kinds of relationships were also defined. In 1992, the *Object-Oriented Software Engineering: A Use-Case Driven Approach* book was published (Jacobson et al. 1993), in which the use-case-driven approach was presented for a wider audience. Another book, *The Object Advantage* (Jacobson, Ericsson, and Jacobson 1994), showed how use cases could be used also for modeling businesses.

After Rational's acquisition of Ivar Jacobson's company, the Objectory process first turned into ROP (*Rational Objectory Process*) and then into RUP (*Rational Unified Process*) (Kroll and Kruchten 2003; Rational Software Corporation 2003). During this period, the development of the *Unified Modeling Language* (UML) was initiated. It implied a very small change of the definition of use cases. The relationship between use cases formerly called *uses* was split into two relationships: *generalization* and *include*. All the other constructs used in use-case modeling, however, remained the same (Object Management Group 1997; Rumbaugh, Jacobson, and Booch 1999). In the latest version of UML, called UML 2.0, the use-case construct is still the same (Object Management Group 2003).

Hence, as Ivar Jacobson points out, most of the definitions of the use case constructs were established by 1992 (Jacobson 2003). The fact that use case is a major construct in UML and a cornerstone in most software development projects, being used by thousands of modelers in hundreds of modeling efforts, makes use-case modeling a reliable technique for modeling how a system is to be used.

Acknowledgments

Many have inspired and encouraged us in the writing of this book. First, we must thank Ivar Jacobson for introducing us to use cases back in the 1980s. We have had many inspiring and stimulating discussions with him about why use cases should or should not be defined, modeled, and described in particular ways. Without his groundbreaking work, modern software development would not be where it is today.

We particularly want to thank Steve Berczuk, Katarina Jönsson, Neil Harrison, and Bengt Övergaard for their many valuable comments and suggestions on how to improve the book and its contents.

We also want to thank Christian Averskog, Karl Dickson, Erik Lindahl, and Dan Ståhlberg for their constructive reviews on earlier drafts of the book, as well as Christina Skaskiw for triggering us to actually write this book.

We are grateful to Gerd Övergaard for her invaluable effort helping us make the text more effective and correct, and to Åke Westin for preparing all nonformal artwork in the book. Without the two, the book would have been much more cumbersome and uninteresting to read.

We are also thankful to the team at Addison-Wesley for all their help and patience, especially John Neidhart, Lori Lyons, and Keith Cline.

Needless to say, we are deeply indebted to all who have provided feedback and shared their experiences in use-case modeling over the years.

Finally, without the patience and support of our families, Maria and Vidar, and Johan, Viktor, and Hanna, there would have been no book about use-case patterns and blueprints.

Gunnar Övergaard and Karin Palmkvist
Stockholm, Sweden
July 2004

Part I

Introduction

This part of the book introduces the reader to the use-case pattern and the use-case blueprint concepts. It discusses the need to gain a knowledge base of what constitutes a good use-case model and how well-proven use-case patterns and blueprints can be useful for individual use-case modelers to speed up the process of acquiring such a knowledge base.

The first chapter of this part also provides an overview of Parts III through V of this book.

Part I ends by guiding the reader through a small use-case modeling example in Chapter 2. This chapter shows how you can use patterns and blueprints when developing a use-case model.

Chapter 1

Use-Case Patterns and Blueprints

Reusing Experience

When developing or building a construction of some sort, such as a house or a machine, we all rely on previous experience from similar work. In this way, we will be more productive and will therefore be able to complete a better construction in less time than an inexperienced person. We will know what solutions work, and can thus avoid pitfalls, and we will know or have qualified guesses about possible ways to tackle arising problems. In some cases, we know how a part, a service, or an assembly was successfully built in another construction, and we can then reuse that solution in the current construction. In other cases, it is not a particular solution that can be reused; instead, it is the underlying design that is relevant when we decide how to solve the current problem. In other words, we reuse both existing solutions as well as techniques that have proved to be well suited and efficient in other contexts.

Use-case modeling does not differ from other kinds of developmental work in the sense that an experienced modeler will reuse solutions that he or she has found useful and efficient. The more experience the modeler has, the more frequently and efficiently will he or she reuse earlier solutions.

The experienced use-case modeler does not focus on a single use case when expressing what the system under development is meant to do. Instead, the modeler knows that a specific problem as a whole should be expressed with a particular set of use cases. The solution to the problem may include several use cases as well as relationships between them. Hence, the modeler will reuse fragments of previous, successful models when producing a new use-case model.

The reused model fragments are seldom identical copies of parts produced in the earlier models. After gathering more and more experience, the fragments boil down to *blueprints* capturing the essence of how a particular service offered by a system should be modeled in general, or how a common use-case modeling problem should be solved. Hence, a blueprint may be a use-case model of security in terms of access control of information in the system, or a use-case model capturing the use of a legacy system.

Blueprints can be more or less directly copied into a use-case model of a system including the service or modeling situation captured by the blueprint. Usually it will be necessary to tune some of the details in the blueprint to the specific needs at hand, such as choosing names that are natural to the stakeholders of the current project, and stating particular sequences of actions that are to be performed in the use-case descriptions.

Similarly, the successful techniques and designs that are used over and over again in the use-case models become formalized as *patterns* expressing good use-case model designs. Such a pattern does not describe a particular usage of the system. Instead, it captures a technique for making the model maintainable, reusable, and understandable. To apply a pattern in a use-case model means structuring a part of the model or describing an individual use case in a specific way. Hence, use-case patterns capture good practice in use-case modeling. For example, a subsequence that must be the same in several use cases should be modeled as a separate use case with explicit relationships to the original use cases, and services that are optional in the system should be modeled separately from the mandatory ones.

As opposed to blueprints, patterns are not just copied into a use-case model. Instead, they are used as templates for how the model should be structured, or, for description patterns, how use-case descriptions should be organized.

What then constitutes a reusable use-case blueprint or pattern? First of all, it describes an understanding of a problem, either a particular usage of a system or an underlying design, and gives a solution that is proven sound and reliable. Second, it includes information on situations when the blueprint or pattern is applicable, and third, it describes what the consequences will be when it is applied. To summarize:

- A *use-case pattern* is a generally proven design in a use-case model together with a description of the context in which it is to be used and what consequences its application will have on the model.

- A *use-case blueprint* is a well-established fragment of a use-case model, modeling a re-occurring usage of systems.

Experienced use-case modelers will not only know how to develop a good use-case model, they will also discover when certain use cases are missing, simply because they know that such use cases will most likely appear in this kind of system. In most systems, for example, the users must be identified before they can use the system—that is, they must log in to the system. This implies that there must be use cases not only for logging in, but also for logging out and for registering and deregistering users. Furthermore, if all the users are not supposed to have the same access rights to everything in the system, there must be use cases for registering and checking their access rights as well. All together, this means that experienced modelers do not look for single use cases; they look for groups of use cases. Therefore, the patterns and the blueprints include not only the significant use cases for the modeling problem, but also the supporting use cases needed to be able to perform the significant use cases. This means that the collection of patterns and blueprints in this book offers a lot of help when producing use-case models by providing comprehensive solutions to modeling problems.

However, other people's experiences as well as our own do not only tell us how things should be done, they also make it clear how things should *not* be done. Experienced use-case modelers can often quickly identify imperfections in use-case models they review. This is not because they have modeled the same system before. Just by studying the structure of the model, they detect common mistakes, such as an abnormally large number of relationships in the model, or functional decomposition of use cases. We have therefore complemented the patterns and the blueprints in this book with a collection of *common mistakes* that we have found over and over again. Use this collection as an indicator that something *may* be flawed in the model, but not as a sharp divider between right and wrong. There *might* be a good reason why a specific model triggers such an indicator and still is acceptable. However, such situations are rare!

Contents of the Catalog

For each pattern, blueprint, and common mistake presented in this book, we provide a thorough description. However, because of their different forms and nature, we have organized them in three different groups and structured their descriptions slightly differently. Within each group, we have organized related patterns or blueprints in chapters, each addressing one specific issue. Although we have described the different solutions to modeling problems as separate blueprints and the different designs of models as different patterns, most real modeling situations are not so precise and clear-cut that only one blueprint or one pattern can be deemed fitting or applicable. On the contrary, in most situations, a combination of several blueprints and patterns will have to be used. In some of the examples in the book, you will find that we have used another pattern or blueprint as well, but we have tried to focus each example on the topic of the chapter. We do, however, for each example suggest other patterns or blueprints that also may be applicable to the specific example at hand.

All the patterns, blueprints, and common mistakes are enumerated here to give an overview of the catalog found in Parts III through V of this book. For each chapter, we give the title and a description of the intent (for patterns), the modeling problem (for blueprints), or the fault (for common mistakes). For pattern chapters and blueprint chapters, the names of the individual patterns or the blueprints in that chapter are also listed.

Use-Case Patterns

Chapter 16, Business Rules: Extract information originating from policies, rules, and regulations of the business from the description of the flow and describe this information as a collection of business rules referenced from the use-case descriptions.

- Business Rules: Static Definition
- Business Rules: Dynamic Modification

Chapter 17, Commonality: Extract a subsequence of actions that appear in multiple places in use-case flows and express it separately.

- Commonality: Reuse
- Commonality: Addition
- Commonality: Specialization
- Commonality: Internal Reuse

Chapter 18, Component Hierarchy: Provide a mapping from top-level use cases describing the system behavior as a whole down to leaf elements in a containment hierarchy realizing the behavior.

- Component Hierarchy: Black-Box with Use Cases
- Component Hierarchy: Black-Box with Operations
- Component Hierarchy: White-Box

Chapter 19, Concrete Extension or Inclusion: Model the same flow both as part of one use case and as a separate, complete use case of its own.

- Concrete Extension or Inclusion: Extension
- Concrete Extension or Inclusion: Inclusion

Chapter 20, CRUD: Merge short, simple use cases, such as Creating, Reading, Updating, and Deleting pieces of information, into a single use case forming a conceptual unit.

- CRUD: Complete
- CRUD: Partial

Chapter 21, Large Use Case: Structure a use case comprising a large number of actions. There are two "dimensions" along which a use case may be large: It may either be "long"—that is, consist of a very long sequence of actions—or it may be "fat"—that is, include many different flows.

- Large Use Case: Long Sequence
- Large Use Case: Multiple Paths

Chapter 22, Layered System: Structure the use-case model so that each use case is defined within one layer and use relationships between the use cases in different layers to allow use-case instances to span multiple layers.

- Layered System: Reuse
- Layered System: Addition
- Layered System: Specialization
- Layered System: Embedded

Chapter 23, Multiple Actors: Capture commonalities between actors while keeping separate roles apart.

- Multiple Actors: Distinct Roles
- Multiple Actors: Common Role

Chapter 24, Optional Service: Separate mandatory parts of the use cases from optional parts that can be ordered and delivered separately.

- Optional Service: Addition
- Optional Service: Specialization
- Optional Service: Independent

Chapter 25, Orthogonal Views: Provide different views of the flows of a system that are perceived differently by different stakeholders.

- Orthogonal Views: Specialization
- Orthogonal Views: Description

Chapter 26, Use-Case Sequence: Express the temporal order between a collection of use cases that must only be invoked in a specific order, even though the use cases are functionally unrelated to each other.

- Use-Case Sequence

Use-Case Blueprints

Chapter 27, Access Control: The system is required to include some kind of access security. Access to the information in the system and to the services of the system is stated by the specific access rights given to the individual user.

- Access Control: Embedded Check
- Access Control: Dynamic Security Rules
- Access Control: Explicit Check
- Access Control: Internal Assignment
- Access Control: Implicit Details

Chapter 28, Future Task: A task is registered in the system at one point of time, although the actual performance of the task is to take place at some later time.

- Future Task: Simple
- Future Task: Specialization
- Future Task: Extraction
- Future Task: Performer Notification

Chapter 29, Item Look-Up: The system is to make it possible for the users to search for items in the system. This look-up procedure can be autonomous, but it can also be used in other use cases.

- Item Look-Up: Standalone
- Item Look-Up: Result Usage
- Item Look-Up: Open Decision

Chapter 30, Legacy System: The system is to include or make use of an already existing system.

- Legacy System: Embedded
- Legacy System: Separate

Chapter 31, Login and Logout: The users must register or identify themselves before using services offered by the system.

- Login and Logout: Standalone
- Login and Logout: Action Addition
- Login and Logout: Reuse
- Login and Logout: Specialization
- Login and Logout: Separate

Chapter 32, Message Transfer: A user uses the system to send a message to another user.

- Message Transfer: Deferred Delivery
- Message Transfer: Immediate Delivery
- Message Transfer: Automatic

Chapter 33, Passive External Medium: The system is to monitor or control an external medium that in itself is passive (for example, the surrounding air or a fluid).

- Passive External Medium

Chapter 34, Report Generation: The system is to contain a collection of templates for generating different kinds of reports that present information in accordance with the definition given in the templates. The templates also define how a report is to be formatted and similar matters.

- Report Generation: Simple
- Report Generation: Specialization
- Report Generation: Dynamic Templates

Chapter 35, Stream Input: An actor provides a stream of input to the system, and the handling of this input is to be described by use cases. The solution to this problem depends on whether the stream consists of discrete values or of continuous values.

- Stream Input: Discrete
- Stream Input: Analog

Chapter 36, Translator: The system is to receive an input stream and produce an output stream based on some translation rules.

- Translator: Static Definition
- Translator: Dynamic Rules

Common Mistakes

Chapter 37, Mistake: Alternative Flow as Extension: Modeling an alternative flow of a use case as an extension of that use case.

Chapter 38, Mistake: Business Use Case: Modeling a business process as a system use case.

Chapter 39, Mistake: Communicating Use Cases: Modeling two use cases with an association between them, implying that the use cases communicate with each other.

Chapter 40, Mistake: Functional Decomposition: One large use case with include relationships to a set of inclusion use cases, each modeling a subfunction of the large use case.

Chapter 41, Mistake: Micro Use Cases: Modeling single operations performed by the users as separate use cases, resulting in a use-case model consisting of a large number of very small use cases.

Chapter 42, Mistake: Mix of Abstraction Levels: A use-case model containing use cases defined at different levels of abstraction.

Chapter 43, Mistake: Multiple Business Values: Incorporating too much in a single use case by capturing several goals or business values in one use case.

Chapter 44, Mistake: Security Levels with Actors: Capturing the security levels restricting who may use the different services of the system only by defining actors corresponding to the security levels.

CHAPTER 2

USING PATTERNS AND BLUEPRINTS IN USE-CASE MODEL DEVELOPMENT

This chapter examines the development of a use-case model for a small Internet bank. The main purpose is to illustrate how the patterns and blueprints in this book can be used for identification of use cases, for structuring the use-case model, and for describing use cases. This chapter explains how useful common solutions actually are, even in very simple use-case models, and how much is to be gained by having knowledge about them. Our intention is not to give a complete understanding of the applied patterns and blueprints, and certainly not to describe the ideal Internet bank, but to provide an appetizer and introduction to the subject. Do not worry if you do not quite get the idea of some particular patterns or blueprints applied in this chapter; they are all to be found thoroughly described in Parts III and IV of this book.

For those not familiar with the use-case concept, the chapter serves as an introduction to use-case modeling by providing an example of a use-case model for a small application. Such a reader should focus on the description of the application found in the next section and on the final model presented in the section, *The Complete Model*, and can skip, or just skim through, the sections in between where the development of the model is presented. However, make sure to return to these sections after reading about use cases in the second part, and read them as an introduction before moving on to the third part of the book!

First, we describe the Internet bank application, its purpose, and how it is to be used. Then follows a description of how the use cases are identified immediately in the first discussion between the system analyst and the system owner. Based on these use cases, we describe how the model evolves when different patterns and blueprints are applied. Finally, we present the complete use-case model.

The Internet Bank System

One day, an existing bank decides to make it possible for their customers to interact with the bank using the Internet. In this first version of the Internet bank, only a few services will be available. The customers will be able to

- View their accounts.

- Transfer money between their own accounts.

- Pay bills using the Internet bank.

However, the bank states that a number of requirements must be met by the Internet bank. First of all, security is important. Before the customers can use the services of the bank over the Internet, they must identify themselves using the identity and the password the bank has provided them. Furthermore, of course, a customer must not be able to access a random account. At first the bank intends to grant customers access only to their own accounts, but the bank soon realizes that this would cause problems— for example, when parents want to access their children's accounts, or when two spouses have granted each other the right to access each other's accounts. Therefore, the requirement is changed to state that customers will be able to access only such accounts to which the account owner has explicitly granted them access rights. Note that no restrictions apply to depositing money on an account, so the access rights involve only viewing the contents of the account and withdrawing money from the account.

Furthermore, the bank wants to make it possible for the customers to register in advance a bill that is to be paid later, upon which date the money will be withdrawn. Such transactions will be performed after office hours, which means that the earliest date a bill can be paid is the day after the day it was registered. For similar reasons, the transfer of money between accounts must also be registered one day before the transfer will take place.

Until now, customers have received account statements every second month. Several customers have expressed a wish to be able to check more often than that as to what transactions have taken place on their accounts. Therefore, the Internet bank will offer a service that enables customers to view the transactions of an account during the past two months.

If the Internet bank is a success, the bank intends to expand its customer services. However, it is important that the look and feel of the first version not be modified in the next few versions unless absolutely necessary, for such a change is expected to be received negatively by the customers after they have learned how to use the first version. The use of some kind of service concept, grouping functions together, seems to be vital in the user interface. In such a way, new functions can be added without affecting the existing functions of the Internet bank. Furthermore, if successful, the Internet bank's collection of functions will be large. It is therefore vital that it be given a clear structure even in the first, simple version.

The bank already has systems for managing accounts and for paying bills, and it is required that these systems be used by the Internet bank—their functionality must not be duplicated in multiple systems. However, because of security reasons, the customers must not be given direct access to these bank systems. Moreover, the customers should perceive a uniform look and feel when they use the services of the Internet bank, and this would not be the case if they had immediate access to the account and billing systems. Hence, the Internet bank must implement some functionality to enable the customers to access the services of the existing systems.

The First Draft of the Model

The system owner of the bank and the system analyst responsible for capturing the functional requirements of the Internet bank in a use-case model meet, and together they soon identify a collection of use cases based on the preceding system description (see Figure 2.1).

Customer Login. The system must handle the situation when the customers identify themselves by providing their identity and secret password, which is captured in this use case.

Change Service. The system owner and the system analyst agree that the service concept presented by the bank is to be implemented by Web pages. Each service will be represented by one Web page from where the functions of that service can be initiated, and this use case is intended to handle the situation when the customer wants to change the service currently used.

Present Accounts. This use case will list the accounts that the customer can access.

Pay Bills. This use case handles payment of bills.

Present Account Transactions. This use case takes an account number as input and lists the transactions that have taken place during the past two months.

Transfer Money. This use case transfers money from one account to another.

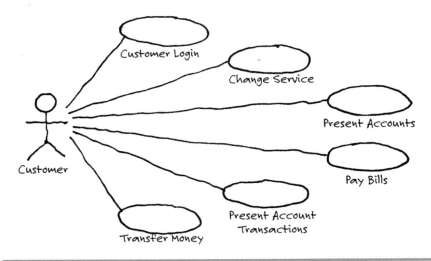

Figure 2.1   The first draft of the Internet bank system use-case model.

Applying Patterns and Blueprints

Login and Logout

When looking at the Customer Login use case, the system analyst realizes that one of the *Login and Logout* blueprints can be applied. These contain different ways to model that users must register themselves to the system before any of the services of the system can be used, which is of course the reason why the Customer Login use case was identified. After evaluating the different blueprints, it is decided that the login procedure will be modeled with one standalone use case and not as an included or an extending use case. (See Chapter 31, "Login and Logout," for details.) Furthermore, both the system owner and the system analyst realize that they have not yet captured logging out from the system. Because security is important, it is vital that the customers be required to log out when leaving the system. The login and the logout procedures are quite straight-forward, so the system owner and the system analyst decide to model the two with one use case, called Customer Login/Logout.

Working with this blueprint, they also realize that yet another use case is missing: the use case that registers the customer in the system and pro-vides the secret password. Hence, the Register Customer use case is added to the model, as is the new Operator actor, performing the new use case (see Figure 2.2).

Figure 2.2   The *Login and Logout: Standalone* blueprint modifies one use
case and adds another use case and an actor to the model.

Use-Case Sequence

The system owner and the system analyst discuss how to express that some of the use cases can be used only after the performance of some other use cases. For example, requesting a list of transactions for an account will be done by the customer clicking a link on the Web page to the account. This will be possible only if the currently active Web page presents the account, such as the page used by the Present Accounts use case. The system owner and the system analyst discuss whether to use an extend relationship between the use cases to model the hierarchy of the services or whether some other kind of relationship should be introduced into the model.

According to the *Use-Case Sequence* pattern, the answer is that neither option is suitable. None of the identified use cases models a sequence of actions that is an addition to another use case. All the use cases in the model are complete in themselves. Instead, the temporal order between different use cases should be stated using preconditions. A precondition of a use case describes the prevalent state of the system when the use case is initiated. The constraint on when the account transaction list can be requested is therefore stated as a precondition of the Present Account Transactions use case:

> The Web page currently presented to the Customer must display the account number of the account that is to be examined.

The system owner and the system analyst describe similar preconditions for all the other use cases in the model that cannot be initiated unless certain conditions are met. These preconditions are not shown in any of the diagrams, but in the descriptions of the use cases.

Legacy System

As described previously in the section *The Internet Bank System*, the bank has existing systems for managing accounts and paying bills, and these systems are to be used by the Internet bank. The system analyst asks the system owner whether the Internet bank is to be viewed as part of the bank's overall system or whether it is a separate system. The system owner replies that the bank views all the application systems as separate systems.

Hence, because the Internet bank is to interact with already existing systems, a *Legacy System* blueprint is applicable to some of the use cases. Because these systems are not to be integrated into the

Internet bank system, the owner and the system analyst decide to select the blueprint where the legacy system is modeled as an actor. The blueprint is first applied to those use cases that use information about accounts, namely Present Accounts, Pay Bills, Present Account Transactions, and Transfer Money. A new actor is identified, called Account System, and associations are defined between the use cases and this actor (see Figure 2.3). Then the blueprint is applied to the Pay Bills use case, which becomes associated with the Billing System.

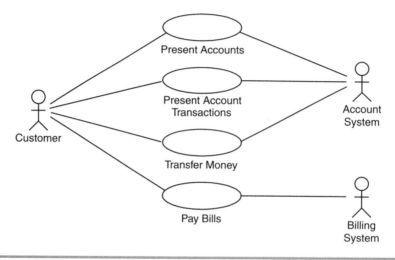

Figure 2.3   A *Legacy System* blueprint is applied twice, which adds two actors and a collection of associations to the model.

Multiple Actors

As soon as more than one actor is associated with a certain use case, there is reason to apply a *Multiple Actors* pattern. The issue is to establish whether the actors play the same or different roles toward the use case in question.

The system analyst realizes that several of the use cases in the Internet bank system involve more than one actor. The initiating actors, among them the Customer, are clearly different from all other actors associated with the use cases. This makes the first *Multiple Actors* pattern applicable, including as it does different actor roles. There is, however, one use case in the model that is associated with three actors, which calls for a closer look.

The `Pay Bills` use case, which is initiated by the `Customer`, is also associated with the `Account System` actor and the `Billing System` actor. Whether
or not, according to the pattern, the latter two actors play the same role
toward the use case is a question of vital importance. Because these two
actors were the subjects of a rather thorough investigation earlier, the system analyst already knows that they play different roles. A double-check
with the system owner establishes that the `Pay Bills` use case interacts
with the `Account System` to retrieve information about the transaction
account, such as the balance, whereas it sends information about the pay-
ments to the `Billing System`. Clearly, these are two different roles, so the
same *Multiple Actors* pattern as the one discussed previously is applicable. The model remains unchanged (see Figure 2.4).

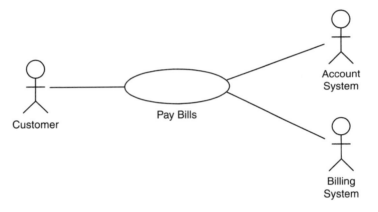

Figure 2.4   The *Multiple Actors* pattern is applied multiple times. Because
all actors play different roles for all use cases, the model need not
be modified.

Future Task

According to the requirements in the section *The Internet Bank System*,
the payment of the bills and the transfer of the money are not to be performed immediately when the `Pay Bills` use case and the `Transfer
Money` use case are carried out. Instead, these use cases just register that
a bill is to be paid and that an amount is to be transferred between two
accounts, respectively, whereas the actual performance of the transaction is to take place after office hours. The transaction performance
implies sending the necessary information to another system, which will
effectuate the transaction.

The system analyst identifies one of the Future Task blueprints as applicable in this situation, choosing the variant that has a generalization to an abstract use case, because both executing a money transfer and executing a payment are of the same kind, namely executing orders. Applying the pattern to the Pay Bills and to the Transfer Money use cases results in three new use cases: Execute Order to Pay Bills, which will inform the payment system that a bill is to be paid; Execute Order to Transfer Money, which will inform the account system that a transfer between accounts is to be performed; and an abstract use case called Execute Order (see Figure 2.5). The abstract use case models how the selection of the order is done, and is inherited by both of the execution use cases. This gives a flexible structure, making it easy to add more kinds of tasks in future versions of the Internet bank system, which is appreciated by the system owner.

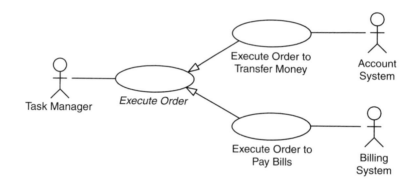

Figure 2.5   A *Future Task* blueprint applied twice adds three new use cases and one new actor to the model.

After introducing the new use cases, the system analyst realizes that the names of the Pay Bills and the Transfer Money use cases are no longer appropriate. Therefore, the names are changed to Register Order to Pay Bills and Register Order to Transfer Money, respectively (see Figure 2.6).

The system owner suggests that another abstract use case be introduced in the model, called Register Order, to be specialized by the two use cases Register Order to Pay Bills and Register Order to Transfer Money. The system analyst recognizes a *Commonality* pattern, but suggests that this decision be deferred until the descriptions of the two use cases have been produced; the fact that their names are similar need not indicate that any commonalities actually exist between them.

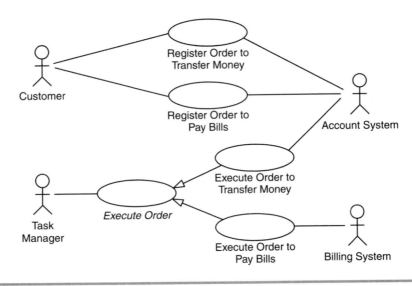

Figure 2.6   The final result of the *Future Task* blueprint application is a model
of five use cases replacing the original two.

CRUD

When looking into the details of the use case `Register Order to Pay Bills`,
the system owner realizes it must cover more than just the registration of
a pay bills order. The customer must of course also be able to modify and
delete registered payment orders. The system analyst then wants to apply
a *CRUD* pattern to the use case, modeling situations when an actor needs to
be able to Create, Read, Update, and Delete information. He suggests
modeling all these operations on payment orders with one use case.

The system owner does not quite approve, however, because this means
hiding the registration of an order to pay bills behind a use-case name such
as `CRUD Order to Pay Bills`. The registration process is far too important
for merging it with another use case. Instead, they agree on using the *CRUD*
pattern in which the CRUD use case is split into two use cases: one use case
for creating a registration order, and one for the modification (including
viewing and deletion) of a registration order.

As a result, the `Register Order to Pay Bills` is left unchanged in the
model and a new use case is introduced, called `Modify Order to Pay Bills`
(see Figure 2.7).

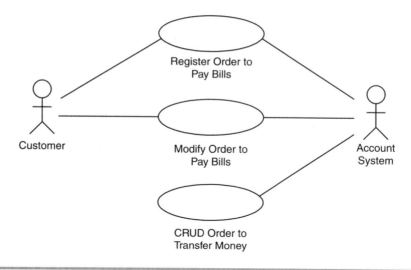

Figure 2.7   Application of two *CRUD* patterns leads to the renaming of one use case and the addition of a new one.

However, the system owner agrees that registering an order to transfer money, viewing it, and deleting it could be modeled as one use case, so the corresponding additional flows are added to the Register Order to Transfer Money use case and it is renamed CRUD Order to Transfer Money.

Access Control

Security is vital to the bank. First of all, the communication link between the Internet bank and the customer must be secure. However, the communication link is handled in the design of the system, and it will not affect the use-case model. Therefore, the system owner and the system analyst leave that issue aside. There is another security aspect, however, that will affect the use-case model: making sure the customers can access only those accounts that they are authorized to access.

The Access Control blueprints suggest two main alternatives. The checking of the access rights can be expressed either explicitly in the use-case model or only in the use-case descriptions. The system owner prefers to have the checking of the access rights expressed explicitly in the model, because security is so important. Therefore, another new use case is introduced into the model: the abstract use case Check Access Rights (see Figure 2.8). Include relationships are defined from the use cases interacting with the Account System, namely Present Accounts, Register Order to Pay Bills, Modify Order to Pay Bills, Present Account Transactions, and Register Order to Transfer Money.

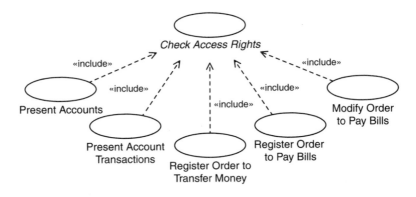

Figure 2.8   Checking access rights explicitly leads to the *Access Control* blue-print, where an abstract use case and a set of include relationships are included.

The blueprint also introduces a use case for adding and removing the right for a customer to access specific accounts, to be initiated by the Operator actor (see Figure 2.9).

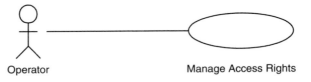

Figure 2.9   The *Access Control* blueprint provides a use case enabling the Operator actor to handle access rights in the system.

Business Rules

The system owner tells the system analyst that the bank has several rules for their software system that must be fulfilled. These rules concern not only a common platform, a common database handler, and so forth, but also rules from multiple sources within the business, such as policy decisions and regulations. The bank is currently discussing whether such rules can be implemented in a central database; so far, however, no such system has been developed, so the rules must be implemented in each software system. However, the rules, which so far are to be found in a set of documents, are imperative. Because this project is a new kind of application, an Internet application, and the bank does not have all the rules in place, the owner and the system analyst must investigate and modify their decisions when new rules are defined.

The system analyst looks up the description of the `Business Rule` patterns and reads that the rules are to be documented separately, to be referenced from the use-case descriptions. For example, the `Register Order to Pay Bills` will have to reference the following rules:

BR1. The registration date of an order must be earlier than its transaction date.

BR2. If an order does not have a transaction date when it is registered, the date of the following day is used.

BR3. An order must have a receiving account number.

BR4. An order must state an amount.

BR5. A transaction text is not mandatory.

The rules will not be visible in the diagrams showing the use-case model. Instead, references to them will appear in the textual descriptions of the use cases.

The following is part of the description of the flow of the `Register Order to Pay Bills` use case:

[...]

A Web page is presented to the Customer where the account number and the balance of the transaction account are shown. This Web page is used for entering the amount of money to be paid, the receiving account, the date the bill is to be paid, and a transaction message.

The Customer enters the requested information. The use case checks the information according to the rules BR1 through BR5. If the rules are fulfilled, the order is stored by the use case together with the account number of the transaction account of the Customer.

[...]

The Complete Model

The diagrams in Figure 2.10, Figure 2.11, and Figure 2.12 together present a use-case model that covers the requirements stated in the section *The Internet Bank System*. As you can see, Customers must log in to the system before using its services as well as log out when they are done. There is a collection of use cases that the Customers can choose between after logging in, such as reading the balances of a set of accounts, checking what transactions have been performed on an account, and registering orders to pay bills as well as to transfer money.

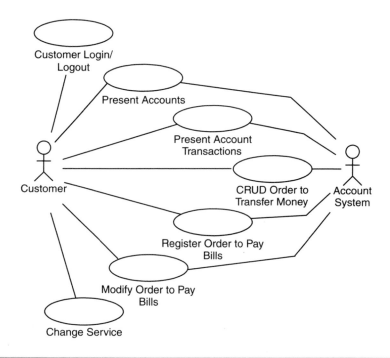

Figure 2.10   Main diagram of the use-case model of the Internet bank system, showing the services directly used by the Customer.

The execution of the orders to pay bills and to transfer money is performed as batch jobs transferring the information to other systems where the actual payment and transfer will take place, as shown in Figure 2.11.

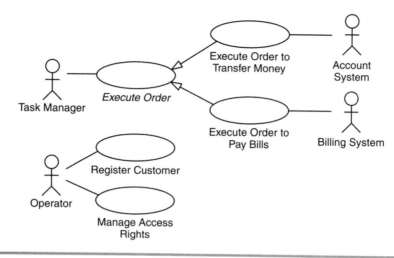

Figure 2.11   This use-case diagram shows what is performed behind the scene from the Customer perspective: background order executions and system management.

Two supporting use cases are also initiated by an Operator. One allows or disallows a customer to use the system, and the other registers what accounts a customer can access.

Finally, the use-case diagram in Figure 2.12 shows the use cases that include checking the access rights of the initiating actor.

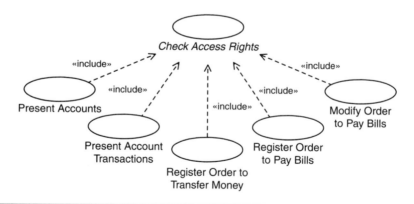

Figure 2.12   The abstract use case Check Access Rights is included in all use cases where security is to be checked.

Hence, the use-case model for the Internet bank system includes the following use cases:

Change Service. The Customer selects a new service and the use case presents the contents of the selected service.

Check Access Rights. This abstract use case checks the right for a Customer to access accounts.

Customer Login/Logout. The Customer logs in to or logs out from the system.

Execute Order to Pay Bills. Registered payment orders are transferred to the Billing System to be executed.

Execute Order to Transfer Money. Registered orders for transferring money between accounts are executed by the Account System.

Manage Access Rights. The Operator registers or removes a customer's right to view an account and to withdraw money from an account.

Modify Order to Pay Bills. The Customer views, modifies, or deletes a payment order.

Perform Task. This abstract use case models selection of a task to be performed and a general description of task performance.

Present Account Transactions. The transactions of an account are presented to a Customer.

Present Accounts. A list of the accounts of a customer is presented to the Customer.

Register Customer. The Operator of the Internet bank registers or removes a customer.

Register Order to Pay Bills. The Customer registers a collection of payment orders.

Register Order to Transfer Money. The Customer registers an order to transfer money between accounts.

Concluding Remarks

In the development of this model, eight different patterns and blueprints were applied, some of them multiple times. None of these were defined specifically for Internet applications or for bank applications. They can all be used in a great number of applications in different kinds of domains. The usage of patterns and blueprints not only increases the quality of the model, but also shortens the time to develop the model, because many necessary use cases will be identified at once, and examples of descriptions as well as a proposal for a platform-independent class model (an analysis model) are provided.

As you become more familiar with the use-case patterns and blueprints, you will see that some other ones can also be used in this application. Also, and more importantly, you will see that you can use them in your own applications.

Part II

Use Cases

This part of the book thoroughly describes the use-case construct as well as other, related constructs needed in a use-case model.

The first few chapters describe use cases and actors, and give the background necessary to understand the descriptions of use-case patterns, blueprints, and common mistakes in Parts III through V of this book. Most of the patterns and blueprints also make use of relationships between use cases and actors. Therefore, this part also includes a collection of chapters describing the different kinds of relationships used in use-case modeling. These chapters can be read more superficially if the only goal is to achieve enough basic knowledge to be able to get a grasp of the patterns and blueprints, but should be studied in more detail by use-case modelers *in spe*.

The part also includes two chapters on how to describe use cases and use-case models. It is not necessary to read these chapters to understand the rest of the book, but they will prove useful to anyone writing or reviewing use-case descriptions.

Part II ends with an introduction to analysis classes used in platform-independent realizations of use cases. This chapter gives basic information on the subject, sufficient to understand the last section of each pattern and blueprint chapter.

CHAPTER 3

USE-CASE MODELING: AN INTRODUCTION

Many different groups of people need to understand the functionality of a system. First, obviously, are the owners of the system. They need to understand the functionality of the system under development, to make sure that the developed system will be the system they want and need. Just as important are the developers of the system, who need to know what system they are to produce. Another important group is the testers, who must verify that what the system offers is in accordance with what was originally agreed on. Other groups that must understand the system include the managers in the organization where the system is to be used, the technical writers who produce user manuals, the service personnel who install and maintain the system, and last, but not least, the users. This list, by no means exhaustive, might be considerably longer depending on the system in question.

What is important is to ensure that all the stakeholders of the system get a common description of the system functionality, one that they all understand and that is detailed enough to make an agreement meaningful and unambiguous. This has made it imperative to find a powerful, well-thought-out and at the same time simple technique to describe the system's functionality. Here the use-case concept has played a major role. This chapter introduces the most important constructs used in use-case modeling. The subsequent chapters provide a more thorough description of the constructs.

A *use case* defines one way of using the system being modeled. All behavior within the system—that is, all the ways the system can be used—is captured by the use cases. The users of the services (persons, machines, and other systems interacting with the system at hand) are modeled as *actors*. Together the use cases and the actors form a *use-case model* of the system. This model describes all the ways the system can be used by its environment—what services the system offers.

For example, in a use-case model of an ATM system (see Figure 3.1), one use case would typically be Withdraw Money, defining what the ATM does when a customer withdraws some money from an account. Another use case would be Transfer Money, which describes the actions of the ATM when money is withdrawn from one account and deposited in another account. The ATM offers both services to its users, here represented by the actor ATM Customer.

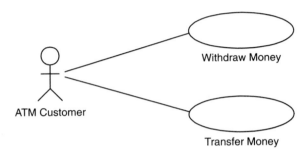

Figure 3.1   A use-case diagram presenting part of a use-case model of an ATM system. The diagram shows an actor associated with two use cases.

To look at another system that we have all experienced as users, we can use the model of a telephone exchange system (see Figure 3.2), where we will find use cases such as Local Call, Long-Distance Call, and Order Wake-Up Call. In some of these use cases, more than one actor is involved, because it takes two to make most telephone calls meaningful.

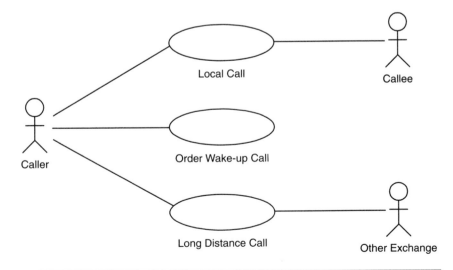

Figure 3.2   A use-case diagram showing some actors and use cases in a model of a telephone exchange.

As we have seen, a use case may involve one or more actors, each capturing a distinct role in relation to the use case. Each role modeled by an actor is played by entities in the system's surroundings, such as human beings, machines, and other software systems. Obviously, the same individual may play different roles, usually at different moments in time. For example, one subscriber may initiate calls as well as answer them (see Figure 3.3).

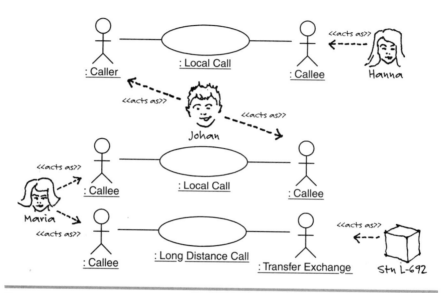

Figure 3.3   The users of a system play the roles defined by the actors. The figure shows instances—that is, actual occurrences of actors and use cases.

Use cases have proved to be easy to understand by different stakeholders of a system. Not only technical people appreciate the concept, but also managers and ordinary software users understand it easily. Use-case modeling has therefore rapidly become one of the more popular ways to capture the functionality of a system. (Unfortunately, this does not mean that everyone produces good use-case models and use-case descriptions!)

By defining the services offered by a system in terms of use cases, we get a comprehensive picture of the functionality of the system. The use cases can be mapped onto the classes in an object-oriented model of the system, showing what objects take part in the performance of each use case, and how these objects interact in doing so. This fills the gap between the user-oriented, outside view of the system functionality and the more technical object-oriented view of the system's interior. (Other implementation techniques, such as procedure/data-oriented implementations, are also possible.)

Use cases are suitable not only for capturing a system's functionality, they are also very useful for defining the boundaries of the system; that is, to express what is inside the system and what is outside. A use case models one way of using the system—that is, it captures everything that happens inside the system—from system boundary to system boundary. The external entities are captured by the actors. This implies that after the use cases and the actors have been identified, the system boundary has also been defined.

Moreover, use cases also prove useful as a basis for a number of other actions related to system development, such as identifying test cases, describing services that can be demanded when buying or configuring a system, planning and estimating the size and cost of a project developing a system, producing a user manual, and describing how different parts of the system interact.

CHAPTER 4

USE CASES

Use Case: A Type of Utilization Providing a Value

Use cases are used for defining how the modeled system is to be used by its surroundings. A *use case* models one usage of the system; that is, it describes what sequences of actions will be performed by the system as a response to events occurring outside the system caused by the users. However, it does not capture actions outside the system; a use case exists only inside the system. A use case constitutes the complete usage of the system in the sense that it starts when someone outside the system initiates it, and it ends when, based on the initial input, no other input is expected and no more internal actions are to be performed.

In the ATM example, the Withdraw Money use case starts when
the customer inserts the card into the card reader of the ATM.
The use case reads the card information and asks the customer
for the PIN code. After the PIN code has been entered, the use
case validates it, and then asks what amount is to be withdrawn. When the amount has been entered, the use case verifies whether the amount may be withdrawn from the account;
if so, it ejects the card, dispenses the cash, and prints a receipt.
This is when the use case ends. All these actions must be performed when money is withdrawn. Inserting the card and
entering the PIN code is not a complete usage of the ATM, nor
is only printing a receipt or dispensing cash. These are just
fragments of behavior that the ATM can perform, but they do
not constitute complete usages of the ATM. Hence, they are not
use cases—they are fragments of use cases.

Every use case has a purpose and provides a value for at least one of the
stakeholders of the system. Often the beneficiary is one of the users
involved in the use case, but other stakeholders are also possible. If no
such stakeholder can be identified, the use case is most likely superfluous
and should be removed, because nobody is interested in it.

In a surveillance system monitoring the traffic, there are a number of surveillance points in the streets registering passing vehicles. Surveillance personnel can request the gathered statistics
to do various kinds of calculations. The use-case model of the
system includes one use case registering vehicles passing the
surveillance point and another use case presenting the statistics.
In the registration use case, there is only one actor (the vehicle).

This actor can hardly be said to take an interest in the use case. (If the collecting of traffic statistics leads to an improved traffic environment in the future, this is good for the driver of the vehicle; to claim that the vehicle benefits from the registration use case is a bit far-fetched, however, to say the very least!) The surveillance personnel and the traffic planners, on the other hand, see the business value of that use case.

Likewise, the use case presenting the statistics has only one actor (the surveillance personnel). Because they need the use case to be able to perform their work, this use case provides a value to its actor.

A use-case name summarizes the usage of the system it models. The name is a verb phrase given in an active present tense form from the system's point of view, and it usually contains several words. For example, Generate Report, Withdraw Money, and Create Order are adequate names of use cases, whereas the following are examples of inadequate, potentially misleading use-case names: Receive Notification (the wrong point of view—should be Send Notification because this is what the system does), Bank Account (not a utilization—should be Handle Bank Account), and Withdrawal of Money (not active—should be Withdraw Money). However, in some cases a usage already has a well-established name, Login and Local Call, for instance. Obviously, these are appropriate use-case names.

Sometimes it is fruitful to classify the use cases in accordance with their importance to the system. This classification can be used, for example, when determining what impact a use case has on the system's architecture. Some of the use cases model the main and important usages of the system. If these use cases were to be excluded from the system, the system would not be meaningful. We call these use cases *primary* use cases. *Secondary* use cases support the performance of the primary use cases. Typically, the latter use cases add and remove such information to and from the system that is needed when the primary use cases are performed. Clearly, the primary use cases are more important than the secondary in the design of the system.

For example, Withdraw Money and Transfer Money are primary use cases of an ATM, whereas Read Transaction Log and Register ATM at Bank are secondary use cases. The latter two use cases are not the primary reason for building an ATM system. Another example is a ticketing system at an airline company, where Order Ticket is a primary use case, and Register Customer is a secondary use case. The reason for developing a ticketing system clearly is not to register customers; it is to handle ordered tickets.

There are also *optional* use cases that model utilizations of the system that might be included in one installation of the system, while excluded in another installation. Obviously, this group of use cases should have less impact on the system design than the other two groups.

A Gray-Box View of the System

The use cases include the actions performed inside the system as well as descriptions of the external events caused by the actors to initiate the performance of these actions, but they do not include actions performed outside the system. The actions included in the use cases can be of many different kinds, such as storing and retrieving information inside the system, performing calculations, as well as sending information, notifications, and requests to actors. However, a use case is independent of the internal structure of the system—the system can be more or less reorganized internally without affecting the use cases, as long as the use of the system remains the same. (Note that the *realization* of a use case is very much dependent on the internals of the system, but that is a separate issue. The use case itself is not. See Chapter 15, "Mapping Use Cases onto Classes.")

This means that a use case's sequences of actions include actions that can be perceived from the outside of the system, but not actions that are dependent on the internal structure of the system—for example, how certain information is represented in the system, what communication takes place between elements inside the system, or which part of the system performs a specific piece of behavior.

Take the use case Withdraw Money in the ATM example and its basic flow, which is described in Figure 4.1. As you can see, the use case includes more actions than just a black-box view, that is, more than just input and output actions. For example, after a user enters the PIN code, the system clearly verifies internally whether the code is correct. Moreover, it is shown that a lot of events are logged, and that different kinds of checks are performed. Even though these are system internal events, they are crucial to the understanding of what takes place in the use case. Therefore, they are of interest to readers of use-case descriptions. However, no parts included reveal how the ATM is structured internally; that is, it is not a white-box description that includes internal communication and shows which part of the ATM does what.

Basic Flow

The use case starts when the ATM Customer inserts the card into the card reader of the ATM. The use case reads the card information and requests the PIN code.

The ATM Customer inserts the PIN code. The use case checks that the PIN code is correct and logs the card information and that the entered PIN code is valid.

The use case checks that there is enough paper for a printed receipt. If not, the ATM Customer is notified. Then, the use case displays the possible kinds of transactions.

The ATM Customer selects to withdraw money. The use case asks for the amount to be withdrawn.

The ATM Customer enters the amount to be withdrawn. The use case sends a request to the Bank System that the amount is to be withdrawn together with the card information, and logs the communication.

The Bank System sends a transaction confirmation, which is logged by the use case. The use case logs that the amount is withdrawn together with a timestamp and the card information, ejects the card, dispenses the cash, and prints a receipt.

The use case checks that there is enough cash for another transaction. If not, an error message is displayed, the ATM changes state to Disabled, and a message is sent to the Bank System. Both of these actions are logged. Otherwise, the welcome message is displayed.

The use case ends.

Figure 4.1   A use-case is a gray-box description of the system. It describes what happens inside the system without revealing the internal structure of the system.

A use-case model gives a "gray-box view" of the system (see Figure 4.1). With such a description, the readers of a use-case model, especially three of the major stakeholders, the users, the customers, and the designers, can understand what the system is to do. They are not only interested in the communication between the actors and the system, but also in what happens inside the system. The former two are seldom interested in the internal structure of the system (or they may lack the competence to understand it), whereas the latter will use the use-case model to *produce* the internal structure of the system. A fourth stakeholder with interest in the use-case model is the test designer, who, among other things, should design tests independent of the internals of the system.

Use-Case Instance: A Specific Utilization

As previously mentioned, a use case describes a *complete usage* offered by the system, including descriptions of external events caused by input from the users and the system's responses to these inputs, possibly also including internal calculations as well as some output to the users. An *instance* of a use case (see Figure 4.2) models the performance of one particular usage described by the use case, carrying out one path through all the sequences of actions described in the use case, triggered by a user playing the role of the initiating actor. The use-case instance takes actual values as input from and output to the environment, it performs actions that cause changes to the system's internal state, and it makes actual decisions during the execution of the actions. The description of such an instance of a use case is by many called a *scenario*, for instance, in UML. For example, one scenario based on the use case `Withdraw Money` is a description of Hanna withdrawing $60 from her savings account at an ATM on November 20.

The advantage of the use-case instance concept is that it makes it possible to discuss different ways to use one use case, for a use case can behave differently depending on the state of the system as well as on the input provided by the actors. Furthermore, the concept can be used to show what happens when different use cases make use of the same information in the system. For example, when modeling a warehouse system, it is important to resolve what is to happen when an order is to be executed and the order is modified at the same time. Use-case instances make it possible to discuss the situation.

: Withdraw Money   Hanna's Withdrawal : Withdraw Money

Figure 4.2   In UML, an instance is denoted in the same way as its classifier, although the name is underlined and preceded by an optional instance name followed by a mandatory colon. The name of a use-case instance is usually omitted.

Multiple Classification of Use-Case Instances

A rarely mentioned but obvious fact about use-case instances is that it is not always possible to state which use case a use-case instance originates from. Use-case instances are not created explicitly like objects, which are created when using a constructor of a specific class. Instead, a use-case instance is implicitly created when a new sequence of actions is performed. If there is only one use case that starts as the use-case instance, then obviously the instance must originate from that use case.

However, multiple use cases can start in the same way. For example, in an ATM both the `Withdraw Money` use case and the `Check Balance` use case start in the same way: the ATM `Customer` enters a card, the use case asks for the PIN code, and the `ATM Customer` enters the PIN code. So far, both use cases are identical, so it is not possible to state from which use case the instance originates. Similarly, in a telephone exchange, it is not possible to state which use case is being performed after the `Caller` has initiated the call by lifting the handset, been registered as busy, and received a dial tone. Making a local call, ordering a wake-up call, and making a conference call all start the same way.

Not even when the instance terminates is it always possible to state which use case it originated from. In the ATM example, if the `ATM Customer` presses Cancel after the PIN code has been verified, the use-case instance ends. At this point, the instance still conforms to both the `Withdraw Money` use case and the `Transfer Money` use case (just as when the `Caller` hangs up after receiving the dial tone).

This classification ambiguity is not a problem as long as there is at least one use case modeling the behavior performed by the use-case instance. If there is not, clearly the use-case model does not model the system correctly, because all the ways the system can be used should be stated in that model.

Here it is relevant to point out an aspect of use cases that some find it difficult to grasp when they start working with use cases. As stated previously, use cases describe, among other things, the interactions between the system and its surroundings. However, instances of use cases do not send messages to each other (see Figure 4.3). What would it mean for a performance of a complete usage of a system to communicate with another complete usage of the same system, because they are both said to be complete? Still, assumed interaction is one of the most common misunderstandings regarding use cases. People are sometimes heard to mention situations when "this use case calls the other one," which is impossible. Instead, if we want to describe that one use case is somehow interleaved with another one, in other words that the sequences of actions of one use case are combined with the sequences of another use case, we are actually describing a third use case. Parts of the sequence of the new use case happen to be described previously in other use cases. Chapter 7, "Include: Reusing Existing Use Cases," and Chapter 8, "Extend: Expanding Existing Use Cases," describe how use cases can be related to each other and how in that way we will reuse descriptions of already existing use cases.

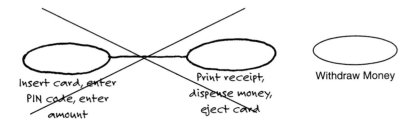

Figure 4.3   Use cases do not communicate with each other.

However, use cases can affect each other indirectly by using the same pieces of information in the system. For example, both `Withdraw Money` and `Deposit Money` will modify the balance of an account, but that does not cause them to communicate with each other by somehow sending messages to each other. Each of them is a complete usage of the ATM, performed independently of whether the other is performed (concurrently) or not.

Why Use-Case Instances Cannot Communicate

There are a couple of reasons why use-case instances cannot be said to communicate with each other:

1. A use case models a sequence of actions in a system, and a use-case instance models the actual occurrence of such a sequence—that is, it models a sequence of events taking place at a certain moment in time. The meaning of a use-case instance sending messages to another use-case instance would therefore be "one sequence of events is talking to another sequence." This is obviously nonsense, like saying, "This chair is talking to that chair." Sequences of events do not communicate; they occur.

2. Use cases model system behavior from a user perspective—that is, a use case represents a complete usage of the system. When tempted to define an association between two use cases, remember the completeness criterion. Apparently, one of the use cases is not enough to capture a complete usage of the system, because it must somehow make use of another use case to fulfill the needs of the user. Obviously, the wanted use case is a combination of the two. Do not confuse two associated use cases with, for example, two use cases with an include relationship between them (see Chapter 7). The latter helps structuring the use-case model at *specification level*; when performed, there is still just *one instance*.

Basic Flow and Variations

A *use-case model* contains all the use cases needed to make up a complete description of the functionality of a system. Because every way to use a system is modeled as a use case, all the behavior of the system will appear in the use-case model (except behavior performed due to the internal structure of the system, such as communication between different parts of the system, or creation and deletion of objects). If not, the system would contain behavior that does not participate in an offered usage, which, of course, would not make sense. Why would behavior not offered by the system to its users be included in the system?

Therefore, if the functionality of a system is to be described completely, the use-case model must capture every sequence that might occur when the system is used. This includes all kinds of flows, also exceptional cases and error cases. In the ATM system, for example, such flows are performed when the PIN code is not correct or the balance of the account does not cover the requested withdrawal. In the telephone exchange example, there would be an exceptional flow describing the case where no lines are available to connect the call.

Other flows that must also be captured include all normal variations of the basic flows. For example, the ATM Customer may or may not want a receipt documenting the withdrawal, or the Callee of the local call may not respond, so the call is not answered. Note, however, that the classification of the flows as basic, alternative, exceptional, and so on has no impact on the system itself. All flows must be identified and described, no matter what they are called. The classification of the flows is just a way for the reader as well as the producer of the model to organize the descriptions of the use cases.

If each such variant were defined by a separate use case, the result would be a very large set of use cases for a single system, so large in fact that the model would be completely incomprehensible. Furthermore, the description of most use cases would be very small because their actual flows would be described in just a few lines. Such a situation would not be manageable in practice, because there would be a lot of overhead handling all the documents for all the use cases, even if each document were to contain very little information.

The solution to this dilemma is to bundle together into one unit a set of sequences that are variations on the same theme—that is, variations, exceptions, and error variants of the same basic sequence of actions. The result is one use case, and this use case includes all the variants of the basic flow. The advantages are numerous. In this way, the total number of use cases for one system is reduced to a fraction of the total number of possible sequences, making the model comprehensible. Furthermore, we treat the basic flow, the alternative flows, and error flows as one conceptual unit; that is, they are to be handled together. By including the use case in the model, we make sure that all its variants are included as well, and by removing it, all the variants are excluded. Moreover, all the variants of one flow are described in one document, although possibly in different sections, which makes the document handling much more viable.

In many cases, it is quite obvious that two sequences should appear in the same use case (see Figure 4.4). For example, if the basic sequence includes a check that should result in *true*, the complement (a check resulting in *false*) should also be included in the same use case as a variant of the first sequence. Other cases are not so obvious. Here, the test is whether the two sequences both contribute to producing the value to the stakeholders. In the ATM example, for instance, the sequence *withdrawing money and printing a receipt* and the sequence *withdrawing money without printing a receipt* both contribute to helping the customer withdraw some money. However, what about the sequence *denial due to too small balance*? Does this sequence also contribute to that value? The answer is probably no, because it is most likely not the customer who wants to prevent the withdrawal in this case; it is the bank. So, do not only look at the actors of the system when verifying the values of the use case; one should also include the other stakeholders of the system.

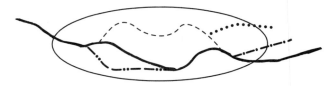

Figure 4.4   There are multiple paths through a use case. An instance of the use case will perform one of these paths.

Of course, if you find a variant flow important enough to promote it to a use case of its own, do so! Just be aware that the size of the model will be increased. However, whether a sequence is to be captured as a separate use case or whether it is to be included in another use case is not the most important question when you create your model. The question is obviously relevant, but whichever you decide, somewhere in your model you will have to model and describe every sequence that is to be performed in the system. Moreover, no matter where you have it in your use-case model, the sequence will be realized in your analysis and design models, and eventually it will be implemented and tested.

Infinitely Large Models?

This leads us to another common misunderstanding. Some insist that it is not possible to describe all the use cases of a system, because any system will contain an extremely large, if not infinite, number of use cases. This is wrong. A normal medium-sized system usually encompasses around 20 to 50 use cases, and to describe them is not a job for Sisyphus—at least not if it is clear what the system is to do; if not, *that* is what is problematic! Of course, the number of use cases increases with the size of the system, but not exponentially. One may think that a very large system would require many more use cases, but in fact, the number is still fairly limited. Remember that a use case includes all the variations of its basic flow, which reduces the number of use cases. The use of include and extend relationships in the model may also reduce the combinatory explosion of the size of a model.

Another reason for the limited size of most use-case models is that when a system is very large or complex, it is not possible to have just one description or specification of the system given at the same level of detail as that of a simpler or smaller system. Instead, the complexity is handled by decomposing the system into subsystems, where the scope is limited to a smaller part of the system and where the functionality can be further elaborated for each subsystem (see Chapter 18, "Component Hierarchy").

As a comparison, just think of all the test cases that are specified for a system. All of them can and must be described; otherwise, it would not be possible to test the system in an organized way. This is also true of the user manual, which describes how the system is to be used. At least the test cases are given at a more fine-grained level than are the use cases, but even if the user manual is not described at that level of detail, it clearly describes all the different ways to use the system. Therefore, we can conclude that it is possible to describe all the functionality of a system with a use-case model.

The next chapter discusses how to model the context of the use cases, focusing on the users of the system. How commonalities, optionality, and the like are to be modeled is described in Chapter 6, "Structuring a Use-Case Model," and the following chapters. How to prepare a detailed description of a use case is discussed in Chapter 13, "Describing Use Cases."

CHAPTER 5

MODELING THE SYSTEM ENVIRONMENT

Actor: An External User

This chapter examines the other parts of a use-case model—that is, the actors of the system and the associations between the actors and the use cases. An *actor* models a role that is played by a user of the system when utilizing the system—that is, when the user interacts with use cases (see Figure 5.1). Because the actors are played by the users of the system, all the actors appear outside the system being modeled. As we are modeling the system, the role of an actor is defined from the system's point of view—the actors model how the *system* perceives its environment.

Figure 5.1   A system perceives its users as playing different roles toward the system. All persons who withdraw money using an ATM act as ATM Customers toward the ATM, whereas one user category of a Sales Management System is represented by an actor called Sales Manager.

Everyone who is using the system is playing a role defined by an actor. An actor can be played both by humans and by machines, like robots and other computer systems. What is important is that the human or the machine is using the services of the modeled system. An actor can interact with several use cases, which means that an individual playing the role defined by the actor uses the system in the way that is modeled by these use cases.

Sometimes a use case in its turn needs to interact with someone outside the system, a person or a machine or so on to complete its task. This someone is also outside the system and is therefore modeled as an actor. It can either be the actor who initiated the use case or another external user. These latter external users are also actors to the system. They may not have been identified at the beginning of the development process, but were added later when the details of the use cases were described and it became clear that a use case must interact with other external users.

One actor can interact with several use cases. This means that a user will interact with instances of one or several of the use cases associated with that actor. Similarly, one use case can interact with one or several actors, which implies that several users are participating in the performance of the use case. For example, two actors will participate in the use case Local Call: the Caller and the Callee. This example makes it obvious that an actor does not model a *user*; it models a *role* played by a user. As a user of a telephone exchange, Jenny will initiate as well as receive calls. When initiating a call Jenny will play the role of a Caller, and she will act as a Callee when receiving a call.

An actor has a name, which is a noun phrase in singular form and usually contains several words. The name should describe the role the actor plays from the system's point of view; that is, when naming an actor, one should move oneself inside the system and describe the role the user is playing. In this way, new kinds of users can be introduced in this role without having to rename the actor.

Actors for whom the system is built are called *primary* actors. These are most likely to be identified when the use-case modeling starts. *Secondary* actors are the external users who use the system so that the primary actors can have their tasks performed. In the ATM example, the ATM Customer is a primary actor, whereas the Bank and the Maintenance Person are secondary actors; they interact with the ATM so that the ATM Customer can use it and perform his or her tasks. Another example is the Clerk of the ticketing system, where the Clerk is a primary actor, and the Airline Company and the Operator are secondary actors.

Primary and Secondary Actors in Another Context

The labels *primary* and *secondary* are very useful in many contexts. Actually, these labels can be used in two different ways with regard to actors. One definition is the one we have discussed previously, which is also the original definition used in Object-Oriented Software Engineering (Addison-Wesley, 1993). Another way of using these labels is to have them denote actors in the local context of one use case.

In relation to a *specific* use case, an actor can be said to be a primary actor if it initiates the use case—that is, it starts the sequence of events. All other actors of that use case are said to be secondary—that is, any communication between such an actor and the use case is a consequence of the primary actor starting the interaction with the use case.

Hence, used in this way, the primary and secondary labels do not define something absolute; rather, such a label characterizes an actor's relation to a specific use case. In other words, one actor can be a primary actor with respect to one use case and a secondary actor in relation to another one.

When identifying actors of a system, it is often useful to think in terms of primary/secondary actors as described in this book—that is, in relation to the system as a whole. This will make it easy to find the actors and it will also help keep focus on the users for whom the system is to be built.

The second meaning of the labeling (the one presented in this box) is often more useful when the attention is focused on single use cases. The primary actor of the use case is often the reason why the use case was identified, and focusing on that use case's need to communicate with external parties will lead to the identification of the use case's secondary actors.

Note, however, no correlation exists between the two ways of using the primary/secondary actor labeling! An actor may be one of the primary actors of a system; from the perspective of one of the use cases, however, it is just the receiver of some information from the use case—therefore, it is a secondary actor of that use case. On the other hand, a secondary system actor, such as a `System Administrator`, is, of course, the primary actor of use cases such as `Register User`, `Check System Log`, and so on.

It is important to understand that an actor models a user from the system's perspective, and not a role in the business where the system is used. Otherwise, you will sooner or later get into trouble when defining what a use case interacts with and how many users will participate in the performance of a use case. Consider a warehouse example. In the business where the system is used, there are, among others, managers and salespersons. Therefore, we have two business roles: `Manager` and `Salesperson`. In the example, both managers and salespersons expedite orders that customers want to place. Therefore, from the business roles' perspective, both of them are performing the `Order Item` use case. However, let us now move over to the system's perspective. How many users participate in the performance of the `Order Item` use case? From this perspective, there is only one, namely the user entering the order information. Therefore, there is only one actor, called Clerk, interacting with the Order Item use case (see Figure 5.2). The use case receives the order information from the Clerk, creates the order, and prints it to the Clerk. From the system's perspective, it is of no consequence whether it interacts with a manager or a salesperson. If we were to model the business roles as actors, we would end up with two actors interacting with the Order Item use case, which is clearly not true. Remember that the actors model the users *from the system's perspective*, not from the business' perspective.

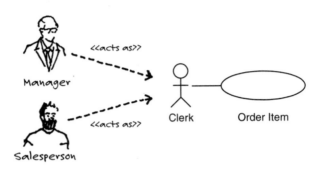

Figure 5.2   Persons acting as Managers or Salespersons in the business act as Clerks toward the Order Item use case.

Consider another implication of the fact that actors are defined from the system's, or the use case's, point of view: As an actor models a role played by an entity external to the system utilizing a use case, *anyone* outside the system utilizing that use case will play the role defined by the actor; that is, it can be a person as well as another system. Therefore, we do not introduce one "person actor" and one "system actor" playing the same role toward the use case, because the use case interacts only with one actor (see Chapter 23, "Multiple Actors"). If different sequences of actions are to be performed depending on whether the user is a person or a system, there should probably be two use cases, possibly interacting with different actors. However, if the sequences of actions are the same regardless of who the user is, there is only one use case and hence only one actor.

At a concrete level, it is likely that the actual messages sent between the system and the external user differ depending on whether the user is a person or a machine. This is not visible at the use-case level, however. Instead, such information is captured in the realization of the use case, where different boundary classes—responsible for transforming messages between user and system (see Chapter 15, "Mapping Use Cases onto Classes")—are used for the different kinds of users (see Figure 5.3).

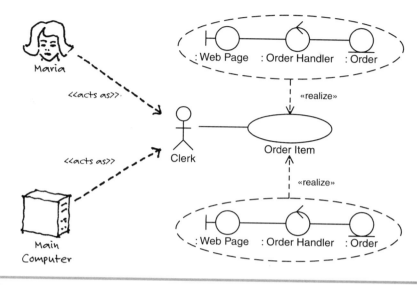

Figure 5.3   One use case can have multiple use-case realizations depending on the external entity playing the role of the actor. Details of the diagram are explained in Chapter 15.

A grave error, although quite common, is using actors to model security levels defined for the users. The problem with using the actors to express the security levels is that no security checks will be performed by the system with this kind of model. All checks that must be performed by the system must be included in the use cases. As we know, actors model how the users of the system are perceived by the system. *Anyone performing a use case associated with an actor will therefore be regarded by the system as an instance of that actor, regardless of whether the person or machine is allowed to use this use case or not.*

Of course, it is not wrong in itself to have actors that correspond to security levels—in some cases this may even make it easier for user representatives to understand the model—as long as it is clear that this does not add any constraints on security checks in the system. This must still be expressed in the use cases! For a more thorough description of the problem and what a correct model would look like, see Chapter 27, "Access Control."

Obviously, the error in capturing security requirements by attaching them to actors is just a special case of a general pitfall: No requirements on the system can be captured by actors! The actors represent the *outside* of the system; hence, they do not pose any constraints on how the use cases *inside* the system are implemented. Anything that the system must fulfill must be expressed in the use cases.

Interaction Between Use Cases and Actors

That an actor and a use case can and will interact with each other is expressed by means of an *association* between the two. However, this association does not state what they communicate, when they communicate, or how they communicate. As with the associations between classes, the *multiplicity* of the association states how many instances of the use case one instance of the actor (one user playing the role defined by the actor) may simultaneously communicate with, and *vice versa*. Similarly, the *navigability* of an association between an actor and a use case describes who initiates any type of communication between the two. Usually, the association is navigable in both directions. These detailed specifications of the associations are often omitted in the use-case models, but if needed, they can be defined (see Figure 5.4).

ATM Customer   Withdraw Money   Bank System

Figure 5.4   One ATM Customer will communicate with one instance of the Withdraw Money use case at a time, and each instance of the Withdraw Money use case will communicate with one ATM Customer and one Bank System. Note that the Bank System may be contacted by several instances of Withdraw Money at the same time.

In some cases, it might be informative to explicitly describe how the use case and its actors interact with each other. This can be done using ordinary UML sequence diagrams, for example.

Draw a sequence diagram with the actors and use case as participants— that is, as columns in the diagram—and then add arrows between the columns representing the interaction between the actors and the use case (see Figure 5.5). Note that this diagram does not describe the use case; it describes how the use case is used by its environment (the actors). More precisely, the sequence diagram describes (a part of) the business use case that is partly automated by the system.

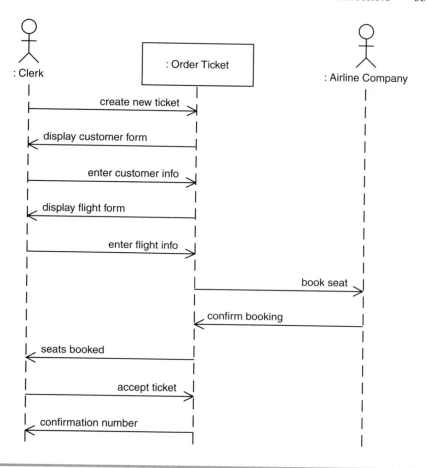

Figure 5.5   Sequence diagrams can be used to describe a use case's interaction
with its environment, i.e. the actors.

CHAPTER 6

STRUCTURING A USE-CASE MODEL

The very first attempt at a use-case model is usually done mainly graphically, in diagrams showing actors and associated use cases (see Figure 6.1). These sketches of a use-case model are complemented by brief descriptions of the use cases and the actors, to make sure that everyone involved in the process understands and agrees on what each actor and use case represents. When these diagrams and descriptions of the model stabilize, more details are provided by means of detailed descriptions of each use case.

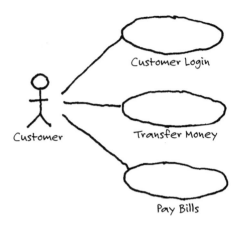

Figure 6.1   The first sketch of a model contains coarse-grained use cases and is very unstable.

During this work, the model is bound to undergo changes, because more details of what actually happens in each use case will be captured. The addition of more details sometimes reveals that the original structure of the model may not have been optimal, or may even have been incorrect. One common type of change involves splitting one use case into two or more use cases, which is necessary when alternative flows prove to constitute completely different flows rather than variants of the basic flow, and hence will be better expressed as separate use cases. At other times, two use cases will be replaced by a single use case—for instance, when detailed descriptions of the flows show that they are in fact very similar and therefore had better be treated as variations of one use case.

Furthermore, parts of some of the use cases may prove to be identical or should be identical, and some parts may be configurable; that is, not all configurations of the system will include these parts. Moreover, some use cases in the system may be mutually exclusive; that is, the system must include either of the two use cases, but not both.

In other cases, mainly when developing a new version of an already existing system, one may want to reuse parts of existing use cases in some of the new use cases, or want to extend already existing use cases with some additional behavior (see Figure 6.2).

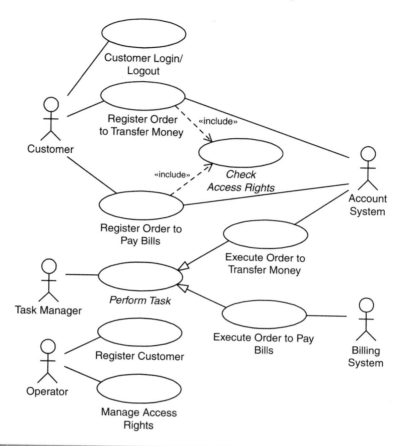

Figure 6.2   Enhancing the model introduces additional elements and modifies existing ones.

The approach described above suggests starting with the identification of the use cases, and then continuing with the identified commonalities found during the description of the use cases. However, the opposite approach is also feasible, which may occur if there is a requirement stating that certain parts of two or more usages must be the same—in other words, when we know in advance that the flows of two or more use cases are to share common parts. Usually, the procedure is a mix of the two alternative approaches. It should be pointed out, however, that the second alternative should be used only when such a requirement has been explicitly stated.

Subsequent chapters describe how such situations can be expressed as well as be prepared for in the use-case model by introducing three different kinds of relationships between use cases: include (Chapter 7, "Include: Reusing Existing Use Cases"), extend (Chapter 8, "Extend: Expanding Existing Use Cases," and Chapter 10, "More on Extend and Extension Points"), and generalization (Chapter 11, "Use-Case Generalization: Classification and Inheritance"). We also discuss how commonalities between actors should be expressed (Chapter 12, "Actor Generalization: Overlapping Roles"). Using these relationships will make the model easier to maintain and usually easier to understand. However, these relationships should not be overused, because this will make the model overly complex (see Chapter 17, "Commonality," Chapter 19, "Concrete Extension or Inclusion," Chapter 23, "Multiple Actors," and Chapter 26, "Use-Case Sequence").

CHAPTER 7

INCLUDE: REUSING EXISTING USE CASES

Include Relationship

In the process of identifying and describing use cases, one might recognize the same subflow in two or more use cases. Obviously, if the purposes and the goals of these use cases are identical, if they interact with the same actors, and if the subflow constitutes most of the use cases, one should consider merging the use cases into one use case or introduce a generalization relationship (see Chapter 11, "Use-Case Generalization: Classification and Inheritance"). If both use cases include a certain subflow that is exactly the same in both flows, but otherwise are disparate and with different purposes and goals, however, it would be a mistake to join them. The resulting use case would not be easily understood, and eventually the merged use case would have to be split because it encompasses disjoint goals.

The issue here is to ensure that the common part-flow stays identical, and to minimize maintenance of the descriptions. The solution is the *include* relationship, which means that one use case includes the flow described in another use case in its own declaration—that is, the sequence of the first use case includes the whole sequence of the other as a subsequence.

In a warehouse system, there is one use case for registering new items and another use case for ordering items (see Figure 7.1). In both cases, the system will check whether the person performing the operation is allowed to do so. The checking of the access rights is therefore extracted and described in a separate use case. This use case is included in the `Register Item` use case as well as in the `Order Item` use case, which implies that the checking procedure is described only once and referenced from all other places where it is to be included.

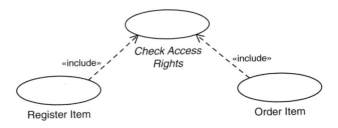

Figure 7.1   In both use cases, the access rights must be checked. herefore, the checking is extracted into a third use case, which is included by the original two.

The include relationship is mainly a reuse mechanism: The flow defined in a use case is reused in the including use case. In this way, a subflow that is common to multiple use cases can be defined just once instead of in all the use cases. Changes to the definition of the common flow will take place in only one use case and then be propagated into all the including use cases.

When discussing the use cases involved in an include relationship, it becomes awkward referring to them as "the included use case" and the "including use case," because the terms are more or less alike, and this might even lead to unnecessary misunderstandings. It is therefore common vocabulary to refer to the including use case as the *base* use case, and the included one as the *inclusion* use case (see Figure 7.2). Note, however, that this labeling is relative to the include relationship at hand; the same use case may be the base use case in one include relationship, and the inclusion use case in another one—that is, it does not characterize the use case itself in any way.

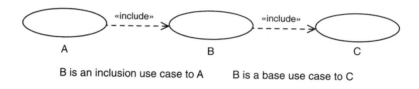

B is an inclusion use case to A   B is a base use case to C

Figure 7.2   The terms *base use case* and *inclusion use case* are relative terms.

Note that an include relationship does not imply communication between instances of the use cases, or the like (which is not possible, as discussed in Chapter 4, "Use Cases," in the section *Use-Case Instance*). It just indicates that a part of the description of the complete flow of a use case is described in the description of another use case. The sequence of actions performed when executing one of the base use cases will include the actions defined in the inclusion use case (see Figure 7.3).

A use-case instance performing the actions of a base use case, like Register Item in Figure 7.3, encounters at some point an instruction to include another use case (Check Access Right, in this case). At that point, the instance performs the actions of the inclusion use case, and then resumes obeying the description of the base use case after the include instruction (see Figure 7.3). Any results from performing the included actions (in this case, the result of checking the access rights) are then available within the use-case instance.

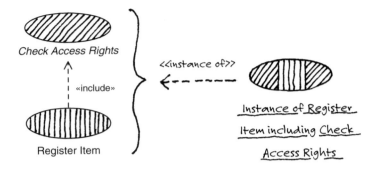

Figure 7.3   The use-case instance to the right follows the description of the
Register Item use case, which includes the description of the
Check Access Rights use case, as indicated by the hatching.

It is usually not possible to perform solely the inclusion use case. Often, such a use case does not define a complete usage offered by the system, but only part of one or several of the ways the system can be used. Inclusion use cases are therefore often declared to be *abstract*.

An abstract use case will never be instantiated; that is, it will never be performed on its own. Its only purpose is to model and describe a (sub-)flow which can be reused by or have other kinds of relationships to other flows—just like abstract classes. In UML, an abstract element is denoted by putting its name in italics. The opposite of abstract is *concrete*; a concrete use case can be instantiated—that is, it is a complete flow that can be performed on its own.

Note, however, that there is no constraint on an inclusion use case that it must be abstract. Situations where a certain subflow of one use case may also be performed on its own are not uncommon, and the include relationship is most useful in these situations as well (see Chapter 19, "Concrete Extension or Inclusion").

Sometimes the include relationship is used to factor out part of a flow, even if it is used in just one use case. This is not always considered bad modeling. Possible reasons for using it are the option to reuse it in later iterations or versions of the system, or the option to make a subflow explicit in the model, which might be important for the stakeholders. However, avoid introducing include relationships that are not prompted by common parts for two or more use cases! The included use case must have some merits as a use case of its own, because it is to be reviewed and maintained and above all because it will increase the size and the complexity of the use-case model and hence often make it more difficult to understand. It is essential to keep the number of include relationships between use cases at a minimum. It is particularly important not to define such relationships too early on in the process of identifying use cases, unless there is an explicit requirement that a subflow be common to multiple use cases. Otherwise, there is a risk that later descriptions will have to be made according to an include relationship that actually should not have been available because later descriptions show that the flows have precious little in common.

Include: A Picture from Real Life

To get an intuitive feeling for the include relationship, consider what happens in a kitchen when a person (let's call him Viktor) is about to prepare a blueberry pie. Viktor is not a very experienced cook, so he will use a cookbook recipe. The blueberry pie recipe can be compared with a use-case description: in this case, Make Blueberry Pie. An instance of this use case will correspond to somebody baking a blueberry pie.

When Viktor reads the recipe, he finds that the cookbook writer has made use of the fact that many kinds of pies are partly made in the same way. In particular, the dough of many of the pies is prepared in the same way. The writer has therefore described the dough in a separate recipe, and the recipes of various kinds of pies refer to it. This is the same mechanism as an include relationship; instead of repeating how the dough is prepared in every pie recipe, this is described once, and this description is to be included in the recipe of the blueberry pie, for example.

When Viktor makes his blueberry pie—that is, when the instance of Make Blueberry Pie is executed—he starts by following the description in the blueberry pie recipe. At some point in this pie recipe, there is a reference to the dough recipe, so he turns the page and continues by following the instructions there. When that is done, he returns to where he was in the blueberry pie recipe and continues making the pie by following that part of the description. This is clearly one flow. The fact that Viktor needs to look at two places in the cookbook does not contradict the statement that baking a blueberry pie is only one sequence of events. There is only one use-case instance performed, regardless of whether the description is to be found in one place or split into two parts to be found in different places. And, obviously, it would not be meaningful to say that the flow of the preparation of blueberry pie communicates with the flow of the preparing of dough.

Documentation of the Include Relationship

The include relationship is documented in the description of the including use case (see Chapter 13, "Describing Use Cases"). The inclusion itself is just stated in the flow of events section of the use-case description, as described in Figure 7.4.

Basic Flow

The use case starts when the ATM Customer inserts the card into the card reader of the ATM. The use case reads the card information and requests the PIN code.

The ATM Customer inserts the PIN code. The PIN code is checked by including the Check PIN Code use case. If the PIN code is correct, the use case logs the card information and that the entered PIN code is valid.

[…]

Figure 7.4   In the description of the Withdraw Money use case, there is an explicit reference as to where to include the Check PIN Code use case.

In principle, the inclusion use case is described as any other use case. However, because it usually models part of a usage and not the complete usage, an inclusion use case is often abstract. This means that it does not necessarily start with an input from an actor, nor is it required to include any output or to have a well-defined end of the sequence of actions. However, an inclusion use case must form a continuous sequence, because the whole inclusion use case is to be inserted at one location of the base use case; it must not be distributed over multiple locations of the base use case.

The start and the end of the description of an inclusion use case differ slightly from the ones of a use case that is not to be included in other use cases (see Figure 7.5). Note that the end section of an inclusion use case explicitly states which information is available in the base use case after the inclusion—that is, the result of the included flow, if any, because this is important information when reusing this use case (see also Chapter 19, "Concrete Extension or Inclusion").

Basic Flow

When this use case is included by other use cases, the use-case instance continues by performing the following actions:

[...]

The subflow ends and the use-case instance continues as described in the base use case after the location where this use case was included. The result of the PIN code check is available in the base use case.

Figure 7.5   The start and the end of the flow description of Check PIN Code are affected by the fact that it is an inclusion use case.

Dependency on Inclusion Use Cases

When two use cases are connected by an include relationship, the base use case is dependent on the inclusion use case, but not the other way around, just as in other reuse situations. This is also shown in the notation of the relationship: The base use case's dependency on the inclusion use case is shown, as always in UML relationships, with the direction of the arrow (see Figure 7.6).

Figure 7.6   The Withdraw Money use case is dependent on the included Check PIN Code use case.

The reuse aspect of the relationship implies some additional constraints on the participating use cases. First, as mentioned previously, an inclusion use case must not be dependent on any of its base use cases. Therefore, it must not be dependent on the structure of its base use cases or on how they are described. For example, an inclusion use case must not depend on a base use case's association to an actor, or on the terminology used in the description of a base use case. If the definition of the inclusion use case were to be dependent on a base use case, it would not be suitable for reuse because all its base use cases would then have to be defined in a specific way. Furthermore, the amount of information in the system accessed both by actions in an inclusion use case and by actions in its base use cases should be minimized, although it is often impossible to make it go away completely.

Moreover, the base use cases must not depend on what is inside the inclusion use case, because any change there would then affect the base use cases. The base use cases must depend only on the result of the execution of the actions defined in the inclusion use case's sequences of actions and not on any specific action or relationship to other elements (for instance, actors). We say that the inclusion use case must be encapsulated—its interior must not be exposed to or used by the base use cases.

However, the definition of the base use case is dependent on the *existence* of the inclusion use case. Remove the latter and the former will break.

CHAPTER 8

EXTEND: EXPANDING EXISTING USE CASES

Extend Relationship

When subsequent iterations in a project are performed or when later versions of a system's use-case model are developed, completely new use cases are often added to the model and new actions are inserted into existing use cases. This means that the existing services are extended with some additional features that did not exist in the previous versions of the model. However, the different stakeholders often do not want to modify the existing use cases because these have already been reviewed and approved. They are only willing to have certain features *added* to the existing use cases. Therefore, the developers will have to express these additions without modifying the existing use cases.

To solve the situation, it is possible to use the extend relationship. An *extend relationship* states that the flow of a use case is extended by the flow defined in another use case. The original use case is often called the *base* use case, and the use case capturing the addition is called the *extension* use case (see Figure 8.1). We can compare these labels to those involved in an include relationship in the sense that this labeling is relative to the extend relationship, and not to the use cases as such.

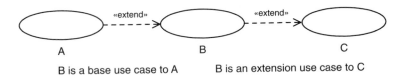

Figure 8.1   The terms *base use case* and *extension use case* are relative terms.

The fact that the relationship is defined *from* the extension use case *to* the base use case—that is, from the new use case to the already existing one—makes it very useful. The direction implies that the extension use case is dependent on the base use case, whereas the base use case is in fact independent of the extension. In other words, the dependency goes *to* the base use case—that is, in the opposite direction compared with the include situation where the dependency goes *from* the base use case. Therefore, an extend relationship can be added to a model without affecting the base use case; that is, the definition of the base use case will not be modified at all when the subflow of the extension use case is added.

> In the warehouse system example, there is a use case `Order Item` that describes how a collection of items is ordered, how the registered numbers of these items are decreased in the system, and how a pick list is generated and sent to the warehouse personnel instructing them to deliver the items to the customer. In the first version of the system, the head buyer of the warehouse must manually check whether the number of an item is running low; if so, it must be restocked. Obviously, it would be desirable that the system automatically informs the head buyer when an item has to be restocked. Therefore, in the next version of the system, a new use case, `Restock Item`, is added to the use-case model. The added functionality implies that when the registered number of an item falls below a specified threshold, a restock order is generated and sent to the warehouse's head buyer. The `Restock Item` use case has an extend relationship to the `Order Item` use case stating that when the latter use case is performed, the actions described in `Restock Item` will be inserted into the performed sequence of actions (see Figure 8.2).

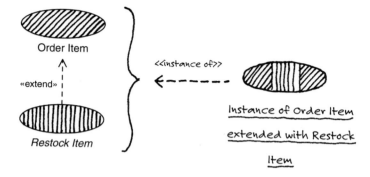

Figure 8.2   The use-case instance to the right follows the description of the Order Item use case extended by the description of the Restock Item use case, as indicated by the hatching.

Note that in the first version of the warehouse system, the use-case instance will perform the actions described in the Order Item use case, whereas in the second, enhanced version, the use-case instance will perform the actions of Order Item *extended by* the actions of Restock Item. There will not be two communicating use-case instances, because use-case instances do not communicate with each other, as was stated in Chapter 4, "Use Cases," in the section, *Use-Case Instance: A Specific Utilization.* Therefore, in both cases, there is only *one* flow of events; in the latter version, this flow will include the actions modeled by two use cases.

The extend relationship is also used when the flow of a use case includes a part that from a conceptual point of view does not belong to the rest of the flow—in other words, when the flow includes a part that, in some sense, is orthogonal to the rest of the flow. This could be logging, for example, which in itself usually has nothing to do with what is being logged; in this sense, it is orthogonal to the rest of the flow. How logging is done can be described separately (see Figure 8.3).

Perform Task   *Log Event*

Figure 8.3   Modeling behavior that conceptually does not belong together with the rest of the behavior of a use case is often done using an extension use case.

Used in this way, the extend relationship makes it easier to read and understand the model. In our telephone exchange system, assume that all telephone calls are to be charged. Hence, the flow of Local Call must include the actions that cause the charging to take place. However, the information about the charging procedure may be distracting to readers of the Local Call use case. Instead, we describe charging in a separate use case extending Local Call (see Figure 8.4).

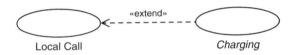

Local Call   *Charging*

Figure 8.4   Extracting behavior into an extension use case may increase readability and understandability.

One important motivation for the extend relationship is that it makes it possible to model services that are optional in a configuration of (an installation of) the system, enabling the customers buying the system to decide whether to include a certain service. In the warehouse system example, there can be one basic version of the system and a collection of additional services, including automatic restocking. Different warehouses can buy different configurations of the system by selecting different sets of use cases (see Figure 8.5). This implies that the inclusion or exclusion of optional services must not affect the other parts of the model. Because we have related Restock Item to Order Item using an extend relationship, we can add as well as remove it without influencing the rest of the model, thus obtaining the desired structure of the model.

If for some reason the use-case model must be modified depending on whether some optional parts are supplied, the model will of course have to be structured differently! For a more thorough discussion of optional services, see Chapter 24, "Optional Service."

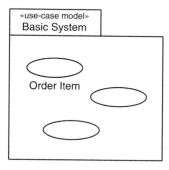 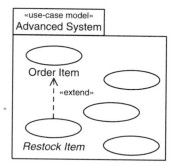

Figure 8.5   In different configurations of the system, optional use cases can be
added. Some of these may expand mandatory use cases using
extend relationships.

One use case may, of course, extend several other use cases—like the
Charging use case, which probably extends all the use cases that model the
performance of some kind of telephone call, as is shown in Figure 8.6.
There will be an extend relationship from the Charging use case to each of
the extended use cases, which means that each of them is extended with
the sequence of actions described by the Charging use case.

Furthermore, one use case may be extended by more than one use case.
The Local Call use case may be extended not only by the Charging use
case but also by, for example, the Call Waiting, the Present Caller Line
Identification, and the Survey Quality of Call use cases.

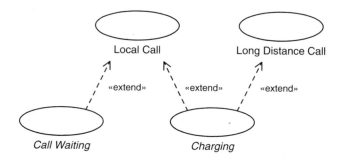

Figure 8.6   One use case may extend several use cases, and several use cases
may extend the same (base) use case.

Extend: A Picture from Real Life

Time to visit Viktor's kitchen again (see Chapter 7, "Include: Reusing Existing Use Cases"). Today's menu includes steak with wine sauce. Because Viktor is not that experienced, he has asked his friend Vidar to help him with the sauce. However, when he tastes the sauce, Vidar realizes that he has used far too much salt. Disaster! Can something be done to save the situation?

In the cookbook, Vidar finds that there might be a solution to the problem: He could peel a raw potato, put it into the sauce, and boil it for a while. The idea is that the potato will absorb salt, which might rescue the sauce. Vidar follows this advice, which makes it part of the use-case instance that is being executed. However, this advice is not included in the recipe of the wine sauce, because this has very little to do with that particular recipe. Instead, it is described in a separate part of the cookbook, where it is stated that this can be done if a sauce proves to be too salty.

This is an analogy to having an extend relationship from the `Fix Too Salty Sauce` use case to the `Make Sauce` use case, where the extension point (see the section *Extension Points*) is "when the sauce has been tasted" and the condition (see the section *Conditional Extensions*) is "the sauce is too salty." Because the raw potato trick can be used not only in sauces, but also for stews, pots, and so on, there will be similar extend relationships to several recipes.

Why not use include relationships in such situations? The reason is that the author of the cookbook does not want to overload the users of the cookbook with all kinds of special tricks to be used in different situations. That a special trick can be inserted should not be visible in the "base" recipes, which would have to be the case if include were to be used. (This analogy has its limits, but hopefully you get the idea!) Instead, the writer prepares a separate section including descriptions of different emergency measures—another useful one being that if a sauce breaks, adding an ice cube and stirring can help! (For a more thorough discussion regarding include *versus* extend, see Chapter 9, "Include vs. Extend.")

Characteristics of the Extend Relationship

As mentioned previously, the relationship is directed from the extension use case to the base use case. This implies that the base use case is independent of the extension. Only the extending use case is dependent on the extend relationship. This means that the extend relationship can be used only to model additional behavior—it cannot be used for modifying or removing behavior within the base use case. The rationale for this restriction is to make sure that the base use case will not have to be reviewed and approved after the introduction of an extension.

When we extract behavior from a base use case and put it in an extension use case, the base use case must still be complete, understandable, and meaningful in itself. There must not be an apparent hole in the sequence of the base use case; that is, it must not be possible to conclude by just looking at the description of the base use case that there has to be an extension of this use case, because something is apparently missing. Remember that the base use case is independent of any extensions and hence, at least in theory, it must be possible to perform just the base use case without any extension. If the base use case is of no value to the stakeholders without the insertion of an extension, it is not a justifiable use case and the model should be restructured.

Similarly, if the description of the base use case necessitates a reference to an extending use case, it is evident that the extend relationship is inappropriate. Again, the base use case must be independent of the existence of extension use cases. In this situation, two straightforward solutions exist. One is to merge the behavior of the extension use case with the behavior of the base use case. In cases where the extension use case is shared with other base use cases, the solution is to use an include relationship instead of the extend relationship. This is appropriate because in this case the additional parts are referenced from the base use case.

Extension Points

Clearly, it is not enough to state only that the behavior of the extension use case is to be added into the sequence of the base use case. The exact location in the sequence of actions where the extending sequence is to be inserted must also be defined.

A straightforward way to do this is to reference an explicit location in the base use case's sequence. This is how this was done in the early days of use-case modeling. It soon became obvious that an indirect reference would be preferable, however. There were two reasons for this change. One was that to understand where to insert the extending behavior, the use-case modeler must read and understand the detailed description of the base use case to find exactly where the extension was to take place, which is not always an easy task. The other reason was that if the base use case were later to be modified, the explicit reference might prove to have become invalid: The referenced location might have been removed or might no longer be the desired location. Therefore, extension points were introduced.

An *extension point* declared in a use case consists of a *name* and a *reference* to a location in the sequence of actions of the use case where it may be extended (see Figure 8.7). Therefore, the extension point belongs to the base use case, implying that the reference to the exact location in the flow is encapsulated within that use case.

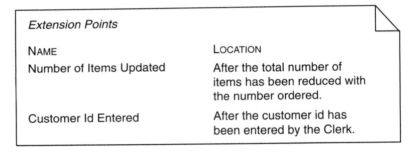

Figure 8.7   Two of the extension points defined in the `Order Item` use case. Each of them has a name and references a location in the flow of the use case.

An extend relationship will now not only identify the extending and the base use cases, but it will also define at which extension point in the base use case the behavior of the extension use case is to be inserted. When an extend relationship is to be added, use-case modelers check the list of extension points declared in the base use case to identify at which point the additional behavior is to be inserted. In this way, they have to read and understand only the extension points, not the complete description of the base use case. Therefore, the use case might be slightly reorganized without affecting the extending use cases. (Of course, a major reorganization of a use case may affect all the use cases that have relationships to it.)

The name of an extension point should describe what happens at this location in the use case, not the actual location in the sequence of actions. In this way, the extension points will be easier to understand and the behavior of the use case will be kept encapsulated. Note that the name of the extension point must not reveal what is to be inserted at that point, because that would make the extended use case dependent on the extending use case!

> In Figure 8.7, the extension points of the use case `Order Item` are enumerated. Assume that this use case is extended with the `Restock Item` use case to check whether the number of items is below a given threshold so that additional items must be purchased. The `Restock Item` use case extends the `Order Item` use case at the point where the total number of the relevant items is updated. A common mistake is to name the extension point *Check for Restocking*, because it indicates what is to be inserted. The proper name states what happens in the base use case, which in this case is *Number of Items Updated*.

Another advantage of extension points, often forgotten, is that they also make it possible in the implementation to prepare for extensions that might occur in the future.

Conditional Extensions

The extend relationship has another useful property: a *condition* is connected to it. This condition determines whether the extension is to be inserted when performance of the use case's flow reaches the extension point referenced by the extend relationship. If the condition then evaluates to true, the extending flow is inserted into the flow of the base use case, and the result is a flow complying with the description of the base use case *and* the description of the extending use case. Again, there is no communication, no calling of other use cases, no delegation, no invoking of other use cases!

The condition can be stated in terms of both values inside the system and events caused by actors of the system. An example of the former is the extend relationship from the `Restock Item` use case in the warehouse model, where the generation of the restocking order takes place only if the number of the specific item is lower than the predefined threshold level (see the left part of Figure 8.8). This indicates that the `Restock Item` extension will not be inserted if the current number of the item exceeds the threshold level.

The warehouse model also contains an example of an extend relationship where the condition is stated in terms of actor interaction. If the customer, when the `Order Item` use case is performed, wants to know the total cost of the items currently ordered, the customer can request that the system calculate the price, for example, by clicking a button. By defining an extend relationship from the `Calculate Price` use case to the `Order Item` use case, and by defining the condition to be *The Customer requests the current total of the order*, we get a model that captures this situation (see the right part of Figure 8.8). If there is a use-case instance performing the sequence of actions described by the `Order Item` use case, and the customer presses the button—that is, requests that the sum total be stated—the condition of the extend relationship is fulfilled, which in turn means that the sequence of `Calculate Price` is inserted into the use-case instance.

The conditions of extend relationships are usually not shown in diagrams, simply because they make the diagrams messy and harder to read, but they may be included if that adds clarity to the diagram.

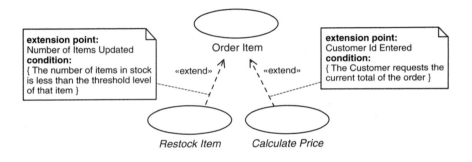

Figure 8.8   An extend relationship has a condition that states under what circumstances the extension is to take place. The condition can include references to information inside the system and to interactions between an actor and the system.

The fact that an extend relationship is conditional has led to the misunderstanding that an extend relationship is appropriate in any situation where the performance of a certain subflow is ruled by a condition. However, a condition is not always as useful an indicator as one might think. Instead, the criterion for determining whether an extend relationship can be used is whether the part proposed to be factored out can be extracted without making the remaining behavior incomplete and therefore not properly expressed as a use case. It turns out that there is often a condition involved where part of the use case can be extracted into an extension use case. For the convenience of the developer, the definition of the extend relationship therefore includes a condition.

Note, however, some extensions' conditions are always true. In the telephone exchange example, `Charging` is always inserted into `Local Call`; therefore, the condition of this extend relationship is *true*. We sometimes see models where the condition in such situations is left out. As always with implicit information like this, the risk for misunderstanding is obvious. We therefore strongly recommend that use-case modelers explicitly state also those cases where the condition is *true*.

Documentation of the Extend Relationship

An extend relationship is documented in the description of the extending use case. Note that this is the only place available, because the base use case must include no information about the extension. The relationship should be documented as part of the flow description, explaining how the insertion is initiated (see Figure 8.9). If the use case is extending several use cases, each extend relationship should be given a paragraph of its own. It should consist of a reference to the use case that is to be extended, a reference to the extension point where the additional behavior is to be inserted, and the condition that must be fulfilled if the extension is to take place.

Likewise, for each base use case the extension use case extends, there is a paragraph at the end of the description of the flow (see Figure 8.9).

Basic Flow

The flow of this use case is inserted into the Order Item use case at the Number of Items Updated extension point if the total number of an item in stock is less than the threshold value of the item.

[…]

The subflow ends and the use-case instance continues according to the Order Item use case after the Number of Items Updated extension point.

Figure 8.9   The description of `Restock Item` includes a description of the extend relationship as a description of where and why the flow is added. The end of the flow description is also slightly affected by the extend relationship.

Apart from the start and the end of the flow, an extension use case is described as an ordinary use case. Note, however, that an extension use case usually models only part of a usage and not a complete usage, implying that an extension use case is often abstract. Just as for inclusion use cases, this means that the flow of an abstract extension use case does not necessarily start with an input from an actor; nor is it required to include any output or to have a well-defined end of the sequence of actions. Just as for include relationships, however, there are exceptions to this rule; see Chapter 19, "Concrete Extension or Inclusion."

The base use case is described as an ordinary use case, and it must not include anything that depends on the fact that there are extension use cases to be inserted into it.

The extension points are defined entirely within the base use case, and they are therefore documented in the description of that use case (see Figure 8.7). This may seem to contradict the fact that the base use case should be independent of any extensions. However, an extension point does not reveal whether something (and if so, what) may be inserted at that extension point. It is therefore very important to assign to extension points names that are completely understandable within the use case itself, and that in a simple way describe their location in the use-case flow.

Dependencies Between Extending Use Cases

As stated previously, the base use case is independent of the extension use cases, and the extension use cases and their extend relationships are defined independently of each other. If more than one extend relationship refers to the same extension point in a use case, it is therefore not possible to deduce in what order the extensions will take place—if at all, depending on the evaluation of their conditions. Consequently, extend relationships can reference the same extension point only if no particular order is required. Otherwise, different extension points must be used, so that the order in which the extension use cases are to be inserted into the base use case is defined by the locations referenced by the extension points (see Figure 8.10).

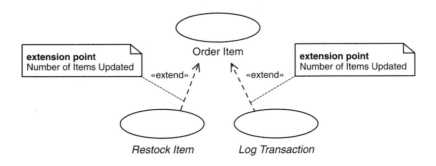

Figure 8.10   The order in which Restock Item and Log Transaction will be inserted into Order Item is not deterministic, because they both reference the same extension point in this model. If the transaction must be logged before the item is restocked, Log Transaction must be inserted at an extension point located at a place defined earlier in the flow than the extension point Number of Items Updated.

CHAPTER 9

INCLUDE VS. EXTEND

It may seem confusing to have two kinds of relationships between use cases that both imply adding a subflow into another flow. However, as described in the two previous chapters, their purposes are very different. The include relationship is intended for reusing behavior modeled by another use case, whereas the extend relationship is intended for adding parts to existing use cases as well as for modeling optional system services.

When modeling behavior common to several use cases, it may at times seem difficult to decide which of the two relationships to choose. The answer to the following question often clarifies whether an include relationship or an extend relationship is to be used: *Which of the two use cases is to be dependent on the other, and which of them must not be dependent on the other* (see Figure 9.1)?

| Log Transaction | Withdraw Money | Check PIN Code |

Figure 9.1   The Withdraw Money use case is dependent on the Check PIN Code use case, but not the reverse. Moreover, the Withdraw Money use case is not dependent on the Log Transaction use case, whereas the latter is dependent on the Withdraw Money use case.

An include relationship is to be used when it must be possible to reuse the extracted behavior in different use cases—that is, when the extracted behavior has to be independent of where it is used. Moreover, the base use case is not complete without the extracted behavior; it is therefore dependent on the existence of the included use case.

The argument for the extend relationship is the opposite: The base use case is complete without the extension use case; it must therefore be defined independently of the existence of the extension use case. Moreover, the extension use case describes an addition to another use case; it is therefore dependent on that use case (the base use case).

The reason for extend being defined with a condition, and include without, is that most cases where include is used are not conditional, whereas most extend situations involve a condition. Therefore, they are defined in this way to support the most common situations.

To sum up the contrast:

- Include is intended for common parts of use cases.
- The base (including) use case is dependent on the inclusion use case, but not vice versa.
- The base use case is not complete without the included use case.

whereas

- Extend is intended for additional parts of use case flows.
- The base (extended) use case is not dependent on the extension, but the extension use case is dependent on the base use case.
- The base use case is—and must be—complete without the extension.

A few words of advice: Do not overuse the extend and the include relationships in your model, because they add to the complexity and to the size of the model. The extension and the inclusion use cases should make it easier to understand and maintain the model. Such a use case should either have an explicit value to the stakeholders, in the same way as ordinary use cases do, or be required by one of the stakeholders. Otherwise, its behavior should be merged into the base use case(s) and the extension/inclusion use case should be removed from the model. Overuse of relationships between use cases results in unnecessarily complex models that are hard to understand.

In the development of a use-case model, postpone all work with the relationships between the use cases until you have produced a first draft of the descriptions of the use cases and therefore can identify the true commonalities (and not imagined ones). Of course, if there are explicit requirements that two services must share a common part, or if you are positive you know what you are doing, add the relationships directly and just make sure to confirm them when you are producing the use-case descriptions. However, we have seen too many examples of projects introducing relationships between use cases just for the sake of it. Our advice is this: When in doubt, skip relationships between the use cases until you have identified and described all the concrete use cases and their actors (see also Chapter 26, "Use-Case Sequence").

CHAPTER 10

MORE ON EXTEND AND EXTENSION POINTS

This chapter describes some additional ways of using the extend relationship that might be relevant for the advanced use-case modeler. If you do not have special needs or a special interest in the extend relationship, it is safe to skip this chapter.

Multiple Fragments of Additional Behavior

When extending a use case with additional behavior, one sometimes becomes aware that it would be a mistake to insert all of it at one location in the flow of the base use case. Instead, only one part of the additional behavior should be inserted at one location of the base use case and the other parts at other locations in the same use case. There are a number of situations that will show the validity of this procedure. The classical situation arises when the additional behavior is to measure a period of time in the performance of the base use case.

For example, consider the Charging use case in the telephone exchange example. Its sequence of actions consists of two subflows. One flow describes the initiation and the start of the time measurement, which should be performed when connection has been established and the subscribers start to communicate. The other describes stopping the clock, calculating the duration of the call, and adding the resulting charge to the balance of the caller. This latter subflow should be performed when one of the subscribers hangs up, thereby interrupting their communication.

It would obviously be pointless to insert all of this behavior at one location so that the second subflow follows directly on the first, because then the clock would stop immediately after starting, which would result in no charge at all. Instead, we need two extension points so that we can separate the two subflows and insert them at the relevant locations (see Figure 10.1).

Charging

Basic Flow

PART 1

The use case is always inserted into the Local Call use case.

This part is inserted at the Callee Answers extension point.

The measuring of time is started.

The subflow ends and the use-case instance continues according to the Local Call use case after the Callee Answers extension point.

PART 2

This part is inserted at the Disconnect Call extension point.

The measuring of time is stopped, the cost is calculated based on the direction of the call, and the caller is charged for the call.

The subflow ends and the use-case instance continues according to the Local Call use case after the Disconnect Call extension point.

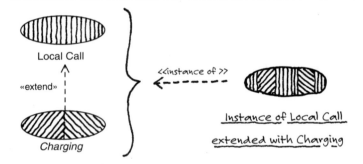

Figure 10.1   The sequence of an extension use case can be divided in several parts, to be inserted at different extension points in the base use case.

Here we have two subflows in the extension use case that are to be inserted at separate extension points—in the general case, there can be any number of subflows that are to be inserted at a corresponding number of extension points. These subflows are dependent of each other in the sense that if we insert the first subflow at the first extension point, all the other subflows must be inserted at their extension points as well, or the extension will not be complete. On the other hand, if for some reason the first part is not inserted, the other parts will not be inserted either. This means that the extend relationship's condition is checked only once: when the use-case instance reaches the first extension point. If the condition is evaluated to *true, all* the subflows of the extension use case are inserted at their extension points. Similarly, if the condition evaluates to *false* at the first extension point, nothing at all will be inserted, not even if evaluation of the condition were to result in *true* at some of the other extension points.

Multiple Insertions

Can one and the same extension use case be inserted at two different places in the same base use case? The answer is quite obvious, although it may come as a surprise to some. Every extend relationship states when and where the extension is to take place. (The time is expressed in the condition and the location in the sequence of references to extension points.) From this follows that one extension use case can be inserted multiple times in the same base use case, but a separate extend relationship must be defined for each insertion (see Figure 10.2).

As mentioned in the section *Documentation of the Extend Relationship* in Chapter 8, "Extend: Expanding Existing Use Cases," each extend relationship is documented in a separate paragraph in the flow of the extension use case.

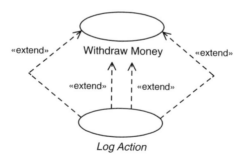

Figure 10.2   The Log Action use case extends the Withdraw Money use case multiple times, each at its own extension point.

In an ATM, most actions are logged. This acts as a precaution-
ary measure in that it makes it possible for the bank to check
what happened in a situation when something went wrong. In
our use-case model of the ATM, there is one use-case Log
Action that models the logging of an action. This use case
extends the Withdraw Money use case at four locations: when the
PIN code has been checked, when the transaction has been sent
to the bank, when the answer is received from the bank, and
when the money has been dispensed. At each one of these locations, the whole Log Action use case is inserted, not just fractions of it.

In our model, we therefore define four extend relationships
from the Log Action use case to the Withdraw Money use case.
Each of these extend relationships references its own extension
point in Withdraw Money and has its own condition stating if the
extension is to take place.

Of course, it is possible to define a graphic shorthand in this situation.
Instead of drawing multiple dashed arrows from the ellipse denoting the
extension use case to the ellipse denoting the base use case, we can draw
just one. To make it clear that this arrow denotes multiple relationships,
the condition and the sequence of references to the extension points of
each extend relationship are stated in a note that is attached to the dashed
arrow. Hence, there will be multiple notes attached to such a shorthand
arrow (see Figure 10.3).

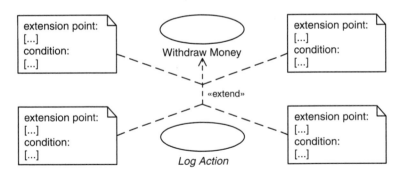

Figure 10.3   A shorthand for the Log Action use case extending the Withdraw
Money use case at multiple extension points.

More on Extension Points

A useful property of an extension point, although no longer defined in UML, is that it can reference a collection of locations in the flow and not only a single location. An extension referencing such an extension point can take place in any of the locations referenced by the extension point; it is not necessary to define one extension point for each of these locations. Without this property, the description of the extend relationship would have to be much more complicated.

In the ATM example, suppose that we want to register every transaction with the bank where the response is not received within 5 seconds. We start by modeling the registration as a separate use case called Log Delayed Transaction.

Let us look at the locations in the Withdraw Money use case where the Log Delayed Transaction can be inserted (refer to Figure 4.1). There are two transactions with the bank, namely when the bank is notified that the withdrawal is to take place, and when the bank is notified that there is not enough cash left for another withdrawal. Do we need two extension points, then? No, we define one extension point called *Bank Transaction* in the Withdraw Money use case. We then let this extension point reference *all* the locations in the use case's sequences of actions where the use case communicates with the bank system. In this case, we do not even have to list them, because we can easily characterize them (see Figure 10.4).

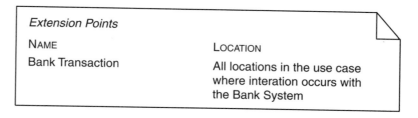

Extension Points

NAME

Bank Transaction

LOCATION

All locations in the use case where interation occurs with the Bank System

Figure 10.4   An extension point can reference several locations in the sequence of actions of the use case.

Finally, we define the extend relationship from the `Log Delayed Transaction` use case to the `Withdraw Money` use case. We state that the condition of the relationship is *The response from the bank is not received within 5 seconds* and that the extension is to take place at the `Bank Transaction` extension point (see Figure 10.5). Because this extension point references multiple locations in the `Withdraw Money` use case, the extension will take place at any of these locations if the condition is fulfilled when the execution of `Withdraw Money` gets there.

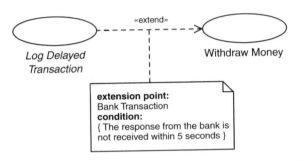

Figure 10.5   `Log Delayed Transaction` extends the `Withdraw Money` use case at one extension point.

In this example, it first seemed as though we would have had to refer to several extension points in the `Withdrawal` use case, but by the definition of the `Bank Transaction` extension point, we need to use only one extension point, and its definition refers to all the locations where the extension can be performed.

Note that an extend relationship referencing an extension point that in turn points to several locations in the flow like this cannot define different conditions for the different locations.

In other words, several extension points are used when an extending use case is to be *split* over several places in the extended flow. When, on the other hand, the *whole* of an extension can be inserted at several places, this can be modeled using only one extension point. The advantage is that we will not have to modify the extend relationship if the base use case is modified so that new locations become relevant insertion points or so that existing locations are removed. We just have to update the definition of the extension point.

In fact, an extension point can even be defined as a region. An extend relationship referring such an extension point implies that the extension may take place whenever the condition is true between two places in the extended flow. For example, in the `Local Call` use case in the telephone exchange example, the `Caller` can hang up and terminate the call at any time before the `Callee` answers the call. If an extension use case is to be inserted if the `Caller` hangs up before the call has been answered, the extension point will reference this region—that is, from the beginning of `Local Call` to the point just before the `Callee` answers the call. In general, an extension point may be a combination of these variants—that is, consist of a set of distinct points and a set of intervals in the extended flow.

When the flow of an extension is to be split over several extension points, only the first of these extension points (the one where the condition is checked) may be referencing more than one location. The reason for this is that as soon as the condition has been checked, all the extension parts are to be inserted at their respective extension points; therefore, all of them must at that moment reference well-defined locations. The location of the first insertion is defined by the condition being evaluated to *true* at that location within the first extension point; as we have seen before, however, no more condition checking is performed. If one of the subsequent extension points were referencing multiple locations, it would not be clear where the corresponding extension part should be inserted.

Multiple Extend Relationships Versus Complex Extension Points

The observant reader may have noticed that a potential overlap exists between using several extend relationships to one use case and using one extend relationship referencing one extension point that will refer several locations in the description of the flow of that use case. This situation occurs when one extension should be inserted at several places in one base use case. In this situation, it is possible to define extension points for each such place and then define an extend relationship for each extension point. However, would not one extend relationship referencing one extension point, which in its turn references all these locations, also do the trick?

The answer is yes, if the condition for the extension to take place is the same for all locations. If there is a different condition for each location, however, there must be one extend relationship for each location, because the condition is connected to the relationship. In the latter case, there will be one extension point in the base use case for each of the extend relationships.

Another situation when several extend relationships are to be used is when extension points are already defined in the base use case for each of the possible insertion locations. In that case, it is normally better to use them as they are instead of defining an extra extension point referencing all the locations. In this way, there will not be an unnecessary change of the base use case. Of course, this has to be weighed against the disadvantage of having several relationships to maintain in the model.

CHAPTER 11

USE-CASE GENERALIZATION: CLASSIFICATION AND INHERITANCE

Generalization Between Use Cases

In a use-case model, sometimes several use cases model the same kind of usages. For example, there will be different kinds of account transactions in an ATM, such as deposit and withdrawal, or different kinds of telephone calls between subscribers in a telephone exchange. To capture that a collection of use cases model the same kind of usage of the system, we introduce a new use case into the model. In this new use case, we provide a general description of this kind of usage, stating that it describes the commonalities and the general pattern of this usage. Then we define generalization relationships from the other use cases to this new use case stating that they are specializations of the new use case (see Figure 11.1). The use case capturing the commonalities is called the *parent* use case, and the specializing use cases are called the *children*, just as with ordinary generalization relationships. However, it is important that all the children express the same kind of usage of the system as the parent, because in UML, generalization is a taxonomy relationship.

Usually such a parent use case is abstract; that is, it is not instantiable on its own. It is only used to capture the common nature of its children.

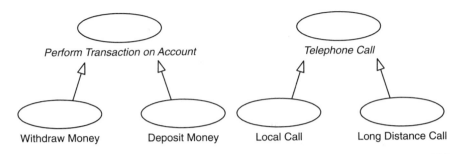

Figure 11.1   Classification of use cases using generalization to the use case
expressing the commonalities. Because the parent use cases are
abstract in these two examples, their names are in italic.

In this way, the model becomes easier for the readers to understand
because they can immediately discern the commonalities. Another
advantage is that the children use cases do not have to duplicate things
described in the parent use case, which means that their definitions do
not have to start from scratch. Another way of putting this is to say that
we enforce the sequence of actions from the parent use case onto the children; that is, the children must exhibit the same kind of usage as the parent. When capturing the requirements of, say, the ATM system, we can,
by use of the generalization, require that the Deposit Money and the
Withdraw Money use cases must follow the same kind of sequence of
actions, and this sequence is defined in the Perform Transaction on
Account use case. This means that the children use cases include the same
behavior as the parent. In the children use cases, we can specialize that
behavior as well as add new behavior, as long as the children are still
modeling the same kind of usage as the parent (see Figure 11.2).
However, on no account must we remove behavior in a child use case or
reorganize the sequence of actions.

Note, finally, that a generalization between two use cases implies that the
whole parent use case is inherited—that is to say, not only the normal
flow, but also all the alternative flows are inherited. If only part of the parent is to be reused, generalization is not the correct relationship. Instead,
consider extracting that particular part into a separate use case and use an
include or an extend relationship between the two old use cases and the
new use case.

Documentation of the Generalization Relationship Between Use Cases

In the description of a child use case, we may choose between two ways of describing the actions defined in the parent. Formally speaking, all the actions of the parent appear in the child as well. However, we do not duplicate the description of what is defined in the parent unless needed (cf. generalization between classes). For use cases, this usually means that the description of the child use case includes some kind of references to the description of the parent use case implying that *this specific piece of behavior described in the parent use case is to be performed here in the child* (see Figure 11.2).

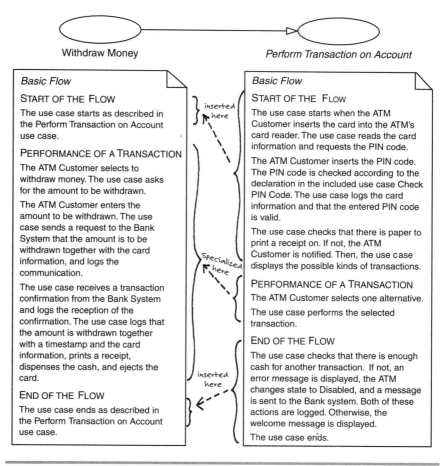

Figure 11.2   The sequence of actions of Withdraw Money starts and ends as described in Perform Transaction on Account, and specializes the middle part. The headings do not add any behavior, but only serve to clarify the structure.

In the use-case descriptions in Figure 11.2, we have included extra headings into the text. These have no formal meaning, and add nothing to the flows themselves, but are added to make it easier to see the common structure of the flows. This is entirely optional, of course, but may in fact prove useful in more situations than just use-case generalizations. When a use-case description is long, for example, inserting headings such as these can be very useful to readers as well as writers of the description.

When the interleaving of reused and new/redefined text is very fine-grained, it is sometimes more efficient for both the reader and the writer if the description of the parent is in fact duplicated in the child, and then any new behavior is inserted into the description, and any specializing behavior replaces corresponding inherited behavior.

CHAPTER 12

ACTOR GENERALIZATION: OVERLAPPING ROLES

Frequently, multiple actors have associations with the same use case. For example, in the ATM example, both the ATM Customer and the Bank System are associated with the Withdraw Money use case. From the use case's point of view, it is clear that there are two external entities interacting with it—these two entities play different roles toward the use case (see Figure 12.1).

Figure 12.1   A use case can have associations with more than one actor.

If only one external user is involved in the usage, however, only one actor is to be associated with the use case. Therefore, as soon as actors overlap—that is, they model the same role toward a specific use case (or a set of use cases) they are associated with—there is need for another actor to represent this overlapping role. This is because, as you may recall from Chapter 5, "Modeling the System Environment," the actors represent how the system perceives its surroundings. Saying that two or more actors play the same role toward a use case is precisely the same as saying that the use case perceives them as one; that is, it is impossible for the use case to see any difference between these actors (see Figure 12.2). Hence, from the use case's point of view, there is just one actor playing this role, implying that the role should be represented by one actor.

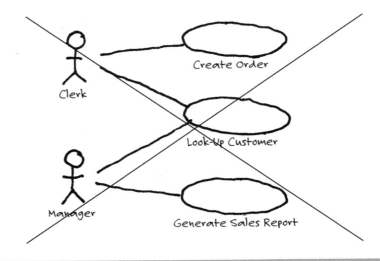

Figure 12.2   This diagram gives the impression that the Look-Up Customer
use case interacts with two different actors when it is performed,
which is not the case.

Generalization is used to express that an actor incorporates the role defined
by another actor. This is, in fact, the only kind of relationship that exists
between actors. The actor modeling the common or shared role is called
the *parent* actor, and the one incorporating the shared role is called the
child. The relationship implies that a user playing the role defined by the
child actor interacts not only with those use cases that the actor itself is
associated with, but also with those use cases that the parent actor is associated with (see Figure 12.3). In other words, a child actor inherits the
capability to communicate with use cases its parent actor is associated
with, according to the description of those use cases (see also Chapter 23,
"Multiple Actors").

A parent actor is more often than not abstract, because there are usually no
individuals playing that specific role; as a rule, only the roles of the children are concrete. However, there are cases in which both the parent and
the children roles are concrete. This usually occurs when the actors are
quite close to business roles. This is in itself no error, but calls for an extra
check that this is not the only way security levels are captured in the model
(see Chapter 5, "Modeling the System Environment," Chapter 27, "Access
Control," and Chapter 44, "Mistake: Security Levels with Actors").

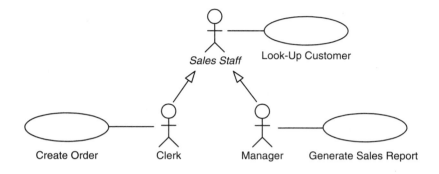

Figure 12.3   Both the Clerk and the Manager can create orders, but from the use case's point of view only one actor is involved.

Generalizations between actors should only be introduced when it is clear that two actors are overlapping—that is, they play the same role toward a specific use case or a group of use cases.

Remember that actors define how the system perceives its surroundings; they do not model the roles of the business in which the system takes part (see Chapter 5). A common mistake is to introduce an actor representing a certain business role with no association of his/her own, but equipped with generalizations to all the actors interacting with the use cases that are of interest to that particular business role. Such an actor only adds to the size of the model.

CHAPTER 13

Describing Use Cases

Documenting Use Cases

After the use cases have been identified, they must be described in detail. It must be stated what sequences of actions they represent, what external events will cause the various sequences to be performed, and so on. Without a more detailed description of the use cases, a use case will not be more than a named ellipse, which in most cases is not enough as a specification of the usage of the system. A Use-Case Description document should be prepared for each use case in the use-case model. How to describe the use-case model as a whole is discussed in the next chapter (Chapter 14, "Documenting a Use-Case Model").

The use cases themselves can be documented in many different ways. The most common way to document a use case is using ordinary text describing the different sequences of actions (the basic flow and the different variants). There are two major reasons for this. One is that this form is the easiest way to present the behavior of a use case to other people, especially to nontechnical people. The other reason is that if a more formal technique is used for documenting the sequences of the use cases, the overall usage may be lost behind the technical details. Furthermore, it is usually more difficult and time-consuming to use such a formal technique. More detailed descriptions of the system are instead provided in the other kinds of models prepared for the system at hand.

Other kinds of description techniques that can be useful for describing a use case include state machines, activity diagrams, Petri net, operations, and sequence diagrams. Also other techniques may prove useful depending on the required level of formalism as well as any specific needs of the readers and other stakeholders. It is the intended use of the use-case descriptions that must guide which technique to use. If in doubt, we recommend describing the use cases with ordinary, structured text.

However, to produce a good description requires some proficiency in writing. Answering a few relevant questions is clearly a good strategy as a starting point for the use-case description. Some of the most important questions for the use-case description writer to bear in mind are as follows:

- **What is the purpose of the use case?** The name of the use case is usually not enough to make people understand which flow is modeled by the use case. Even though most people will get a general idea of the use case by just reading the name, their interpretations might differ considerably. A short description (two to five sentences) will serve as an overview of the use case and help focus on what is important in the full description.

- **Which is the audience of the description?** Depending on the background of the reader, different amounts of detail and explanation must be included in the description. An experienced user of a similar system will probably need less explanation than a newcomer. A developer will need more details than a user representative.

- **How many descriptions will there be of the use case?** If only one description is to be produced, it must include all the information that anyone might be interested in. On the other hand, the description can be more focused on a subset of the stakeholders if multiple descriptions are to be used (see also Chapter 25, "Orthogonal Views").

- **Which level of abstraction is to be chosen?** It is quite possible to include all the minor details of the flows in the description, but who will be interested in them at this stage? In our experience, you should include only those details that the reader will need to grasp what the use case does. It is therefore important that you know whom you are addressing. Will the description be used when realizing the use case? If so, all the actions performed by the system must be included, such as business logic, error cases, and information handled in the use case. If the use case is to be mapped onto a collection of subsystems, the description can be given at rather a high level of abstraction because more detailed use cases will be identified and described within each subsystem (see also Chapter 18, "Component Hierarchy"). Is the description meant to be used only in discussions with management and users of the system? Then most details of what happens inside the system may be left out, and only details that can be perceived from the outside of the system should be described.

- **Is a black-box, gray-box, or a white-box description to be produced?** This is similar to the preceding point. Should the description only describe the actions that can be perceived by the actors (black-box), should all actions except those having to do with the internal structure be captured (gray-box; the most common one), or should every action performed by the system be described (white-box)? For example, in the `Withdraw Money` use case in the ATM example, the user is aware of actions regarding validating the card and the PIN code, reducing the balance, and dispensing the money. However, the system will in fact also log every transaction, so that, in case something goes wrong, the bank will be able to track what happened, which may be of little or no interest to the user of the ATM when withdrawing money. At the most detailed level (white-box), the creation and deletion of instances inside the system as well as their interaction can also be captured. However, the white-box view is usually a description of the realization of the use case. Chapter 25 contains a more thorough discussion.

- **How formal should the description be?** Here the term *formal* is not used about a type of language. Instead, it refers to the manner in which the text is presented. In a small project where a one-time application is developed with project members who are familiar with each other, a more informal manner of style can be used. In large projects with distributed development and multiple iterations in which is developed a product that is to exist in many different versions, a much more formal style must be used, to make sure that all of its information is captured and available to all the team members. Another parameter is whether this is the first time the team is developing this kind of product (in which case, all the details must be captured) or if they have produced use-case models earlier (in which case, the descriptions can be made more abstract—but bear in mind that the next version of the product may be developed by another, less-experienced team).

After these questions have been answered and documented in a style guide, possibly accompanied by an example of a use-case description and a glossary, it is time to start writing. Unless the use case is very short and can be described right away, it is generally considered helpful to start by enumerating the major actions of the normal performance of the use case, beginning with what the actor does to start the use case. Next comes the system's response to that initiating stimulus, which is to be followed by the descriptions of the main actions and the communications from the system to the environment. All the details do not have to be included at this stage; the goal is an outline (see Figure 13.1).

In a ticketing system for airline tickets, a clerk can use the system to register information about customers, to find information about flights, and to register payment and issue tickets. One of the use cases is called Order Ticket, which assists the clerk in registering the flights requested by a customer, assigning seats, and creating the corresponding ticket.

- The Clerk registers the information about the customer.
- The Clerk enters the requested flights and their departure dates.
- The use case checks that there is a seat available. If so, it is booked.
- The Clerk accepts the order, and the use case creates a new ticket and presents a confirmation number to the Clerk.

Figure 13.1   An example of the first draft of the description of the use case Order Ticket in an airline ticketing system.

After the first draft has been produced, it should be discussed with the different stakeholders to make sure they all agree on the purpose of the use case and the intended sequence of actions.

After this discussion, the description can be expanded with additional details. This also includes handling all the complementing alternatives to the choices made in the flow. If the basic flow includes what is to be done if a check evaluates to *true*, there must also be a description of what happens if the check evaluates to *false*. Unless the alternative flow is very short, it should be placed in a separate subsection.

Following is an example of a use-case description, including a summary of the use case in the Brief Description section, a Basic Flow description, and descriptions of Alternative Flows.

Note that the purpose of the use-case descriptions in this book is to provide an understanding of the use-case concept and how to describe use cases as well as an understanding of the different patterns and blueprints. These use-case descriptions are what we would expect to find in an industrial project, although they are somewhat simplified regarding details and functionality unnecessary for understanding the pattern or blueprint. In addition, the alternative flows are often fewer and shorter than normal because we do not want the examples to diverge because of exceptions and error handling.

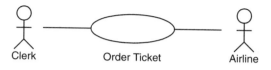

Figure 13.2   The Order Ticket use case interacts with two actors.

Use Case: Order Ticket

Brief Description

The Clerk registers a new ticket in the system, and the included flights are booked at the Airlines.

Basic Flow

The use case starts when the Clerk chooses to register a new ticket. The use case asks the Clerk for the name and address of the customer.

The Clerk enters the requested information, and the use case checks whether the customer is already registered. If so, the Clerk is notified if the customer is a VIP customer and how many tickets the customer has bought in the past 12 months.

The use case asks what flights are to be included in the ticket, their origin and destination, or whether a search for a flight should be made.

- The Clerk enters the selected flight number, the origin and the destination, and the departure date and time.
- If the Clerk instead chooses to search for a flight, the Look Up Flight use case is included.

For each flight:

The use case sends a booking request to the Airline.

If the Airline returns a confirmation number, the use case includes it in the reservation. If the Airline instead returns a reservation failure, the Clerk is notified and the flight is not included in the reservation.

The use case presents the complete reservation to the Clerk, and asks for a confirmation from the Clerk.

The Clerk confirms the reservation. The use case registers a new ticket and stores the name and address of the customer together with the flights, the dates, and the seats. The name of the Clerk is retrieved from the system and stored. Finally, a reservation number is displayed to the Clerk, and the use case asks the Clerk for acknowledgement.

The Clerk acknowledges the reservation number.

The use case ends.

Alternative Flows

NO CONNECTION WITH AIRLINE

If the connection with the Airline cannot be established, the Clerk is notified and the flight is not included in the ticket. The use case continues with the next flight.

NO FLIGHT

If no flights have been included in the ticket when it is to be registered, the Clerk is notified and no reservation is created. The use case continues by asking what flights are to be included.

RESERVATION CANCELED

If the Clerk chooses not to confirm the reservation, the use case asks for a confirmation of the cancellation.

If the cancellation confirmation is received from the Clerk, the reservation is removed from the system, any booked flight is canceled, and the use case ends. If the cancellation is discarded, the use case continues by asking for confirmation of the reservation.

It is important to remember to include exceptional cases, for example, if no communication connection can be established with an actor, perhaps because the network suddenly breaks down, or if part of the information could not be stored in the system, perhaps because the database management system times out, and so on. Situations of this type are often forgotten in the description of the use cases. Obviously, it will cause the implementer a great deal of trouble to decide how to solve them. Even worse, they could even cause the system to break down because no solutions have been implemented. A typical example of such an exceptional case is the flow *No Connection with Airline* in the preceding description.

What most people experience when they start describing their use cases is that the work often comes to a halt. They do not know what to write! This has nothing to do with being uncomfortable writing descriptions (although that might be a problem as well). Instead, they are—far too often—not clear about what the system should actually do. The paramount need of having access to people with the right business expertise and the authority to make decisions cannot be stressed enough!

When producing the first draft, the main focus should be on describing the flow of the use case and possibly identifying any questions, not to answer them. Experts on the business and its usage of the system as well as experts on technology should also be brought into the project at this stage to answer questions that arise. It is much easier to schedule meetings with these persons at this stage instead of trying to find them and have them answer single questions on a number of occasions during the project. If proper use-case descriptions are not produced, most problems will not pop up until at a late stage in the project. Then, usually an implementer writing the code must solve the problem, while the deadline is approaching quickly.

After description of the use case has been produced, it must be reviewed to make sure it captures the correct flow. Obvious reviewers are the end users and the customer (or the product owner, if the system is developed by the same organization that will use it). Other reviewers who are relevant in the review process include developers and testers to make sure the description includes enough details, architects to make sure the use case utilizes the different parts of the system in a correct way, and usability experts to ensure that the interaction between the actors and the use case is suitable and satisfactory.

Guidelines for Writing

This section provides some guidelines to be used when writing a use-case description. You can use them as a starting point for a project style guide.

- **Use a consistent style**—Use common words and phrases in short sentences when describing the flow. The text will be easier to read and understand.

- **Prepare a template and an example**—It will be easier to produce uniform descriptions.

- **Use subsections**—When organizing the text, use subsections in the same way as you do when writing other text. The text will be much easier to read.

- **Describe the flow as something that actually happens**—Even if the system has not been built yet, describe the flow as something that actually happens to make it easier for the reader to get an idea of the system.

- **Use the active voice**—To make it clear who initiates the interaction, the system or an actor, use an active voice writing style.

- **Always use the name of the actor in the interaction**—Do *not* just write "the actor." This makes it clear which actor is involved.

- **Capitalize the names of the actors**—This will make it clear that you are referring to an actor and not to some information about the actor inside the system.

- **Use short paragraphs with one input**—A paragraph should contain no more than one actor input, which should be given as the first sentence. This makes the text more structured and readable.

- **Be explicit about what information is sent, received, stored, and so on**—Never use phrases such as *store the information about X* unless you are referring to information explicitly stated one or two sentences back. Otherwise, the reader will have no clue what information you are referring to.

- **State business rules explicitly**—In a separate section in the use-case description or in a separate document to be used in all use-case descriptions, state business rules explicitly. Reference these business rules in the description of the flow. This will make the text much easier to read, and the business rules can be maintained and enhanced separately.

- **Create separate sections for details**—If there are many information attributes, list all the details in a separate section of the use-case description that can be referenced from the description of the flow. In this way, the description of the flow will not be cluttered with a lot of details that disturb the understanding of the flow. If the same information attributes are used in several use cases, put them in a separate document and treat them in the same way as business rules.

- **Identify nonfunctional requirements**—State nonfunctional requirements explicitly in a separate section of the use-case description or in a separate document to be used in all use-case descriptions.

- **Do not mention GUI design details in the flow**—For example, do not identify characteristics of the GUI such as drop-down lists, lists of radio buttons or check buttons, or text fields. The GUI design will most likely be changed in a later version of the system, and if no mention is made, the use-case descriptions need not be modified.

- **Do not mention design or implementation details in the flow**—Avoid using terms such as *applet*, *database*, and *process*. This would restrain the designers using the use-case model as input to making design decisions. Changing the implementation technology should not imply changes in the descriptions of the use cases. Furthermore, the use-case model will become more general this way. For example, the same use case can be used for presenting information on a web page as well as on a mobile phone screen.

- **Specify information retrieval and calculation means**—Be explicit about how information handled in the use case is retrieved or calculated.

- **Confirm enough details are included**—Make sure the description contains enough details so it is possible to produce a use-case realization based on it, to estimate time and resources, and to identify all major architecture components.

- **Describe long loops separately**—Describe the body of a loop directly in the flow only if it is short (less than half a page). Otherwise, put it in a separate subsection. If not, the overview of the flow will be lost.

- **Define long alternatives separately**—Describe the alternatives in a condition in the flow only if they are short (less than a third of a page). Otherwise, put them in separate subsections.

- **Specify where use case ends**—Explicitly state that the use case ends at the appropriate place(s) in the flow description.

- **Avoid cross-references**—*Never* reference (sub-) sections in other use-case descriptions. These may be modified later, which will make references outdated.

- **Reference extension points of other use cases**—When defining an extend relationship to another use case, only reference extension points of that use case. The flow or the description of the flow of that use case might be reorganized later, which will make other references obsolete.

- **Reference logical locations within a use case**—Never reference paragraph numbers or line numbers. These will be modified. Reference locations defined by the state of the use case or (sub-) sections within the use-case description instead; these are more stable.

- **Do not use explicitly tagged keywords**—The text will be harder to maintain, and the reader is most likely not a programmer and therefore not used to the notion of keywords.

- **Prepare a glossary of words and terms**—This glossary is to be used by persons producing use-case descriptions, which means that the same terminology will be used in all the descriptions. Furthermore, the reader can look up the precise meaning of a word in this particular model and project.

- **Diagram complex flows**—If the flow is complicated, prepare a state diagram or activity diagram to make it easier to follow the text.

- **Diagram nontrivial cases**—In nontrivial cases, prepare one diagram for each use case, showing the use case in the middle of the diagram and all the elements it has relationships with in a circle around it together with the relationships. Put the actor initiating the use case on the same side of the use case from which you start to read. Included and parent use cases are normally put at the top of the circle.

How include, extend, and generalization relationships to other use cases affect the description of the flow is described in the *Documentation of . . .* sections of the chapters presenting these relationships.

Sections of a Use-Case Description

The core of a use-case description is, of course, the description of the sequences of actions. What else is to be included in the document depends largely on the needs of the project, the documentation standard of the organization, and so forth. Therefore, it is difficult to present a universal template for this kind of document. However, some sections tend to occur in most use-case descriptions, as shown in Figure 13.3.

```
1.  Brief Description
2.  Relationships
3.  Extension Points
4.  Basic Flow
5.  Alternative Flows
6.  Special Requirements
```

Figure 13.3   Commonly used sections of a use-case description.

The *Brief Description* consists of two to three sentences that summarize the usage modeled by the use case. Apart from the flow description itself, this is the most important section of the document, and must not be excluded. Mention at least the initiating actor so that the reader understands the context of the use case. If the use case is abstract, this should be stated here.

The next section, *Relationships*, presents the context of the use case in the use-case model—that is, what relationships the use case has to other use cases and to actors. Often this is done by including a diagram showing the use case surrounded by all use cases and actors it has relationships with.

This kind of diagram, showing the use-case model as seen from the viewpoint of one of its elements (in this case, a use case) is sometimes called a *local diagram* of the model.

The diagram may be replaced by a textual description, in which case this section usually has subsections for the different kinds of relationships the use case has with other elements.

For extend relationships, not only the use case at the other end of the relationship should be stated here but also the condition and the extension point of the base use case. Note that an extend relationship is documented only in the description of the extension use case—that is, not in the base use case because this is to be independent of the extension!

Of course, the opposite goes for include relationships, which are documented only in the base use case, not in the inclusion use case. An include relationship is fully described here by just stating which use case is included.

The description of associations with actors should include multiplicities, if such are to be used in the project (see the section *Interaction Between Use Cases and Actors* in Chapter 5, "Modeling the System Environment").

Different conventions for the *Relationships* section can be applied, such as not including the section at all for use cases with a very simple context (for example, consisting of only one association to an initiating actor). On the other end of the scale, for use cases with extremely complex surroundings, it might be convenient to include both a diagram and a textual list of the relationships with their characteristics. The drawback is that there will be more documentation to maintain and keep in sync. Another option is to skip the *Relationships* section and instead include a diagram as an appendix of the use-case description.

The *Extension Points* section is used when relevant, defining all extension points in terms of name and location in the flow. Remember to keep the extension point locally defined; that is, the name must not indicate what is expected to be added at the extension point. Also avoid referring to labels such as numbered sections in the flow description.

There may be multiple flows in the *Basic Flow* section of a use-case description. These flows are of the same significance, which will make it impossible or inappropriate to refer to one of them as basic and to the others as alternative. Instead, you can number them Basic Flow 1, Basic Flow 2, and so on. Even better would be to name the different flows in a descriptive manner (for example, Update Order and Delete Order). It is also wise to enumerate all those flows at the top of the *Basic Flow* section so that it becomes clear to the reader from the start that there are multiple basic flows.

Depending on the characteristics of the different flows of a use case, you can use different headings in the subsequent sections, such as *Alternative Flows, Exceptional Flows,* and so forth. Use only necessary headings and exclude the rest!

Use-case descriptions often include a final section called *Special Requirements*. Any requirements regarding this use case that are not naturally included in the flow descriptions can be listed here. In particular, this includes nonfunctional requirements, such as requirements on response time, time out, number of concurrent users, and so on. Many projects prefer to collect all such requirements in a separate document; if so, this section is excluded.

Apart from the sections listed here, which are used in most use-case descriptions, you can add others when needed. One example is to include sections for pre- and postconditions. A *precondition* describes in which state the system is when the use case is to be initiated. Its purpose is to set the context for a reader of a use-case description. Note that it does not state a condition that the system will check before enabling the use case. All actions to be performed by the system, including checks whether a condition is fulfilled or not, must be included in the flows of the use case. A *postcondition* is similar to a precondition, but it tells the reader the state in which the system is after the use case ends.

Note that the postcondition describes all possible end states of the use case, including the error states, and not only the state reached when ending successfully; whereas the precondition describes the state in which all possible flows of the use cases can be initiated. Obviously, you can use pre- and postconditions when describing single sequences within a use case.

Another example is a section enumerating all outstanding issues that are to be resolved. With this section, you can keep all questions together with the description without cluttering up the description of the flow. At the end of the project, the section is (hopefully) empty, and you can remove it when finalizing the documentation.

In general, additional techniques like using paragraph numbers in the description of the flow can be used during the development of a use-case description.

CHAPTER 14

DOCUMENTING A USE-CASE MODEL

Because the behavior captured by a use-case model is made up of its contained use cases, it will be fully documented by the descriptions of these use cases (see Chapter 13, "Describing Use Cases"). However, mainly for practical reasons, the documentation of a use-case model as a whole is usually complemented by a few more documents.

In general, the purpose of these documents is to give an overview of the model, both its structural and behavioral contents. It is therefore customary to produce a Use-Case Model Survey document as well as a set of Use-Case Diagrams.

Use-Case Model Survey

A Use-Case Model Survey is a text document whose main part consists of brief descriptions of each use case contained in the model, as well as of all its actors. The Use-Case Model Survey should also contain a concise *Introduction* to the model as a whole, describing the purpose of the system and pointing out the core use cases matching the main purpose of the system being modeled (see Figure 14.1). This is normally given in terms of half to one page of text in a separate section at the beginning of the document. Therefore, when approaching a system modeled with use cases, this is the first document to read; it gives a brief introduction to the system and to its use cases.

```
┌─────────────────────────────────┐
│  1.  Introduction               │
│                                 │
│  2.  Actors                     │
│                                 │
│  3.  Use Cases                  │
│                                 │
└─────────────────────────────────┘
```

Figure 14.1   The main sections of a Use-Case Model Survey.

Actors, the next section of the document, includes brief descriptions of all the actors in the model. Because actors represent entities outside the system in focus, in other words by definition outside our control, there is not much that can be said about them. However, it is very important to capture for each of them precisely what their role is toward the system, so that there is no risk of ambiguity. Therefore, we should provide a paragraph consisting of one to three sentences for each actor, always remembering to focus on its role toward the system. This is not as easy as one might think. Often these short descriptions tend to describe the role in the organization as a whole represented by the actor, which is in fact more or less irrelevant in our case because we should focus on the system. It is possible to avoid this error by writing two paragraphs for each actor, one focusing on the role in the organization and one on the role we are actually interested in. Normally, the former can be omitted in the final document, but in some cases it provides information to the readers of the document that will make the model easier to understand. It is important, however, to make sure that the difference between the two roles is made clear.

The last section, *Use Cases,* which makes up the bulk of the Use-Case Model Survey, contains brief introductory descriptions of each use case in the model. This is also where we describe the pattern and blueprint usage in the model. As an introduction to this section, we list the use-case patterns and blueprints that have been applied, together with explanations when appropriate. This will give the reader a better understanding of the rationale behind the structuring and descriptions of the model.

The description of a use case in the Use-Case Model Survey document and the brief description in the Use-Case Description document of that use case should be identical. This section of the Survey will therefore, in essence, be a compilation of all the brief descriptions of all the included use cases. It therefore functions as a convenient introduction and overview of the model. Obviously, it is very helpful if a tool can assist in keeping these texts identical, for it is a well-known fact that it is cumbersome to maintain two different descriptions of one and the same thing, especially if their purposes coincide. Note, however, the point here is not that the two texts are identical, but that they express the same information.

The use cases in this section may be organized in groups according to different criteria, for example, in service areas and/or in alphabetic order. The latter may be convenient for small systems with no particular logical order between the different use cases. However, for medium-sized models, just ordering the use cases alphabetically usually makes it hard for readers to get a clear overview of the system behavior. It is then better to identify various service areas, grouping use cases together, and presenting them in separate subsections. If the use cases are presented in subsections, you may consider listing the used patterns and blueprints in the subsections rather than in the introduction to the use-case section as a whole. With the intended readers in mind, choose what would seem to be the more suitable alternative.

In rare situations, where the use-case model consists of a very small set of use cases, the use-case descriptions may be included in the Use-Case Model Survey directly, making this the only text document describing the model. This has one obvious advantage—there will be only one document to read and maintain—as well as a number of obvious drawbacks—the Use-Case Model Survey will have to be revised, reviewed, and approved whenever there is a change in one of the use cases.

Use-Case Diagrams

One of the first things a reader will look for to get an overall picture of a use-case model is the use-case diagrams depicting the model. These may be presented in the existing sections or in a separate section of the Use-Case Model Survey, as appendices of the Use-Case Model Survey, or handled separately.

However, it is practically impossible to create a single diagram showing all the use cases of a model. Instead, the model will be graphically documented in a set of diagrams, each of them showing a subset of all the actors and use cases in the model, selected according to some given criterion (see Figure 14.1). These criteria should be given by the different kinds of designated readers of the model.

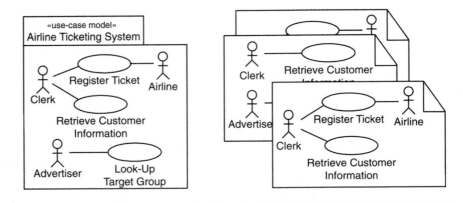

Figure 14.2   The elements in a use-case model are usually presented in a collection of diagrams. Some elements, such as the use case `Retrieve Customer Information`, participate in several diagrams, whereas others, such as the use case `Register Ticket`, appear in only one diagram.

There are mainly three different kinds of readers of the Use-Case Model Survey: those interested in a particular part of the system, those representing the users of the system, and those interested in a particular use case. It is therefore a good policy to prepare three different kinds of diagrams. Obviously, the diagrams will vary considerably depending on the size and complexity of the system and who the target readers are and so forth. The different kinds of diagrams are as follows:

- *Overview,* or *global, diagrams*—An overview or global diagram presents the use cases and the actors of one of the (functional) areas of the system. If the diagram becomes too crowded, it should be split up into multiple diagrams. All these global diagrams together show all the actors and use cases of the model, including all their relationships. Some of the elements may be presented in multiple diagrams to make them easier to understand.

- *Actor,* or *local, diagrams*—A local actor diagram presents one actor and all the use cases the actor is associated with, all the parent actors of the actor, as well as the generalizations between them.

- *Use case,* or *local, diagrams*—A local use-case diagram presents one use case and all the actors the use case is associated with as well as all the use cases to which it has generalizations, include, and extend relationships.

The use-case diagrams may well overlap; that is, a use case (or an actor) may be shown in several diagrams. Sometimes some relationships involving a certain use case are not relevant in the context depicted in a certain diagram, but are better shown in another diagram where this use case also appears. Therefore, just because a use case is present in a diagram, the whole truth about that use case is not necessarily shown there! It is important to make sure the diagrams together show every use case, every actor, and every relationship to be found in the model.

Supplementary Documents

Apart from the core use-case model documents, which consist of a Use-Case Model Survey, Use-Case Descriptions, and Use-Case Diagrams, other documents may be prepared. Which of them will be needed depends on the type of project and the kind of system to be developed.

Often it is necessary to compile a Glossary to make sure that the terminology used in the use-case descriptions is consistent. In some cases, it is even appropriate to complement the Glossary, or even replace it, with a Domain Model. This is a model of the concepts used in the business domain of the system, including relationships relevant within the project.

Another document usually produced when a use-case model is being developed is a document where all the nonfunctional requirements are captured. These are requirements that are not easily expressed as use cases, such as response times, volumes to handle, regulations to adhere to, security requirements, architectural requirements, and standards to use.

Some systems are highly dependent on a set of business rules, guiding the procedures of the system. These may of course be included in the affected use cases, either directly in their flow descriptions or in a separate section of the description document, but it is often more convenient to keep them in a separate Business Rules document. See Chapter 16, "Business Rules."

Other kinds of rules affecting the performance of the use cases in the models, such as algorithms, printout templates, and so forth, may be treated in the same way as business rules, which means that they may be documented in the same document as the business rules, under separate subsections, or in separate documents, whichever is more convenient.

CHAPTER 15

MAPPING USE CASES ONTO CLASSES

Kick-Starting the Class Modeling

One of the reasons for using patterns and blueprints when developing a use-case model is to speed up the development of the model. With pre-defined use-case models, it is also possible to provide standard realizations of these models. This gives a kick-start when designing the system—that is, when mapping the use cases onto classes. Another effect of providing such mappings is that it becomes clear what the effects of different modeling decisions in the use-case model are in the subsequent models.

In Part III, "Use-Case Patterns," and Part IV, "Use-Case Blueprints," we have therefore included ideal class models—models that are independent of implementation technologies. These models present initial attempts at the classes needed to perform the use cases. This chapter provides the background you need to understand such ideal class models, or analysis models as they are often called.

You can find an introduction to class modeling and object orientation in *Object Technology: A Manager's Guide*, by D. Taylor (Addison-Wesley, 1998) and in *Object-Oriented Software Engineering: A Use-Case Driven Approach* by I. Jacobson et al. (Addison-Wesley, 1993).

Analysis Models and Design Models

Use cases model how a system is to be used. However, they do not capture how the system is structured internally in terms of classes, components, subsystems, and so forth. The internal structure is stated in a class model, such as an analysis model or a design model, modeling the realization of the use-case model. Usually the difference between these two kinds of models is that an *analysis model* describes how the system ideally ought to be structured so that it can be easily maintained, whereas a *design model* describes how the system is actually structured.

The analysis model expresses the platform-independent, ideal design of the system and can therefore be given a straightforward structure. In contrast, the design model has to be adjusted to constraints imposed by performance requirements, implementation standards, security requirements, existing code, volumes to be handled, what can be implemented efficiently in the programming language at hand, and so forth. In some situations, the maintainability might have to be partly sacrificed to meet the design constraints.

There is a never-ending discussion whether to use an analysis model when developing a system. Many agree, and we certainly share their opinion, that it is wise to develop the design model in two steps. The first step involves preparing an initial version of the model not taking into account implementation constraints. The goal here is to prepare a model that is resilient to future changes and additions. For this reason, this task is sometimes referred to as *robustness analysis* (Jacobson et al. 1993; Rosenberg and Scott 1999). In the second step, this ideal model is adjusted and adapted to the implementation environment at hand, which results in an ordinary design model.

In this sense, the developers will actually have an analysis model at some stage in their work (even if the work is done incrementally). The remaining question to answer is this: Should the analysis model be maintained, be discarded after the design model has been produced, or be refined and transformed into a design model? Different persons have different views on the subject; we only want to stress that we do not think that the development team should have the final say in the matter. The product owner ought to decide which types of models should be developed and maintained, because he or she is responsible for the maintenance and the enhancement of the system.

The following sections first describe what different kinds of classes we use in the analysis models, and then describe how the mapping from use cases onto analysis classes is expressed.

Analysis Classes

Analysis classes are ordinary classes; they declare the structure and the behavior of the *instances*, or *objects*, that appear in the analysis model. However, the declaration is often not as detailed and explicit as are those for design or implementation classes. The focus is more on the responsibilities of the instances of the classes than on how these responsibilities are to be realized. Typically, the behavior is described in ordinary text (rather than in algorithms expressed in a language with precise semantics such as a programming language). Furthermore, parameter lists are seldom complete (if they exist at all), and rather than following an implementation standard the name of a signature focuses on understandability. Similarly, many of the details about the information expressed as attributes in the classes and associations between the classes are abstracted away. All of these details must be provided at some point, but most of them can safely be left to the design model, thereby preventing wasted time and effort in making preliminary decisions in the analysis model that later have to be changed in the design model.

We favor a paradigm with three kinds of analysis classes: *entity class*, *control class*, and *boundary class*, each with its own notation icon (see Figure 15.1). We originally used this paradigm in OOSE (Jacobson 1993), and it is now used in other books and processes (Jacobson, Booch, and Rumbaugh 1999; Rational Software Corporation 2003; Rosenberg and Scott 1999). The idea is to look at the system in terms of three dimensions, which helps to keep each class more focused on one subject—a class should not be an assembly of independent things; remember that maintainability is a primary goal of the analysis model. The advantage of organizing the system according to these dimensions is that the classes can often be modified independently of each other. Hence, a class focused on displaying information is not modified if the procedure of how to perform a task is modified. (Of course, the world is seldom ideal, so at times a fourth concept might also be useful: *service package*, which is a package grouping modeling elements that model a whole service offered by the system. A modification of that service should only affect the classes in the corresponding service package.)

If you are not interested in using these kinds of classes, they can simply be replaced, in this chapter as well as in the pattern and blueprint descriptions, with ordinary nonclassified (nonstereotyped) UML classes.

The meanings of these kinds of classes are as follows (see Figure 15.1):

- **Entity class**—Models a concept managed inside the system. The focus of the entity classes is on the information the system needs about various concepts, but they also contain the behavior relevant for these concepts. Instances of entity classes are passive in that they provide other instances in the system with information, but they do not initiate communication with other instances than entity objects. The instances usually live longer than a use-case instance (they are often said to be persistent), but longevity is not a firm requirement. One entity class usually participates in multiple use cases and one entity object in multiple use-case instances.

- **Control class**—Models a task or a job to be performed in the system; it coordinates what takes place in a use case. The task originates from one or a few use cases in which the task is performed. Instances of these classes are active in the system because they perform the tasks and coordinate the actions in the system. The instances normally live only during the lifetime of one use-case instance; they are said to be transient. A control object usually participates in one use-case instance, but a control class may participate in the realizations of a few use cases.

- **Boundary class**—Models a transformer of the interaction between the interior of the system and the system's environment; the boundary classes appear only on the system boundary. This implies that communication between actors and the system is handled by instances of boundary classes. Instances of a boundary class are normally active, because they initiate actions in the system. The instances can both be short-lived and long-lived. In the realization of one use case, there must be at least one boundary class for each actor associated with the use case. However, the same boundary class may participate in the realization of multiple use cases, and one boundary object may participate in multiple use-case instances.

The properties of the different kinds of analysis classes imply that associations connected to entity classes should be navigable only *to* the entity class, but not *from* an entity class to a boundary class or a control class. (Passive instances should not initiate interaction with active instances.) However, entity classes may have associations with other entity classes, and these associations may be navigable in both directions.

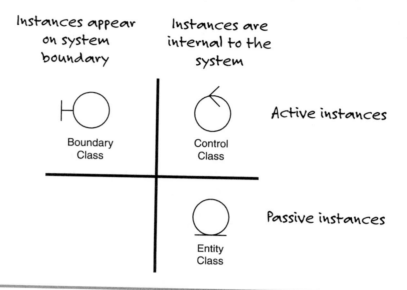

Figure 15.1   Matrix displaying some of the properties of the analysis classes.

Classification of classes like this is expressed with stereotypes in UML. This implies that all these three kinds of analysis classes have all the features of ordinary classes, such as attributes and operations, but they have been given specialized purposes as well as icons of their own.

Use-Case Realization: How Objects Perform a Use Case

The use-case model and the analysis model model different aspects of the same system. Therefore, in the analysis model it must be possible to perform all the usages of the system expressed in the use-case model; otherwise, these two models are not harmonized. (In fact, the reverse is also a requirement, although this is seldom mentioned: All the ways the system can be used according to the analysis model must be modeled as use cases in the use-case model.) For each use case, we create a *use-case realization* that states what roles are to be played by instances, or objects, of the classes in the analysis model when they cooperate to jointly perform an instance of the use case. Such a use-case realization is usually documented in what in UML is called a *communication diagram* (previously called collaboration diagram) or a *sequence diagram*, stating what participants take part and what their interactions will be when performing the use-case instance.

Assume that we have a task management system where work tasks are registered. The registration of a task includes what is to be done, when to do it, and any other information needed. At some other point in time, on a command, the system retrieves the registered work tasks that are to be performed at this moment in time, and these selected work tasks are then executed by the system (see also Chapter 28, "Future Task").

The realization of the Perform Task use case—the realization of the latter use case described previously—consists of a set of roles that are played by a collection of objects when they together perform one instance of the Perform Task use case (see Figure 15.2).

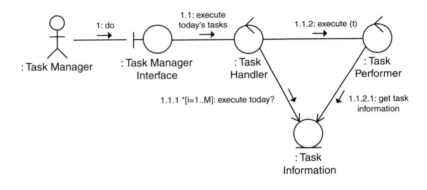

Figure 15.2   A communication diagram presenting the use-case realization of the Perform Task use case.

Figure 15.2 shows the realization of the Perform Task use case. Because the use case starts when the Task Manager causes an external event (in this case, by giving a command to execute the relevant work tasks), there must be a boundary object between the actor and the rest of the system. Therefore, we introduce the Task Manager Interface. An object of this boundary class will transform the external event into an internal stimulus sent to a control object responsible for identifying what work tasks are to be performed at this moment in time. This control object is an instance of the class Task Handler, which models how the retrieval of tasks is performed.

We can conclude that the system also needs to handle information about the work tasks, so we identify an entity class, the Task Information class. After the Task Handler object has identified what work tasks are to be performed, these work tasks will be executed. Because this is another job to be performed within the use case, we identify another control class, Task Performer. (That it is another control class can easily be seen by just analyzing the cardinalities: There is one instance identifying the work tasks, but there are many work tasks to be executed in each use-case instance.) The Task Performer is responsible for executing a work task, so it will contain a description of how this is done. Any task-specific information it will need for the execution is to be found in its instance of Task Information.

Multiple use-case realizations can be used when realizing a use case. If some of the alternative flows depart significantly from the basic flow—that is, if a partly different collection of roles is used—the realization of the alternative flow is best captured in a separate use-case realization. Together, these two use-case realizations then realize the complete use case. Furthermore, nothing prevents using multiple communication or sequence diagrams when documenting a use-case realization. If, for any graphical reason, the diagram becomes difficult to read, split it into two or more diagrams; by doing so, you will make the use-case realization more easily understood by the reader.

A more lightweight alternative to producing communication or sequence diagrams for the use-case realizations is to leave out the dynamics from the diagram and let it show only the roles the objects are to play and their relationships (see Figure 15.3). The diagram may be complemented by one or a couple of sentences written for each participant, describing its responsibility in the performance of the use case. In this way, the dynamics are described textually, which is often preferred for use-case realizations during analysis; the details of the communication being excluded to be worked out as part of the design work.

The use-case realizations form a basis for identification of the classes. Each realization identifies what roles are to be played by instances when they jointly perform an instance of the realized use case and hence what requirements the use case poses on the instances. By analyzing one realization, or a group of related realizations, we can identify classes or associations that are needed in the analysis model, or features that have to be added to the description of the existing analysis classes. Based on this information, we can extend our model with new classes, new associations, and new features so that it will be possible for the analysis model to perform the realized use case.

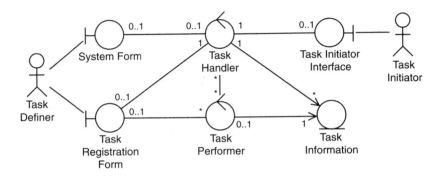

Figure 15.3   A diagram showing some of the classes in an analysis model.

Sometimes it becomes necessary to go back and modify some of the use-case realizations because they might impose contradictory requirements on the analysis model, but that is at least a localized problem. We will not have to start all over again. Nevertheless, it is necessary to iterate back and forth between the use-case realizations and the analysis classes, all the time making sure that the use-case realizations and the use cases synchronize. When both sides have stabilized, we can describe the classes in more detail and continue with the design model.

Experience shows that it is most helpful to prepare a class diagram for each use case, presenting the static structure of all the classes that somehow participate in the realization of the use case. This is particularly true when multiple sequence diagrams are used to document the use case's realization. In this way, the reader will get an overview of the subset of the classes in the analysis model that is relevant for this use case. In the early days, we called such a diagram a *VoPO*, an acronym for *View of Participating Objects*, because we then used the term *object* in a much broader sense than today (the term meant both classes and instances). Today, a more proper acronym would be *VoPC*, which obviously has not caught on, probably because it is hardly pronounceable.

In the descriptions of the patterns and modeling problems in the next part of this book, we have chosen to include an analysis model consisting of the classes needed for realizing the use cases. We have also added a textual description of how the classes are used in that context.

Part III
Use-Case Patterns

This part of the book presents a collection of use-case patterns proven useful when developing maintainable and reusable use-case models. These patterns focus on designs and techniques used in high-quality models, and not on how to model specific usages. Each chapter in this part presents and discusses a group of related patterns.

All chapters in this part are organized in the same way:

- **Name of group**—A descriptive name of the patterns in a few words

- **Intent**—Captures what the intent is of applying one of these patterns

- **Characteristics**—States whether the patterns are simple or complex, common or infrequent

- **Keywords**—A list of keywords characterizing the patterns

- For each pattern

  - **Name**—A descriptive name of the pattern

  - **Model**—A use-case model of the pattern

  - **Description**—A description of the pattern model

  - **Applicability**—States when the pattern should be used

  - **Type**—States whether the pattern affects the structure of the use-case model or the description of a use case

- **Discussion**—A comprehensive discussion on the patterns in this chapter

- **Example**—An example where one or more of the patterns is applied, including use-case descriptions
- **Analysis model**—A platform-independent class model providing a realization of the use cases in the pattern models

The chapters containing the use-case patterns are sorted alphabetically within this part. For each chapter, we list its contained patterns together with their intent.

Chapter 16. Business Rules: Extract information originating from policies, rules, and regulations of the business from the description of the flow and describe this information as a collection of business rules referenced from the use-case descriptions.

- Business Rules: Static Definition
- Business Rules: Dynamic Modification

Chapter 17. Commonality: Extract a subsequence of actions that appear in multiple places in use case flows and express it separately.

- Commonality: Reuse
- Commonality: Addition
- Commonality: Specialization
- Commonality: Internal Reuse

Chapter 18. Component Hierarchy: Provide a mapping from top-level use cases describing the system behavior as a whole down to leaf elements in a containment hierarchy realizing the behavior.

- Component Hierarchy: Black-Box with Use Cases
- Component Hierarchy: Black-Box with Operations
- Component Hierarchy: White-Box

Chapter 19. Concrete Extension or Inclusion: Model the same flow both as part of one use case and as a separate, complete use case of its own.

- Concrete Extension or Inclusion: Extension
- Concrete Extension or Inclusion: Inclusion

Chapter 20. CRUD: Merge short, simple use cases, such as Creating, Reading, Updating, and Deleting pieces of information, into a single use case forming a conceptual unit.

- CRUD: Complete
- CRUD: Partial

Chapter 21. Large Use Case: Structure a use case comprising a large number of actions. There are two "dimensions" along which a use case may be large: It may either be "long," that is, consist of a very long sequence of actions, or it may be "fat," that is, include many different flows.

- Large Use Case: Long Sequence

- Large Use Case: Multiple Paths

Chapter 22. Layered System: Structure the use-case model so that each use case is defined within one layer and use relationships between the use cases in different layers to allow use-case instances to span multiple layers.

- Layered System: Reuse

- Layered System: Addition

- Layered System: Specialization

- Layered System: Embedded

Chapter 23. Multiple Actors: Capture commonalities between actors while keeping separate roles apart.

- Multiple Actors: Distinct Roles

- Multiple Actors: Common Role

Chapter 24. Optional Service: Separate mandatory parts of the use cases from optional parts that can be ordered and delivered separately.

- Optional Service: Addition

- Optional Service: Specialization

- Optional Service: Independent

Chapter 25. Orthogonal Views: Provide different views of the flows of a system that are perceived differently by different stakeholders.

- Orthogonal Views: Specialization

- Orthogonal Views: Description

Chapter 26. Use-Case Sequence: Express the temporal order between a collection of use cases that must only be invoked in a specific order, even though the use cases are functionally unrelated to each other.

- Use-Case Sequence

CHAPTER 16

BUSINESS RULES

Intent

Extract information originating from policies, rules, and regulations of the business from the description of the flow and describe this information as a collection of business rules referenced from the use-case descriptions.

Characteristics: Very common. Simple.

Keywords: Definitions, legislative requirements, parameter list, policies, regulations, rules, standards.

Patterns

Business Rules: Static Definition

Model

Description

This pattern is applied to all use cases modeling services that are affected by the business rules defined in the organization. However, this pattern does not influence the structure of the use-case model; it deals with the description of use cases. The rules are described in a separate document, referenced by the relevant use-case descriptions.

Applicability

This pattern is appropriate when there is no need to dynamically change the business rules while the system is in use.

Type

Description pattern.

Business Rules: Dynamic Modification

Model

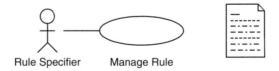

Rule Specifier   Manage Rule

Description

This pattern model contains one use case, called Manage Rule, which creates, updates, and removes business rules (see also Chapter 20, "CRUD").

Applicability

This pattern is useful when the collection of rules will be modified dynamically; that is, they can be modified while the system is up and running.

Type

Structure and description pattern.

Discussion

Most businesses and organizations, such as banking, medicine, and insurance, have rules, regulations, policies, and best practices that are to be followed by the business. These can be defined by the company itself as well as by governments, by customers, by general standards and so on, and any computer system developed to support the work within the company must respect them. For convenience, we use the term *business rule* to refer to any of these kinds of rules, because they can be treated the same way in the use-case model.

In a post-order company there are several business rules concerning orders; some of them are as follows:

1. An order is an official agreement between a customer and the company stating that the customer is buying a collection of items from the company to be delivered and paid for at a specific date.

2. An order can consist of multiple items.

3. An order must consist of at least one item.

4. The value of an order is the sum of the values of the included items plus shipping costs plus tax.

5. A rush order is an order that is placed before 6:00 p.m. EST and is to be delivered before 4:00 p.m. EST the next day.

6. An invoice is to be produced and sent after an order has been delivered.

These rules can be organized and described in many different ways. The simplest way is to enumerate them in a document and give each of them a unique name or identity. Another way, which we have found fruitful, is to define the business rules in a class model. In such a model, rule 1 in the preceding example would be manifest as a class, whereas rule 2 would be expressed as an association in the model. (The actual rules may of course also be explicit in the description of the class and the association, respectively.) The remaining rules would be defined as features of the elements in the model. For a more thorough discussion about business rules, refer to *Business Rules Applied* (von Halle 2001).

The business rules state facts about the business, regardless of whether they will be fulfilled manually or by a computer. By separating the specification and the implementation of the business rules from the rest of the software, the business becomes much more agile, because it can be modified without being hampered by rigidly defined software systems. It will also be easier to change the software systems, and they will adapt more readily to a changing business because the actual use of the business rules is stated explicitly rather than buried in the code and interleaved with unrelated actions.

When developing a use-case model of a system constrained by business rules, the use cases are identified in the usual way. However, the descriptions of the use cases will have to be slightly modified. First, instead of describing the different business decisions in the description of the flow, references are made from the description to the collections of business rules formulating the decisions. Second, the business rules will not be described in the same document as the use case from which the rules are referenced. Instead, the rules are described in a separate document or repository. In this way, the business rules will be described only once even if they are to be applied in several use cases.

In the post-order company, a complete shipping address must be supplied when a new order is registered. The following is a fragment of the description of the Create Order use case in the company's order management system:

When the order is to be saved, the shipping address is checked according to rule BR68. If it is fulfilled, the information about the order is stored; otherwise, the Clerk is requested to enter a new, complete shipping address.

The business rule is defined as

BR68.   A shipping address consists of the name, delivery address, city, zip code, and state of the receiver.

With this approach, the business rules can be reviewed and updated separately from the use cases. It also implies that the use-case descriptions can be reviewed and approved independently of the approval of the rules. This as an advantage from a project management perspective, because the descriptions of the business rules and of the use-case model usually have different development cycles, and the approval of the former usually involves business persons who are not deeply involved in the project (for example, lawyers and experts on standards).

The first *Business Rules* pattern assumes that the business rules are hard-coded in the system, and the second pattern includes a use case for updating the rules while the system is up and running. Which pattern is preferable depends on whether it should be possible to modify and update the rules dynamically. A use case that models creation and maintenance of the business rules is described using ordinary techniques (see Chapter 20).

To benefit fully from their business rules, some companies not only describe these rules separately, they also implement them separated from the code implementing the applications that depend on the rules. The implementation of the business rules can be made in separate components, in repositories, in existing rules products, or even in the databases storing the data used in the applications. In this way, a rule can be updated without modification of all the applications in which the rule is used. The benefits are obvious: For example, each time the interest on a loan or the salary threshold for some pensions is modified, all applications using these values must be updated, and in a bank or an insurance company, the number of applications depending on these values can be enormous. If the rules are implemented in one central repository (which, of course, can be replicated multiple times for efficiency and accessibility), the updating of the rules is simple (from a technical point of view) and all applications depending on the rules will become updated immediately.

The *Business Rules* patterns are also applicable to other kinds of reoccurring information, or that is repeatedly referred to in use-case descriptions. Examples include lists of information attributes, parameter lists, definitions, information to be printed in headers, process algorithms, and so forth.

Example

This section provides an example of a use case containing references to business rules (see Figure 16.1), and a fragment of the document containing descriptions of the business rules. The example is valid for both `Business Rules` patterns; the `Manage Rule` use case in the `Business Rules: Dynamic Modification` pattern is described using ordinary techniques (see also Chapter 20).

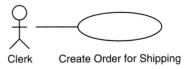

Clerk   Create Order for Shipping

Figure 16.1   The `Create Order for Shipping` use case depends on business rules.

In the post-order company, the shipping department must have a complete shipping address before the package can be delivered. Furthermore, to prevent empty packages from being delivered, the logistics department requires that each package must contain at least one item. To cover the shipping cost of a package, the finance department has stated that if the value of the ordered items exceeds $10, the shipping is free; otherwise, a shipping fee of $2 is added.

Use Case: Create Order for Shipping

Brief Description

The use case registers the information about an order to be shipped based on the information received from the Clerk.

References

The Business Rules document.

Example   137

Basic Flow

The use case starts when the Clerk chooses to register a new order. The use case presents a form to the Clerk requesting the shipping address of the order, and for each item to be shipped also the ID and the quantity of the item.

The Clerk fills in the requested information. For each item, the system retrieves information about the item according to Shipping-1 and presents it to the Clerk.

The Clerk asks that the system save the order. The use case checks the shipping address according to rule Shipping-2 and checks the number of items of the order according to rule Shipping-3.

For each ordered item, the use case checks that the number of items in stock is greater than or equal to the number of ordered items.

For each ordered item, the use case reduces the number of items in stock with the number of ordered items.

The use case adds the shipping cost to the order according to rule Shipping-4, and the order is given an identity according to rule Shipping-5.

Finally, the order is saved, and the order identity is presented to the Clerk.

The use case ends.

Alternative Flows

CANCELING

The Clerk can, at any time, cancel the order registration. If the Clerk chooses to cancel the operation, the gathered information is discarded and the use case ends.

INCORRECT SHIPPING ADDRESS

If the shipping address is incorrect, the Clerk is notified and requested to provide a correct shipping address.

The Clerk enters a new shipping address, and the use case continues where the check of the shipping address is performed.

Missing ID or Quantity

If the ID or the quantity of an ordered item is missing, the Clerk is notified and requested to enter the missing information.

The Clerk enters the missing information and the use case continues where the items are entered.

Too Few Items in Stock

If the number of items in stock is less than the number of ordered items, the Clerk is notified and requested to re-enter the information about the item. The use case continues where the items are entered.

Too Few Items in Order

If the order does not contain enough items to be shipped according to the Shipping-3 when the order is to be saved, the Clerk is notified and requested to enter at least one item. The use case continues where the items are entered.

Business Rules

Introduction

This document defines the business rules to be used within the PO Company.

[. . .]

Shipping

1. The information presented about an item consists of its name and description, and of the number of instances available.

2. A shipping address consists of the name, delivery address, city, zip code, and state of the receiver.

3. A package to be delivered must contain at least one item.

4. If the total shipping value of a package to be delivered is less than or equal to $10, there will be a surcharge (an additional shipping fee) of $2.

5. An order identity is generated by incrementing the previous identity by one and then appending a dash at the end followed by the identity of the shipping site.

[. . .]

Analysis Model

There are two ways to realize the `Business Rules` patterns in an analysis model, depending on which pattern is applied: The business rules are either modeled as separate classes or hard-coded into other classes of the system. In the following model, we have modeled them as separate classes that can be dynamically updated. The other alternative is easily derived: Replace a call from a general class to the business rule class with a hard-coded implementation of the rule.

The analysis model of the `Business Rules: Dynamic Modification` pattern contains five classes (see Figure 16.2). One is an entity class, called `Business Rule`, which contains the information about one business rule. Apart from ordinary initialization operations, this class defines two major operations: `checkRule` and `deriveValue`. The former returns a Boolean value stating whether the rule is fulfilled (applicable to Shipping-3 and Shipping-4 in the example), whereas the latter calculates a value according to the rule (Shipping-2 and Shipping-5). Specific kinds of business rules can be defined as subclasses of this class.

The second class, the control class `Rule Handler`, is used for creation, modification, and deletion of rules, whereas the boundary class `Rule Definition Form` is used when the actor is to view or enter the information about a rule. The `General Class` is any class in the system that uses a business rule, and `System Form` is the boundary class from where different use cases are initiated.

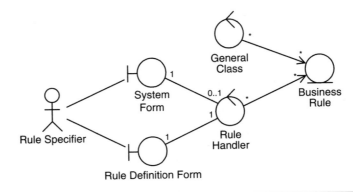

Figure 16.2   An analysis model of a system for business rules. The model
allows dynamic modification of the rules.

The Manage Rule flow starts in the System Form where the Rule Specifier
selects to operate on a business rule. An instance of Rule Handler is created, which opens a Rule Definition Form to the Rule Specifier. In this
form, the actor enters the information about a new rule, modifies the
information about an existing rule, or deletes an existing rule. Instances of
the Business Rule entity store the definitions of the rules. General Class
represents any class in the system whose instances apply business rules.

CHAPTER 17

COMMONALITY

Intent

Extract a sub-sequence of actions that appear in multiple places in use-case flows and express it separately.

Characteristics: Common. Basic.

Keywords: Common type of usage, reuse, same sub-sequence, similarities between flows.

Patterns

Commonality: Reuse

Model

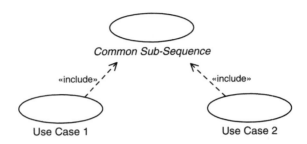

Description

The Commonality: Reuse pattern consists of three use cases. The first, called Common Sub-Sequence, models the sequence of actions that is to appear in multiple use cases in the model. The other use cases model usages of the system that share the common sub-sequence of actions. Obviously, there will be at least two of them.

Applicability

In this pattern, the sub-sequence must be in one piece; that is, all of it must be included as one whole. Furthermore, no references must be made from the sub-sequence to where it is to be used, because the inclusion use case must be independent of the base use cases.

Type

Structure pattern.

Commonality: Addition

Model

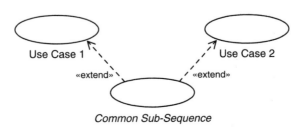

Description

In an alternative pattern, the Common Sub-Sequence use case extends the use cases sharing the sub-sequence of actions. The other use cases model the flows that are to be expanded with the sub-sequence.

Applicability

This pattern is preferable when other use cases are complete on their own; that is, they do not require the common sub-sequence of actions to model complete usages of the system.

Type

Structure pattern.

Commonality: Specialization

Model

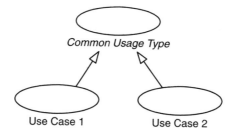

Description

Another *Commonality* pattern contains use cases of the same kind. In this case, they are modeled as specializations of a Common Usage Type use case. All actions in the Common Usage Type use case are inherited by the child use cases, where other actions may be added or the inherited actions may be specialized.

Applicability

This pattern is applicable when the usages modeled by the use cases are of the same type, and this type should be made visible in the model.

Type

Structure pattern.

Commonality: Internal Reuse

Model

Description

If the sub-sequence of actions is used in multiple places in only one use case, there is no need to extract the sub-sequence into a separate use case. Instead, it should be described in a separate sub-section in the description of the use case. This sub-section will be referenced from the different locations in the description of the use case where the sub-sequence of actions is to be performed.

Applicability

This pattern is preferred when the common sub-sequence appears in multiple places in only one use case.

Type

Description pattern.

Discussion

In many systems, some use cases partly overlap; that is, a sub-sequence of actions is the same in several use cases. If this is a coincidence, and the sub-sequences are unrelated to each other and will be modified independently, no additional measures are needed. However, if it is required that these sub-sequences of actions must be the same, this requirement should be expressed in the model. This is done by modeling the common sub-sequence of actions, including its alternative flows, in a separate use case. When the performance of the sub-sequence is to be modified, only this use case will be updated.

It is important that the commonality encompasses a sequence of actions and not just a single action. Furthermore, if there is no explicit requirement stating that the sub-sequence must be the same in the overlapping use cases, there must be another significant reason for introducing the additional use case into the model (for example, to enable future reuse). If not, the complexity of the model will be increased without any defendable cause.

Obviously, the use-case model must comprise relationships of some kind between the use case modeling the common sub-sequence of actions and the use cases in which the sub-sequence is to appear. Which kind of relationship to use depends on the situation (see also Chapter 7, "Include: Reusing Existing Use Cases," Chapter 8, "Extend: Expanding Existing Use Cases," and Chapter 11, "Use-Case Generalization: Classification and Inheritance").

Sub-Sequence Independent of Context

If the sub-sequence must be independent of in which context it is used, an include relationship should be used, as in the *Commonality: Reuse* pattern. In this case, the base use cases will have include relationships to the use case modeling the common sub-sequence of actions. The description of the flow of the base use case will incorporate a reference to the included use case where the common sub-sequence is to be performed, but there will be no references in the other direction because the common sub-sequence is independent of its context (see Chapter 7). Reuse of the same sequence of actions in multiple use cases is a typical example of when to use the include relationship (see Figure 17.1).

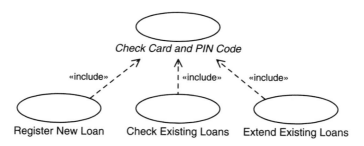

Figure 17.1   The PIN code is checked in multiple use cases.

In a library system, the borrower must always present the library card and a corresponding PIN code when registering a new loan, checking the existing loans, or extending an existing loan.

The sub-sequence checking whether the card is valid and whether the PIN code matches the card will be modeled in a separate use case to be reused in all the different loan-handling use cases (see Figure 17.1). When adding a new type of loan transaction to the library system, the new use case will have an include relationship to the existing Check Card and PIN Code use case. Hence, that sequence of actions will be reused when defining the new use case.

Note that the whole sub-sequence is to be performed at a single location in the base use case. It is not possible to split the sub-sequence in parts where one is to be performed at one location and the other at another location. If this is required, one include relationship must be defined for each sub-sequence part.

Additions to Existing Use Cases

When a new sub-sequence of actions is to be added to multiple already existing use cases, or when the same sub-sequence can be extracted from already existing use cases without breaking them or making them incomplete, an extend relationship is to be used. This is the Commonality: Addition pattern. In this case, the existing use cases will be independent of the common sub-sequence of actions, so their descriptions will not contain any references to the use case modeling the commonality. Hence, this use case can be added or removed without affecting the definition of the existing use cases (see Chapter 8).

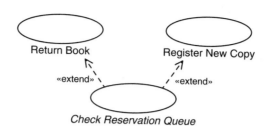

Figure 17.2   The check if someone has pre-registered to be the next borrower of a book is inserted into multiple use cases.

Each time a book is returned to the library, the library system checks whether someone has pre-registered to be the next borrower of that book. If so, a notification is sent to that person and the book becomes unavailable for any other borrower within the next seven days.

The same check is also performed when the librarian registers that the library has bought a new copy of a book.

Because the Return Book use case and the Register New Copy use case are both complete in themselves, we can model this check in a separate use case, called Check Reservation Queue, that will have extend relationships to the other two use cases (see Figure 17.2).

Although all the behavior modeled by the extension use case will be added to the base use case, it is not required that all is added at the same location in the base use case. Instead, one part of the extension use case may be added to one location and another part be added to another location. However, if the parts have an internal order in the extension use case, they must be inserted in that order into the base use case (see Chapter 10, "More on Extend and Extension Points").

Similar Use Cases

Some systems include several use cases that perform similar tasks. One example is a warehouse management system where each type of order is carried out in a similar way. An automated production system is another example, where the different kinds of production directives are executed similarly but not identically. Because all the use cases modeling the performance of tasks are of the same kind, this commonality should be captured in the model. It is done by introducing a new use case that will model how a task is to be performed in general, including all the actions common to all kinds of tasks. The specific performances of the tasks are captured in separate use cases with generalization relationships to the new use case, as in the *Commonality: Similarities* pattern. The child use cases may specialize actions defined in the parent use case as well as add new ones (see Chapter 11).

Commonality Within a Single Use Case

In one use case, the same sub-sequence of actions may appear several times, typically in different alternative flows, but sometimes even in the same flow. In such cases, the common sub-sequence should not be extracted into a separate use case, because it only adds to the complexity of the model. Instead, the sub-sequence is described in a separate section in the description of the use case according to the *Commonality: Internal Reuse* pattern. When describing the flow of the use case, this section will be referenced from all the locations where the common sub-sequence is to be performed.

Example

This section provides an example of the *Commonality: Specialization* pattern. The example consists of three use-case descriptions: Perform Task, Generate Pick List, and Generate Invoicing Basis (see Figure 17.3). The abstract use case Perform Task models how a task is performed in general, that is, how it is selected, the fact that it is performed (but not how; this is left to be defined in specializing use cases), and what happens to the task when it is completed. The other two use cases are specializations of Perform Task. Generate Pick List models how the information about what items to be picked in a warehouse is compiled, whereas Generate Invoicing Basis models how the information about all noninvoiced orders is compiled and sent to the Financial System actor. (For the registration of tasks, see Chapter 28, "Future Task.")

Apart from the *Future Task* blueprints, the *Report Generation* blueprints are also useful in this example.

For examples of the *Commonality: Reuse* pattern, see Chapter 29, "Item Look-Up," and Chapter 27, "Access Control." For examples of the *Commonality: Addition* pattern, see Chapter 31, "Login and Logout," and Chapter 19, "Concrete Extension or Inclusion." For an example using subsections for extracted subflows as in the *Commonality: Internal Reuse* pattern, see Chapter 21, "Large Use Case."

Example   149

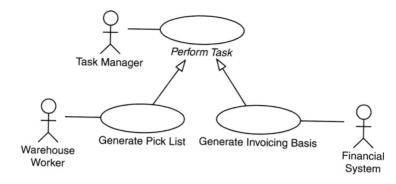

Figure 17.3   The Generate Pick List use case and the Generate Invoicing Basis use case are specializations of the Perform Task use case, which models how a task is performed in general.

Use Case: Perform Task

Brief Description

When initiated by a Task Manager, the use case retrieves a pre-registered task and, based on the registered information, performs it.

The use case is abstract.

Basic Flow

START OF THE FLOW

The use case starts when the Task Manager requests it. The use case collects all the tasks that are to be performed at this time and that have not been registered as *active, failed,* or *postponed.* The task with the highest priority is selected and marked as *active.*

PERFORMANCE OF THE TASK

The use case performs the task.

End of the Flow

If the task is performed successfully, it is removed.

The use case ends.

Alternative Flows

Failure of Task

If the performance of the task fails, the use case changes the status of the task to *failed* and stores it again together with the reason for failure. The use case ends.

No Task

If there is no task to be performed, the use case ends.

Use Case: Generate Pick List

Brief Description

The Generate Pick List use case, which is a specialization of the Perform Task use case, generates a list of items to be picked in the warehouse when compiling a shipment. The generated list is sent to a Warehouse Worker.

Basic Flow

Start of the Flow

The use case starts as described in the Perform Task use case.

Performance of the Task

The selected task being a *generate pick list* task, the use case collects all the orders that have been assigned to this pick list.

For each of these orders, the use case retrieves where in the warehouse the ordered items are to be found.

The use case calculates the total number of each ordered item.

Example   151

The use case prints a list to the Warehouse Worker with all the items, the quantity of each item, and the location in the warehouse where each item is to be found.

The use case marks the collected orders as *collected*.

END OF THE FLOW

The use case ends as described in the Perform Task use case.

Alternative Flows

LOCATION NOT FOUND

If the location of an item cannot be found, all orders containing the item are marked as *special* and removed from the shipment. The use case continues with the remaining orders.

NO ORDER

If no order is assigned to the pick list, the performance of the task fails.

Use Case: Generate Invoicing Basis

Brief Description

The Generate Invoicing Basis use case, which is a specialization of the Perform Task use case, generates a basis for invoicing that is sent to the Financial System actor.

Basic Flow

START OF THE FLOW

The use case starts as described in the Perform Task use case.

PERFORMANCE OF THE TASK

The selected task being a *generate invoicing basis* task, the use case collects all the orders that are marked as *shipped*.

For each of these orders, the use case retrieves the customer's name and address, as well as the order number and the ordered value, including discounts and tax. The collected information is sent to the Financial System.

The Financial System acknowledges the invoicing information. The use case marks the collected orders as *invoiced*.

END OF THE FLOW

The use case ends as described in the Perform Task use case.

Alternative Flows

NO ORDER

If no orders are marked as *shipped*, no information is sent to the Financial System.

INFORMATION NOT RETRIEVABLE

If the required information cannot be retrieved from an order, the status of the order is set to *manual invoicing*. The use case continues with the remaining orders.

NO ACKNOWLEDGEMENT

If no acknowledgement is received within two minutes, or if a message stating that something went wrong is received from the Financial System, the status of the orders is left unchanged and the performance of the task fails.

Analysis Model

Standard techniques are used for realizing the use cases in the `Commonality` patterns. The relationships between the use cases are also realized using the normal techniques.

- **Include**—The relationship is usually realized with an association navigable from a class in the realization of the base use case to a class in the realization of the inclusion use case.

- **Extend**—The standard way of realizing an extend relationship is the same as for an include relationship, that is, with an association from a class in the realization of the base use case to a class in the realization of the extension use case. Note that this association has the opposite direction compared to the extend relationship. However, if more special kinds of relationships are available for use between classes, such as *extend* (Jacobson et al. 1993), the direction of the relationship can be the same as for the extend relationship between the use cases. A third alternative is to use the Observer design pattern (Gamma et al. 1995) where a class in the realization of the base use case plays the role of the Subject and a class in the realization of the extension use case plays the role of Observer.

- **Generalization**—The realization of the child use case will most likely include classes being specializations of classes in the realization of the parent use case. Of course, additional classes and associations may also appear in the realization of the child use case.

- If the commonality is expressed in a separate section in the description of the use case, it can be realized either as a separate operation or as a separate class (or classes) that is to be called when the subsequence is to be performed.

CHAPTER 18

COMPONENT HIERARCHY

Intent

Provide a mapping from top-level use cases describing the system behavior as a whole down to leaf elements in a containment hierarchy realizing the behavior.

Characteristics: Common. Advanced.

Keywords: Addition to existing flow, component, decomposition, encapsulation, subsystem.

Patterns

Component Hierarchy: Black-Box with Use Cases

Model

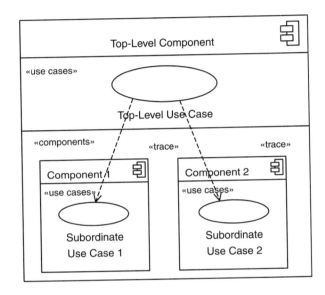

Description

The `Component Hierarchy: Black-Box with Use Cases` pattern consists of a top-level component containing an arbitrary number of use cases. These use cases state how the component is to be used and how it will act without revealing its internal structure. Each of the top-level component's use cases is mapped onto a subset of the components contained by the top-level component; that is, instances of this subset of components will jointly cooperate in the performance of that use case.

In this pattern, each lower-level component provides a black-box specification of its behavior given in terms of use cases, to separate how it is to be used from how it is realized internally.

Applicability

This pattern is preferable when the contents of a lower-level component should be hidden from the users of that component. Hiding the internals of a component is important when, for example, it should be possible to replace a component with another one or to restructure the internals of the component. Furthermore, the usages of the lower-level component should involve sequences of messages and not only single operations.

Type

Structure pattern.

Component Hierarchy: Black-Box with Operations

Model

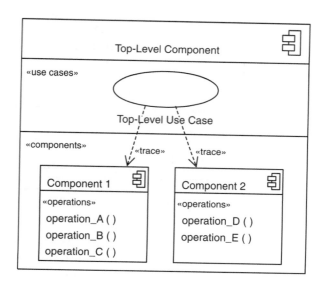

Description

In an alternative pattern, the lower-level components are specified with operations instead of using use cases. The lower-level components will still be replaceable and modifiable as in the previous alternative, because their operations constitute black-box specifications and hence hide the internals of the lower-level components.

Applicability

This alternative is preferable when the instances of the lower-level components will be used by their environments in a simple and straightforward way, and the operations are not necessarily performed in a specific order.

Type

Structure pattern.

Component Hierarchy: White-Box

Model

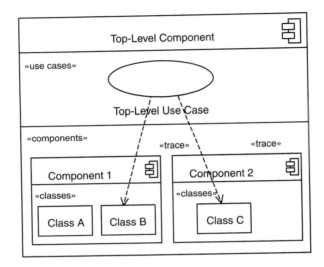

Description

Another alternative is to use a white-box specification of the contained components. In this case, the top-level use cases are mapped directly onto the leaves of the component containment hierarchy.

Applicability

This pattern is applicable when the contents of the lower-level components should not be encapsulated. The advantage is that it is easy to understand the mapping of the top-level use cases to the leaf components, and to trace the requirements from the top-level component down to the detailed realizations and back. The disadvantage is that modifying a component or replacing a component with another one requires the mapping of the top-level use cases (which are defined outside the component) onto the leaf elements to be changed.

There are several reasons why this alternative should not be used for large systems. The essence of them all is that in practice it is not possible to create and maintain the dependencies between the top-level use cases and the leaf elements.

Type

Structure pattern.

Discussion

Most systems, except very small ones, are too big to be developed in one chunk. Instead, a top-down development technique can be used where the system will be divided into smaller parts that each can be designed using traditional techniques. If a part is still too big, it can be further divided into even smaller parts, until a manageable size is reached.

In other cases, the system will be designed in a bottom-up fashion. New parts will be constructed by assembling existing ones, and in the end, the whole system will be an assembly of parts. Typically, these parts are called *components* or *subsystems*.

The exact semantics of these concepts vary between different projects because of their different needs as well as because of the chosen modeling and programming languages. However, regardless of the approach chosen, all functionality expressed by the use cases of the overall system must be implemented by the leaf components or the leaf classes inside the system; that is, the leaf elements must realize the top-level use cases. Hence, it must be possible to map the use cases of the overall system onto the leaf elements in the system's containment hierarchy to be able to trace the requirements all the way down to the code and back up again. This mapping can either be done in multiple steps, where there is one mapping from one level's use cases to the next level's components and so on, or it can be done directly between the top-level use cases and the leaf elements (see Figure 18.1).

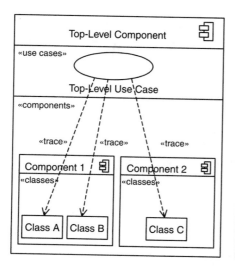 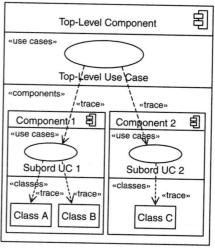

Figure 18.1   The mapping from the use cases onto the leaf components can be done in one step or in multiple steps.

The major advantage with mapping the top-level use cases onto the leaf elements in several steps is that it is possible to replace or to modify one component in the hierarchy without affecting the mapping of the top-level use cases down to that component. The drawback is, of course, that the complete mapping is more complex and therefore harder to understand. If a direct mapping is used from the top-level use cases onto the leaf elements, the arguments are reversed.

Replaceable Components: Black-Box Components

One requirement of many component-based systems is that it should be possible to replace one component with another one, without requiring changes to the environment in which the original component exists. If the components are to be replaceable, it must be possible to use the new component in exactly the same way as the old one was used, and the new one must not require any other features of the environment than the old one did. A fundamental characteristic of the new component is therefore that it must offer at least the same collection of operations to its environment and at the same time use at most the same operations as its predecessor.

A logistics system consists of multiple subsystems, each with its own responsibility (see Figure 18.2). There is, for example, one handling the information about the shipments, such as their sizes, weights, and delivery addresses and dates. Another subsystem manages the information about the transporters, such as their capacities, and their current loads and locations. A third subsystem encapsulates a huge database with geographical information. One of the more complex subsystems in the system is the scheduler, which assigns the shipments to the transporters. It interacts with the other subsystems and uses their information to schedule the transporters in an optimal way. The scheduler subsystem is used by a subsystem publishing the schedules of the individual transporters.

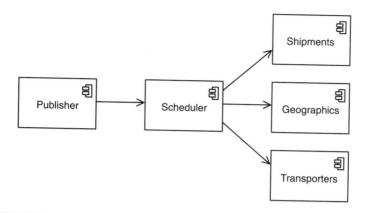

Figure 18.2   Interacting subsystems in a logistics system.

Different strategies can be applied when generating the transportation schedule, and different implementation techniques can be used. A logistics company might start with a simple version of the scheduler in their system and upgrade to a more efficient one later when the size of the business increases. Hence, to guarantee that a new version of the scheduler subsystem can function in the same environment as the existing one, the new one must use (at most) the same operations as the old one to access the information in the other subsystems. Furthermore, the environment of the scheduler must be able to use the new version of the scheduler in the same way as it used the old one to be able to operate as it did before.

Another characteristic of a replaceable component is that no element outside the component must be dependent of a specific element inside the component. Replacing the component with another one implies the removal of that internal element, which, of course, will cause the dependent external element to break. Similarly, if the component is to be used in different environments, the internals of a component must not be dependent of an external element.

Hence, the interior of a replaceable component must be hidden from its environment. This means, for example, that there must not be an association between classes defined inside two peer components; that is, an association must not cross component boundaries, because changing or replacing one of the two peer components will affect the definition of the class contained in the other component (see Figure 18.3).

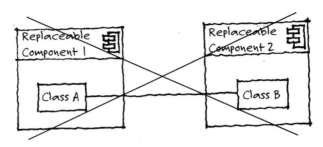

Figure 18.3   A replaceable component must not be dependent on the contents of another component.

(In UML, there is a *port* concept specifying interaction points between an element and its environment. An internal element connected to one of the container's ports may interact with the environment via this port without knowing what external element it interacts with. Similarly, an external element connected to one of an element's ports will not know which internal element it interacts with. The element is completely encapsulated by the port.)

To really achieve the advantages of black-box specifications, not even the mapping of the specification of a component onto its realization is allowed to make use of elements not immediately contained within that component, because this will also prevent the so-called plug-and-play possibilities of the contained components. Therefore, each use case in the specification of a top-level component should be mapped only onto the components directly contained by that component and not onto components further down the containment hierarchy. Mapping a use case onto components further down in the hierarchy would prevent modification or replacement of a component contained directly by the top-level component. At least the mapping itself would have to be modified.

Black-Box Components Specified with Operations

When the operations offered by the components are atomic in the sense that their descriptions are uncomplicated and they are used independently of each other—that is, they can be applied in an arbitrary order—the operations are sufficient as a specification of the components (see Figure 18.4). In these cases, the `Component Hierarchy: Black-Box with Operations` pattern is applicable. After the operations have been identified, it is possible to "move inside" each component and proceed with its interior design and implementation, using the operations as a requirements specification.

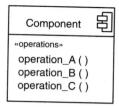

Figure 18.4   A black-box component can be specified with operations.

Note that if an existing component is to be used in the realization of the use case, its existing operations must be taken into account. For example, when defining the interaction between peer components that describe the realization of the use case, only operations already defined in the existing component may be applied. This may also imply that the use case itself might have to be modified to adhere to the behavior of the existing component.

Black-Box Components Specified with Use Cases

If a component's behavior is complex, it is always used in specific sequences, it has a compound interior, or it is to be designed and implemented by someone else, it is often useful to specify that component using use cases (see Figure 18.5). After the use cases of the component have been identified and described, the component may be seen as a system on its own and a traditional development technique can be used within the component. Therefore, if one of the components contained by the top-level component has some of the characteristics just mentioned, it should not be specified using operations; instead, use cases should be applied, according to the *Component Hierarchy: Black-Box with Use Cases* pattern.

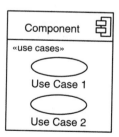

Figure 18.5   A black-box component with, for example, more complex behavior may be specified with use cases.

As we know, an actor models someone or something outside the system using the system. How the system is to be used is expressed with the use cases. This means that for the use cases at the system level, the actors will appear outside the system. However, when modeling the use cases for a component contained inside the system, the actors of those use cases do not necessarily appear outside the *system* boundaries, although they must always appear outside the *component*. A component may be used by other peer components, which implies that these peer components will act as actors of the first component's use cases; that is, instances of the peer components will play the roles modeled by actors of the first component (see Figure 18.6).

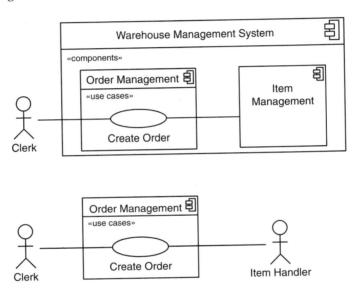

Figure 18.6   The actors of a component appear outside the component, but not necessarily outside the system. From the viewpoint of `Order Management`, an instance of `Item Management` will act as an actor.

In a diagram showing only one component, you may include the actors of that component's use cases. However, when showing a collection of components being wired together, no actors should be included except possibly the actors outside the collection. Because the instances of the components will play the roles of each other's actors, it makes no sense to show an actor and at the same time a component playing the role of that actor.

After the mapping of all fragments of the top-level use cases to the contained components has been established, the fragments mapped onto each of the contained components will be used as a basis for identification of that component's internal use cases. Remember that the focus is now on the contained component, so its internal use cases will describe how that component is to be used, regardless of in which context the component will appear. This implies that not all fragments originating from one of the top-level use cases will necessarily be captured in one internal use case (see Figure 18.7); instead they might be expressed by a few internal use cases. However, we have not seen any examples of one external use case being mapped onto more than three internal use cases of one component. Furthermore, each of the internal use cases may also participate in multiple of the top-level use cases.

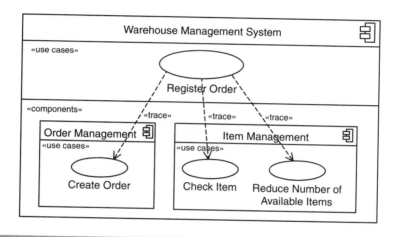

Figure 18.7   Fragments of one top-level use case is mapped onto two use cases of the same component.

Similar to the case where components are specified using operations, an already existing component that has been specified with use cases may be used in the realization of a top-level use case. The top-level use case may then have to be adapted to the existing component's internal use cases. The other components contained by the top-level component must also adhere to the existing component's interfaces.

If some of the identified components will have simple interiors and some will be more complex, it is of course possible to mix the two alternatives described so far. However, it is not recommended to mix black-box approaches with white-box approaches (as described next) because this will cause some parts of the system and its models to be tightly coupled and others to be more loosely coupled.

White-Box Components

The black-box patterns imply that the components may be replaced by others as long as their interfaces and their behaviors match. The drawback is that it will be more complicated to trace between the system requirements and the code because the system's use cases will be mapped onto components which, in their turn, will be mapped onto their contents, and so on (see the right part of Figure 18.1). If the price for having a more complex mapping becomes too high, it is possible to apply the `Component Hierarchy: White Box` pattern instead, and map the system use cases directly onto the leaf components (see Figure 18.8).

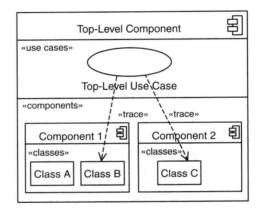

Figure 18.8   The mapping of a system use case to the leaf classes is done in one step.

However, there is a price to pay when using this alternative, too. The components in the system's component hierarchy will not be as easy to replace as those in the black-box alternatives. If one of the components is to be replaced by a new one, it will no longer be enough that the new component offers and uses the same interfaces. The mapping from the use cases onto the leaf elements must be updated because the leaf components of the original component will be replaced by the ones in the new component (see Figure 18.9).

The advantage with this alternative is that it is easier to overview the complete mapping at once; the drawback is that changes to any of the components in the hierarchy require more work.

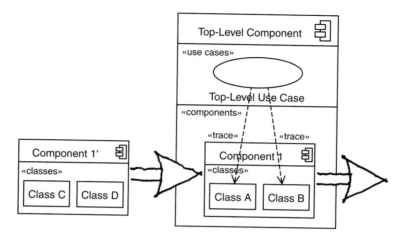

Figure 18.9   Replacing Component 1 with Component 1' requires updating of the trace relationships from the top-level use cases to the leaf classes, because the contents of the components differ.

Common Mistakes

We have seen examples where the top-level use cases have been traced down to the leaf components by include relationships from the top-level use cases to the use cases inside the components; that is, they are all defined within the same use-case model. However, this is nothing we recommend for several reasons:

- In general, all use cases in a use-case model should be at the same level of abstraction (see Chapter 42, "Mistake: Mix of Abstraction Levels"), but in this case the component use cases and the system (top-level) use cases are given at different levels of abstractions, although they have include relationships to each other and, hence, somehow are defined in the same use-case model.

- Replacing a component with another one does not only affect the mapping *from* the top-level use case, but it also affects the definition of the top-level use case *itself* because it has include relationships to use cases defined in the component that was just removed.

- A system use case will be nothing but an assembly of other, lower-level use cases and will not have any behavior and value of its own.

Using generalization or extend relationships like this is even worse. A system use case is very seldom of the same type as the component use case (keep in mind that generalization is a classification relationship), which means that the semantics of the relationship does not match that of generalization.

In the extend case, the system use cases are given their contents by the component use cases having extend relationships to them. This is semantically wrong, because the base use case of an extend relationship must be a complete, standalone use case in itself. In this case, the base use case would be completely empty!

Example

This example shows how the *Component Hierarchy: Black-Box with Use Cases* pattern is applied. The example is a warehouse management system keeping track of the customer orders and the items in the warehouse. The system consists of two subsystems: one for managing the orders and one for managing the items (see Figure 18.10).

There is one top-level use case, called `Register Order`. This use case is realized by the two subsystems together. Part of it is mapped onto the `Create Order` use case in the `Order Management` subsystem, and parts of it are mapped onto the `Check Item` and the `Reduce Number of Available Items` use cases in the `Item Management` subsystem.

In this example, also the *CRUD* patterns and the *Item Look-Up* blueprints may prove useful.

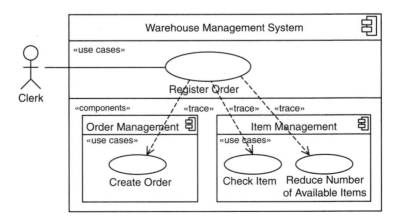

Figure 18.10   The `Clerk` registers an order in the system. The top-level use case is mapped onto the use cases inside the subsystems.

Example   169

Use Case: Register Order

Brief Description

The use case registers an order based on the information received from the Clerk and checks that the ordered number of items exists in the warehouse.

Basic Flow

The use case starts when the Clerk chooses to register an order. The use case requests the name and the address of the customer.

The Clerk enters the required data, and the use case checks that the requested information has been provided. The use case creates a new order and initializes it with the entered information.

The use case requests the identities of the ordered items together with the number of each ordered item.

The Clerk enters the required information. For each ordered item, the use case retrieves the description of the item and presents it to the Clerk and checks that the ordered number of the item is available.

When all items have been entered, the Clerk submits the order. For each ordered item, the use case reduces the number of available items with the number of ordered items.

Finally, the order is stored and the use case ends.

Alternative Flows

MISSING NAME OR ADDRESS

If the Clerk has not entered the name or the address of the customer, the use case asks the Clerk for the missing information. When the information is entered, the use case continues as if the information had been entered from the beginning.

CANCEL THE ORDER

If the Clerk selects to cancel the order when the use case is waiting for an input, all entered information is discarded and the use case ends.

MISSING ITEM

If one of the items is not registered in the system, the use case notifies the Clerk and the item is discarded from the order.

NOT ENOUGH NUMBER OF ITEMS AVAILABLE

If the number of available items is less than the ordered number of that item, the Clerk is notified and the number of available items is presented.

- If the Clerk enters another number of items to be ordered, the entered number is used and the use case continues as if that number had been given from the beginning.

- If the Clerk chooses to cancel the item from the order, the item is discarded from the order. The use case continues with the next item.

Use Case: Create Order

Brief Description

The use case creates an order based on the information received from the Clerk and interacts with the Item Handler to retrieve information about the ordered items and to reduce the number of items available.

Basic Flow

The use case starts when the Clerk chooses to register an order. The use case requests the name and the address of the customer.

The Clerk enters the required data, and the use case checks that the requested information has been provided. The use case creates a new order and initializes it with the entered information.

The use case requests the identities of the ordered items together with the number of each ordered item.

The Clerk enters the required information. For each item

The use case asks the Item Handler to check whether the item exists.

If the Item Handler confirms the existence, the use case asks the Item Handler for the description of the item.

Example 171

The Item Handler sends the description of the item to the use case, which presents it to the Clerk. Then, the use case asks the Item Handler for the number of instances available of that item.

The Item Handler sends the requested number to the use case. The use case checks that the number of available items is greater than or equal to the number of ordered items.

When the Clerk submits the order, the use case sends the identities of the ordered items together with the ordered number of each of them to the Item Handler and asks it to reduce the number of items available.

Then the use case updates the stored order with the identity and quantity of each ordered item. Finally, the use case ends.

Alternative Flows

Missing Name or Address

If the Clerk has not entered the name or the address of the customer, the use case asks the Clerk for the missing information. When the information is entered, the use case continues as if the information had been entered from the beginning.

Cancel the Order

If the Clerk selects to cancel the order, all entered information is discarded and the use case ends.

Missing Item

If the Item Handler informs the use case that an item is not registered in the system, the use case notifies the Clerk and that item is discarded from the order.

Not Enough Number of Items Available

If the number of available items is less than the ordered number of that item, the Clerk is notified and the number of available items is presented.

- If the Clerk enters another number of items to be ordered, the entered number is used and the use case continues as if that number had been given from the beginning.

- If the Clerk chooses to cancel the item from the order, the item is discarded from the order. The use case continues with the next item.

Use Case: Check Item

Brief Description

The use case checks whether there is an item with the identity provided by the Requestor and if so provides the description of the item.

Basic Flow

The use case starts when the Requestor asks whether there is an item with the provided identity.

The use case checks whether there is an item with that identity. If there is an item with the provided identity, the use case sends a confirmation back to the Requestor.

The Requestor requests the description of the item. The use case retrieves the description and sends it to the Requestor.

The Requestor asks for the number of available instances of the item. The use case retrieves the number and sends the result to the Requestor.

The use case ends.

Alternative Flows

ITEM DOES NOT EXIST

If there is no item with the given identity, the use case notifies the Requestor. Then the use case ends.

Use Case: Reduce Number of Available Items

Brief Description

The use case reduces the number of available items requested by the Requestor.

Basic Flow

The use case starts when the Requestor sends a list of items and numbers and asks the use case to reduce the stored number of available items of each of the items in the list with the provided number.

The use case reduces the number of available items of each type.

The use case ends.

Analysis Model

There is no analysis model for the `Component Hierarchy` patterns, since they describe the mapping of use cases defined at one level onto use cases or operations defined at lower levels. The realization of the leaf use cases, and therefore the higher-level use cases, is done in the normal way.

CHAPTER 19

CONCRETE EXTENSION OR INCLUSION

Intent

Model the same flow both as part of one use case and as a separate, complete use case of its own.

Characteristics: Rather common. Basic solution.

Keywords: Addition to existing flow, complete subflow, extend, include, reuse, subflow.

Patterns

Concrete Extension or Inclusion: Extension

Model

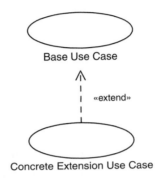

Description

The *Concrete Extension or Inclusion: Extension* pattern consists of two use cases and an extend relationship between them. The extension use case is concrete; that is, it may be instantiated on its own as well as extend the base use case. The latter can be either concrete or abstract.

Applicability

The pattern is applicable when a flow can extend the flow of another use case as well as be performed on its own.

Type

Structure pattern.

Concrete Extension or Inclusion: Inclusion

Model

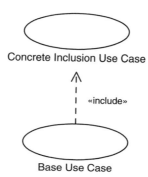

Concrete Inclusion Use Case

«include»

Base Use Case

Description

In this pattern, there is an include relationship from the base use case to the inclusion use case. The latter may be instantiated on its own. The base use case can be either concrete or abstract.

Applicability

The pattern is used when a flow can be included in the flow of another use case and also be performed on its own.

Type

Structure pattern.

Discussion

Sometimes the same subflow is found in multiple use cases. If the flow is substantial enough, we extract it from those use cases creating a separate use case and we define an include or an extend relationship between the initial, but now smaller, use cases and the new use case (see Chapter 17, "Commonality"). This modification does not affect the instances of the use cases but only the declarations in the model; that is, the use-case instances in the original model and the instances of the use cases in the modified model will be the same (see Figure 19.1). This is described more thoroughly in Chapter 7, "Include: Reusing Existing Use Cases," and Chapter 8, "Extend: Expanding Existing Use Cases."

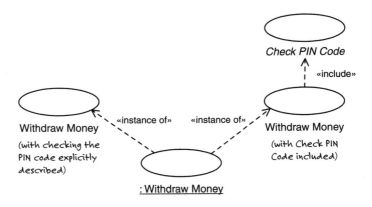

Figure 19.1   Extracting parts of a use case into another use case and defining a relationship between the modified use case and the new one will not affect the use-case instance.

Normally the extracted flows are just parts of other use cases, so the new inclusion and extension use cases are abstract. This means that they are not to be instantiated; that is, there will be no use-case instances that perform only the behavior declared in these use cases. Their flows will only be performed in conjunction with what is declared in other use cases. This implies that an abstract use case does not have to provide a complete declaration of a use case. For example, it does not have to declare a proper start, and it does not necessarily have to include interaction with actors. An abstract use case is just a declaration of some structure and behavior, in the same way as an abstract class is never instantiated but only declares some structure and behavior.

But what if the flow that is extracted from other use cases into a separate use case is actually to be performed separately as well? What if this new use case, apart from having include or extend relationships with other use cases, is to be instantiable? In principle, there is nothing odd about this. Just compare the situation with what happens with a class that is inherited by other classes so that its structure and behavior is reused in the inheriting classes, while the class is also instantiable on its own; that is, new instances of that class can be produced at the same time. Such classes are not uncommon, and they are no different from other classes. The same is true about use cases. A use case can have include relationships from other use cases, as well as extend relationships to other use cases, and at the same time be instantiable (see Figure 19.2).

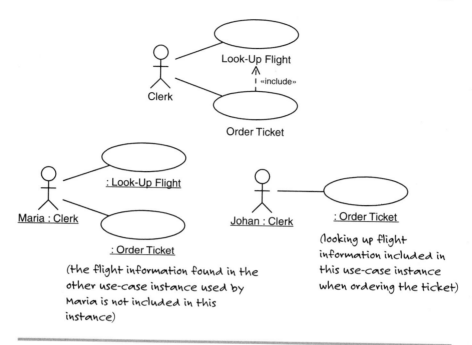

Figure 19.2   A use case can at the same time be a concrete full use case and an inclusion or an extension use case. (Note that the Look-Up Flight use case is concrete, which is, according to UML, why its name is not in italics in this figure!)

In an airline ticketing system example, there is one use case for ordering a ticket and one use case for looking for a suitable flight. The former includes entering the name of the traveler, the chosen flights, and finally booking the airline tickets. The latter use case provides a list of available flights between two airports at a given date. Naturally, both of these use cases have to be concrete, as it must be possible to use either one of the services independently of other use cases. The use-case instances are independent of each other and are just performed in parallel.

However, if a flight selected from the result of a flight request is to be automatically inserted into the ticket by the system, the use case listing available flights must be included in the flow of the use case for ordering a ticket. Otherwise, the result—the preferred flight—cannot be used in the flow of the ordering use case, because ordering the ticket and requesting a suitable flight is performed by two different use-case instances. In general, it is only when the two flows are merged into one that one part of the combined flow can make use of or affect anything defined in the other flow. Therefore, the use case that models selecting a suitable flight must also be included in the ordering use case. Hence, the use case selecting a flight is both concrete and included in another use case.

Therefore, having a relationship between two concrete use cases does not make the model obscure; in fact, it is sometimes necessary. The only intricacy is how to describe the use case. We solve this problem by making use of the fact that use cases can have alternative flows and that, if necessary, these alternatives can be described in separate paragraphs or sections of the description of the use case.

We describe the initial part of the use case as a flow with alternatives by creating one section called, for example, Start, which enumerates all the alternatives by describing each one of them in one paragraph. One of the alternatives is when the use case is performed as a separate instance; that is, a use-case instance is created that follows the flow declared by the use case. This flow always starts when an actor performs a specific action, such as choosing to select a flight matching a specific requirement. Another alternative of the initial part of the use case, described in another paragraph of the Start section, is when the use case is to be included in other use cases (as in the `Concrete Extension or Inclusion: Inclusion` pattern). Then we simply state

`When the use case is included in other use cases . . .` or something similar.

However, we must not mention in what other use cases the use case is included, because the inclusion use case must be independent of use cases where it is included.

In the `Concrete Extension or Inclusion: Extension` pattern, the use case is instead extending other use cases. The description of the flow starts with one paragraph for each extend relationship—normally one for each extended use case. There we state the following:

In use case XYZ, if the condition P is fulfilled at the extension point EP, the flow of this use case is inserted into the use-case instance.

Then follows an enumeration of the locations where the different parts of this use case are to be inserted. (For examples, see below.)

The end of the use case is structured similarly. In a separate section called End, the same alternatives as in the Start section are represented by one paragraph each. If the use case is performed as a separate use-case instance, we state the following:

If the use case is performed as a separate instance [and the actor ABC does X] the use case ends.

(Text within brackets is used only when appropriate.)

Next, in the `Concrete Extension or Inclusion: Inclusion` case, we state the following:

> When the use case is included in other use cases, the subflow ends and the use-case instance continues as described in the base use case after the location where this use case was included [where the R value is available].

In the `Concrete Extension or Inclusion: Extension` case, for each of the extend cases we instead state this:

> If this use case is extending the XYZ use case, the subflow ends and the use-case instance continues according to the base use case after the EP extension point.

Note that this is the last extension point in the sequence describing where the parts of the extension use case are inserted into the base use case (remember, we are talking about the End section); see the section *Multiple Fragments of Additional Behavior* in Chapter 10, "More on Extend and Extension Points." Note also that no value retrieved or calculated in the extension use case becomes available in the base use case, because the base use case must be independent of the extension use case.

So, when do we use an include or an extend relationship between two concrete use cases? This is done only when the base use case is somehow to be affected—for instance, when it is to use a value retrieved by the other use case (include relationship) or when a value in the base use case is to be used by the other use case (extend relationship). If no information retrieved in the inclusion (the base) use case is to be available in the base (the extension) use case, no relationship is needed between the use cases. (This has to do with the definition of the use-case construct. As we know, use-case instances do not communicate with each other, and therefore information in one use-case instance cannot be communicated to another use-case instance. Therefore, when information is to be shared, there must be only one use-case instance, and this instance follows the declarations in two use cases with a relationship—include or extend—between them.)

An include or an extend relationship should not be used between two concrete use cases just because they are to be performed in parallel. Nothing prevents an actor from using two use cases simultaneously, by switching between two windows on the computer screen, for example.

The situations described above deal with concrete inclusion and extension use cases, but note that a use case can also have generalizations to it from other use cases and still be instantiable. Figure 19.3 shows an example of this.

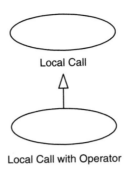

Figure 19.3   Both the use cases Local Call and Local Call with Operator can be instantiated, and hence the specialized use case Local Call is concrete.

Example

This example provides three use cases that all are concrete: Look-Up Flight, Order Ticket, and Present Help. There is an include relationship between Order Ticket and Look-Up Flight, and an extend relationship between Present Help and Order Ticket; that is, both *Concrete Extension or Inclusion* patterns are illustrated (see Figure 19.4).

The first two use cases have been discussed in the previous section. The third use case models what happens when the Clerk requests some help. If the request is done within another use case, the help is "context sensitive"; that is, the help provided is relevant to the current situation, whereas the help index is presented if the help is requested through the "main window."

Apart from the *Concrete Extension or Inclusion* patterns, the *Item Look-Up* blueprints as well as the *Optional Service* patterns are also relevant in this example.

Example 183

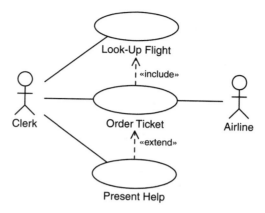

Figure 19.4   There is an include relationship between two of the use cases and an extend relationship between two of them. All the use cases in this example are concrete.

Use Case: Look-Up Flight

Brief Description

The use case looks for a flight that matches a search criterion given by the Clerk.

Basic Flow

START

- The use case starts when the Clerk requests information about a specific flight. The use case, in turn, requests the origin and the destination of the flight as well as the preferred time for take off from the Clerk.

- When the use case is included in other use cases, the Clerk is requested to give the same information as in the paragraph above. However, if a flight has been selected in the base use case, the use case presents its destination as a suggestion for the origin of the flight to be looked for and suggests its arrival time plus one hour as departure time. If no flight is selected, no suggestions are made.

MAIN FLOW

The Clerk enters the values, and the use case retrieves all the flights between the origin and the destination that leave within a three-hour time difference from the given departure time.

The use case presents the flight number, the departure time, and the arrival time for each retrieved flight to the Clerk.

END

- If the use case is performed as a separate instance and the Clerk acknowledges the presented information, the use case ends.

- When the use case is included in other use cases, the subflow ends and the use-case instance continues as described in the base use case after the location where this use case was included. Information about the retrieved flights is available in the base use case. If no flight is found matching the requested criterion, no information is available in the base use case.

Alternative Flows

If the origin, the destination, or the departure time is missing when the Clerk has entered the requested information, the use case asks the Clerk to enter requested values again. The use case continues from where the Clerk enters the requested values.

Use Case: Order Ticket

Brief Description

The Clerk registers a new ticket in the system and the included flights are booked at the Airlines.

Example   185

Extension Points

Input—At each location in the use case where the Clerk is to fill in a request.

Basic Flow

The use case starts when the Clerk chooses to register a new ticket. The use case asks the Clerk to fill in the name and address of the customer.

The Clerk enters the requested information and the use case checks whether it is a registered customer. If so, the Clerk is notified whether the customer is a VIP customer and how many tickets the customer has bought in the past 12 months.

The use case asks what flights are to be included in the ticket, their origin and destination, or whether a suitable flight should be found.

- The Clerk enters the selected flight number, the origin and the destination, and the departure date and time.

- If the Clerk instead chooses to ask for a suitable flight, the Look-Up Flight use case is included. If the result consists of several possible flights, the use case asks the Clerk to select one of the flights. The Clerk selects a flight.

For each flight:

The use case sends a booking request to the Airline.

If the Airline returns a confirmation number, the use case includes it in the reservation. If the Airline instead returns a reservation failure, the Clerk is notified and the flight is not included in the reservation.

The use case presents the complete reservation to the Clerk, and asks for a confirmation from the Clerk.

The Clerk confirms the reservation. The use case registers a new ticket and stores the name and address of the customer together with the flights and their departure and arrival dates and times. The name of the Clerk is retrieved from the system and stored. Finally, a reservation number is displayed to the Clerk, and the use case asks the Clerk to acknowledge it.

The Clerk acknowledges the reservation number.

The use case ends.

Alternative Flows

No Connection with Airline

If the connection with the airline cannot be established, the Clerk is notified and the flight is not included in the ticket.

No Flight

If no flights have been included in the ticket when it is to be registered, the Clerk is notified and no reservation is created. The use case continues by asking what flights are to be included.

Reservation Canceled

If the Clerk chooses not to confirm the reservation, the use case asks for a confirmation of the cancellation.

If the cancellation confirmation is received from the Clerk, the reservation is removed from the system, any booked flight is canceled, and the use case ends. If the cancellation is discarded, the use case continues by asking for confirmation of the reservation.

Use Case: Present Help

Brief Description

The Clerk asks for help, and assisting information is displayed.

Basic Flow

Start

- The use case starts when the Clerk requests help. The current page is set to the General Help page.

- In use case Order Ticket, if the Clerk requests help at the Input extension point, the flow of this use case is inserted into the use-case instance at that extension point. The current page is set to the Order Ticket page.

MAIN FLOW

The use case retrieves the help index and the current page, and then opens the Help window to the Clerk and displays the help index and the current page.

The Clerk may, any number of times, select a new page in the help index. The use case retrieves the selected page and presents it to the Clerk in the Help window.

END

- If the use case is performed as a separate instance and the Clerk closes the Help window, the use case ends.

- If this use case is extending the Order Ticket use case and the Clerk closes the Help window, the subflow ends and the use-case instance continues according to the base use case after the Input extension point.

Analysis Model

Whether or not a use case is abstract does not have any impact on the structure of the analysis model. The difference is visible only in the user interface in terms of what services are offered to the user, which implies that only a boundary class is affected if an inclusion or an extension use case is made concrete.

CHAPTER 20

CRUD

Intent

Merge short, simple use cases—such as Creating, Reading, Updating, and Deleting pieces of information into a single use case forming a conceptual unit.

Keywords: Create data, delete data, information handling, merge use cases, read data, short flow, short use case, simple operation, update data.

Patterns

CRUD: Complete

Model

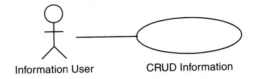

Information User   CRUD Information

Description

The *CRUD: Complete* pattern consists of one use case, called CRUD Information (or Manage Information), modeling all the different operations that can be performed on a piece of information of a certain kind, such as creating, reading, updating, and deleting it.

Applicability
This pattern should be used when all flows contribute to the same business value and are all short and simple.

Type
Structure pattern.

CRUD: Partial

Model

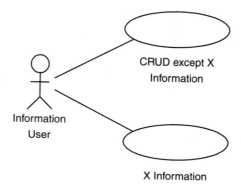

Description

An alternative pattern models one of the alternatives of the use case as a separate use case.

Applicability

This pattern is preferable when one of the alternatives of the use case is more significant, longer, or much more complex than the other alternatives.

Type

Structure pattern.

Discussion

Quite often systems handle information that, from the system's viewpoint, is very easily created in the system. After a simple syntax or type check, and perhaps some trivial calculation or business-rule check (see Chapter 16, "Business Rules"), the information is simply stored in the system. No advanced calculations, verifications, or information retrieval will have to be performed. The description of the flow is only a few sentences long, and there are probably not more than one or two minor alternative paths in the flow. Reading, updating, or deleting the information are equally simple operations. Each of them can be described in a few sentences.

Should such operations be modeled as use cases and, if so, must they be included in the use-case model? The answer to both questions is yes. They are indeed use cases because something is to be performed in the system; someone is to use the system to create (read, delete, update) some piece of information in the system. Moreover, they must be included in the use-case model, or the model will not be complete. If these use cases are not included in the model, some stakeholder will probably miss them; otherwise, the functionality should not have been included in the system in the first place.

Luckily, this does not necessarily mean that this kind of functionality should be expressed as separate use cases. Instead, according to the *CRUD: Complete* pattern, we group them together in so-called CRUD use cases, including all four types of operations on some kind of information—creation, reading, updating, and deletion of any such information.

This procedure has a few obvious advantages. First, the size of the model will be reduced, which will make it easier to grasp because the number of use cases will be reduced. Second, nobody will be interested in a system containing only a subset of these use cases (for example, read and delete, but not create and update). Grouping these flows together in a single use case called something like CRUD X ensures that all four are included in the model, and makes it clear to every reader of the model that this is the use case where all this functionality is captured. Third, the value of each of the separate use cases is very small (if any) for the stakeholders; it is the whole collection of them that gives a value to the stakeholders. Together these use cases form one conceptual unit (see Figure 20.1).

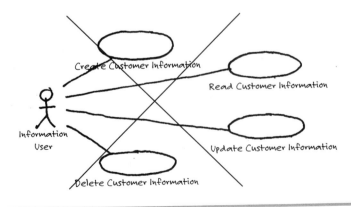

Figure 20.1   The four simple operations should not be modeled as separate use cases. Instead, they should be merged into one use case including all four operations as separate flows.

Example 193

Note that if only some of the four operations are simple while others are complex, you can group the simple operations into one use case and let the other ones be modeled as separate use cases, according to the CRUD: *Partial* pattern.

Note also that this is a typical situation where a use case does not have only one basic flow. None of them can be said to be more "basic," or "normal," than the others. Therefore, a CRUD use case will typically have four basic flows, and possibly a few alternative flows, as is shown in the following example.

An instance of a CRUD use case will perform either a creation, a reading, an updating, or a deletion, and after that it will cease to exist. This instance will not continue to live and wait for the next operation to be performed. That operation will be performed by another instance of the same use case.

A so-called CRUD use case may of course include other (basic) flows than the four common ones, such as searching for an item, or performing some simple calculation based on an item.

It is important not to merge advanced or complex operations into one use case. They should remain separate use cases instead, because they will probably be developed, reviewed, designed, and implemented separately.

As a general rule, when not sure whether to merge the different usages into one use case or to keep them as separate use cases, they should no doubt be kept apart. This decision will not affect the functionality of the system, only the model structure and hence its maintenance.

Example

This section provides an example of the CRUD: *Complete* pattern. It models the registration of a new task to be performed sometime in the future, the modification of a registered but not performed task, the cancellation of such a task, and the presentation of tasks that either failed during their execution or have not yet been performed (see Figure 20.2). As you can see, the four different alternatives are quite simple and short, and they are expressed as four basic flows, because none of them can be said to be superior to the others. Therefore, this is an application of the CRUD: *Complete* pattern even if some of the four basic flows in this case are different from the standard ones.

Error handling and exceptional flows are expressed as alternative flows of the use case.

The *Item Look-Up* and the *Future Task* blueprints are also useful in this example.

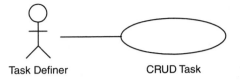

Task Definer   CRUD Task

Figure 20.2   The CRUD Task use case models the creation, modification, presentation, and cancellation of a task.

Use Case: CRUD Task

Brief Description

The use case registers, modifies, or cancels the information about a task to be performed as stated in information received from the Task Definer.

Basic Flow

The use case has four different basic flows:

- Register Task

- Modify Existing Task

- Cancel Task

- View Tasks That Failed

REGISTER TASK

The use case starts when the Task Definer chooses to register a new task. The use case presents a list of possible kinds of tasks to the Task Definer, and asks what kind of task is to be registered, what name it is to be assigned, and when it is to be performed.

The Task Definer enters the required information. The use case checks whether the specified time is in the future and whether the name of the task is unique.

The use case registers a new task in the system and marks the task as *enabled*.

The use case ends.

Example 195

MODIFY EXISTING TASK

The use case starts when the Task Definer chooses to modify an already registered task. The use case retrieves the names of all the tasks not marked as active and presents them to the Task Definer.

The Task Definer selects one of the tasks. The use case retrieves the information about the task and presents it to the Task Definer.

The Task Definer modifies any of the presented information except the name of the task.

The Task Definer accepts the information. The use case checks whether the specified time is in the future and, if so, stores the modified information.

The use case ends.

CANCEL TASK

The use case starts when the Task Definer chooses to cancel a task. The use case retrieves all the tasks not marked as *active*.

The Task Definer selects one of the tasks. The use case retrieves the information about the task and presents it to the Task Definer.

If the Task Definer confirms the cancellation, the use case removes the task; otherwise, no modifications are made.

The use case ends.

VIEW TASKS THAT FAILED

The use case starts when the Task Definer chooses to view a list of all the tasks that have failed. The use case collects all the tasks with the status *failed* and presents their names to the Task Definer.

The use case ends.

Alternative Flows

CANCEL OPERATION

The Task Definer may choose to cancel the operation at any time during the use case, in which case any gathered information is discarded, and the use case ends.

INCORRECT NAME OR TIME

If the name of the task is performed not unique or the time is not in the future, the Task Definer is notified that the information is incorrect and is requested to re-enter the incorrect information.

The Task Definer re-enters the information. The flow resumes where the check of the information is performed.

Analysis Model

The analysis model of a CRUD use case is based on all the flows of the use case. It must include the realization of all the basic flows as well as the realization of the alternative flows.

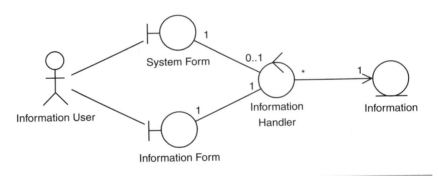

Figure 20.3   An analysis model of a CRUD use case.

However, because the flows are quite simple in this case, the model usually contains one boundary class for presentation and modification of the information, one control class to handle any checks, and one entity class (or perhaps a few) to store the information (see Figure 20.3). The flow starts in the System Form when the Information User requests to create, read, update, or delete the information. An instance of the Information Handler is created, which opens an instance of the Information Form to the Information User.

Depending on the chosen operation, the actor enters information about a new piece of information, or the Information Handler retrieves existing information and asks the Information User via the Information Form to select one item. The Information Form sends the new information or the identity of the selected item, respectively, to the Information Handler which performs the chosen operation. Finally, the Information Form and the Information Handler are removed and the use case ends.

CHAPTER 21

LARGE USE CASE

Intent

Structure a use case comprising a large number of actions. There are two "dimensions" along which a use case may be large: It may either be "long"—consist of a very long sequence of actions—or it may be "fat"—include many different flows.

Characteristics: Moderately common. Basic solution.

Keywords: Alternative flow, large use-case description, long use case, multiple paths, structuring use-case descriptions.

Patterns

Large Use Case: Long Sequence

Model

Description

The first *Large Use Case* pattern contains a use case consisting of a very long sequence of actions that is always to be performed as one unit.

Applicability

This pattern must be chosen when splitting the large use case would result in two use cases where one of them is always to be performed immediately after the other; hence, at least one of them will not model a complete usage of the system. The inevitable drawback is that the description of the use case becomes very long, calling for clever text structuring.

Type

Description pattern.

Large Use Case: Multiple Paths

Model

Fat Use Case Flow 1

Fat Use Case Flow 2

Description

An alternative pattern models the large usage with multiple use cases, each of them modeling one alternative of the usage of the system.

Applicability

This pattern is applicable when the usage to be modeled consists of multiple alternative flows. In this case, each of the longer flows can be modeled as a separate use case. This will keep the description of each use case shorter and more manageable instead of merging them all into one huge description.

Type

Structure pattern.

Discussion

A surprisingly common question is "How large is a use case?" Unfortunately, there is no simple answer, like "a description of a use case is two to three pages," "a use case comprises four to seven stimulus-response transactions," or "in a use case there are at most 10 actions per input stimulus." These numbers can vary a lot and still be reasonable. In some systems, the use cases are very short and simple. For example, one use case may receive an input stimulus carrying some information that is only checked for completeness and then stored in the system, or it may receive a request from an actor and as a response retrieve some information stored in the system and present it to the actor. In other systems, the use cases will receive very few stimuli but perform hundreds of actions as the response to each of these stimuli. Hence, the proper answer to the question is this: *A use case and its description are as large as they must be.*

Many use-case modelers have been told that a use-case description should be kept rather short and that one should watch out for descriptions being more than three pages long. This is good advice, because a long use-case description can be a warning sign that too much is covered by that use case (see Chapter 43, "Mistake: Multiple Business Values") or the use case is described at too low level of detail (see Chapter 42, "Mistake: Mix of Abstraction Levels"). However, sometimes a use-case description has to be long, simply because the use case will perform many actions or it will have multiple alternative flows. In neither of these cases should the description be condensed so that it will fit into, say, three pages, because this would reduce the number of necessary details so the description will not be understandable or it will cease to be useful for the designers of the system. Therefore, a use case that is perceived as large is not necessarily an incorrect use case.

When the flow of a use case is long, as in the *Large Use Case: Long Sequence* pattern, its textual description must be structured wisely. Apart from describing the alternative flows in separate subsections, a few other structuring techniques may be applied. The first one is to organize a description of a flow that is long by introducing headings, just like in ordinary text. In general, however, we do not recommend using more than two levels of headings within the description of the flow, because this would make the structure of the text overly complicated and fragmented.

The description of the basic flow of a use case ordering flight tickets can be structured as follows:

Basic Flow

INITIATE TICKET

The use case starts when the Clerk chooses to register a new ticket. The use case asks the Clerk to fill in the name and address of the customer.

The Clerk enters the requested information and . . .

REGISTER FLIGHTS

The use case asks what flights are to be included in the ticket . . .

REGISTER TICKET

The use case presents the complete reservation to the Clerk, and . . .

The use case ends.

A second option is to extract descriptions of coherent subflows into subsections of their own, to be referenced from the main description (see the *Example* section, below). Together with a reference to the separate subsection, a short summary of the extracted text should be provided in the main description to give the reader an indication of its contents. In this way, the reader will get an overview of the complete flow and can study the detailed descriptions when needed. This proves particularly useful if the use-case description includes technical details of little or no interest to some categories of readers (see also Chapter 25, "Orthogonal Views").

Of course, these two techniques can be combined. However, remember to keep the overall goal in mind: Use-case descriptions should be easy to understand and to review by all relevant stakeholders. Therefore, the level of abstraction in the description should not be modified just to make the

Example   201

description short. Instead, to make them effective, the same level of detail should be used in all descriptions for the same use-case model (see Chapter 13, "Describing Use Cases," Chapter 30, "Legacy System," and Chapter 42, "Mistake: Mix of Abstraction Levels").

When two or more equally important variants of a use case can be distinguished, it is possible to split the use case and promote the variants into use cases of their own, according to the Large Use Case: Multiple Paths pattern. If the variants have different business values, they should be modeled as separate use cases; even if they have the same business value, the variants may be split into separate use cases just to make the descriptions easier to handle and understand. Of course, it is never a good idea to make a separate use case of a small alternative flow or of an exceptional flow, because this would make the descriptions of the use cases as well as the use-case model as a whole more difficult to understand.

If the same short alternative flow is to be used in several of the use cases, it can be extracted into a separate inclusion use case (see Chapter 17, "Commonality"). Similarly, if the same statements, rules, and regulations about the business are valid for several of the use cases, these facts should be expressed as business rules and be referenced from the descriptions of the use cases (see Chapter 16, "Business Rules").

Example

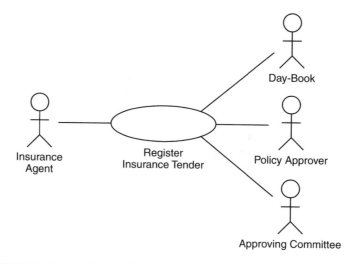

Figure 21.1   The example consists of one use case and four actors.

In this example, there is only one use case, named `Register Insurance Tender` (see Figure 21.1). In this use case, the `Insurance Agent`, most likely sitting together with the policyholder to be, will register all the information about the policyholder, the beneficiaries, and so on. When all information is entered, the use case will check whether the tender can be sent for immediate approval or whether a more thorough evaluation of the tender must be done (if the policyholder practices sky diving, for example).

This is an example of the *Large Use Case: Long Sequence* pattern. The basic flow gives an overview of how the use case is usually performed. The description includes references to other subsections of the use-case description that contain the detailed descriptions of the flow.

Other useful patterns in this example are the *Business Rules*, the *CRUD,* and the *Multiple Actors* patterns.

Use Case: Register Insurance Tender

Brief Description

The Insurance Agent submits a tender for a life insurance. The use case registers the tender in the Day-Book and informs the Policy Approver or the Approving Committee about the new tender.

Basic Flow

The use case starts when the Insurance Agent chooses to register a tender for a new life insurance. The use case asks whether it is a new tender or whether a draft already exists.

The Insurance Agent either enters the identity of an existing draft or selects to create a new one. If an identity is entered, the use case retrieves the existing draft; otherwise, a new tender is created and its identity is presented to the Insurance Agent.

The use case presents the registered name, address, and so on about the policyholder to the Insurance Agent, who can modify the information (see the section *Register Policyholder Name*).

The use case presents the registered status of the policyholder to the Insurance Agent, who can modify the information (see the section *Register Policyholder Status*).

Example   203

The use case presents the registered information about the beneficiaries to the Insurance Agent, who can modify the information (see the section *Register Beneficiaries*).

The use case calculates a preliminary payout based on the input from the Insurance Agent (see the section *Calculate Preliminary Payout*) and presents it to the Insurance Agent.

The use case presents the registered information about how the insurance is to be paid to the Insurance Agent, who can modify the information (see the section *Register Payment Information*).

The use case displays the stored information about the tender to the Insurance Agent and requests an acceptance of the tender.

The Insurance Agent accepts, postpones, or deletes the tender:

- If the Insurance Agent chooses to delete the tender, all the information about the tender is removed and the use case ends.

- If the Insurance Agent chooses to postpone the tender, the use case ends.

- If the Insurance Agent accepts the tender, the use case sends it to the Day-Book system. Then, the use case checks that the values describing the status of the policyholder are within the approved limits. If so, the status of the tender is set to *to be approved* and a notification carrying the identity of the tender is sent to the Policy Approver. If some of the status values are outside the limits, the status of the tender is set to *to be evaluated* and a notification carrying the identity of the tender is sent to the Approving Committee. Finally, the use case ends.

Alternative Flows

Illegal Identity

If no tender is registered with the provided identity, the use case will ask the Insurance Agent to provide a new identity or to choose to create a new tender. The use case continues where the Insurance Agent is to provide the identity of the tender.

Subflows

REGISTER POLICYHOLDER NAME

[. . .]

REGISTER POLICYHOLDER STATUS

[. . .]

REGISTER BENEFICIARIES

[. . .]

CALCULATE PRELIMINARY PAYOUT

[. . .]

REGISTER PAYMENT INFORMATION

[. . .]

Analysis Model

There is no analysis model for this chapter because the size of the use-case description does not affect the structure of the analysis model. However, if the system as a whole is large, it might be good to organize it in subsystems (see also Chapter 18, "Component Hierarchy").

Chapter 22

Layered System

Intent

Structure the use-case model so that each use case is defined within one layer, and use relationships between the use cases in different layers to allow use-case instances to span multiple layers.

Characteristics: Common in mid-size and large systems. Advanced solution.

Keywords: Accessing lower layers, application-specific functionality, dependency direction, directed dependency, domain-specific functionality, level of abstraction.

Patterns

In each of the *Layered System* patterns, there are two packages modeling two layers, and a package import relationship from the package representing the upper layer to the package representing the lower layer. The relationship implies that the (public) contents of the lower-layer package become available inside the upper-layer package. All relationships between elements defined in different layer packages are defined within the upper-layer package.

According to UML, a plus sign (+) in front of the name means that the element is public (that is, it can be used outside the package), whereas a minus sign (–) means that it is private (that is, it must not be used outside the package).

Note that in the pattern models that follow, the use case defined in the lower layer is public in that layer and hence imported into the upper layer. However, because this very same use case is defined to be private in the upper layer, it will not be imported into another layer on top of the upper layer.

Layered System: Reuse

Model

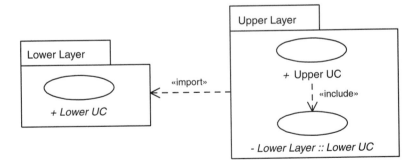

Description

The *Layered System: Reuse* pattern contains two use cases and two packages with a package import relationship between the packages. The use case defined in the upper layer has an include relationship to the use case that is defined in the lower layer and imported into the upper layer. The use case defined in the lower layer is often, but not always, abstract (see Chapter 19, "Concrete Extension or Inclusion").

Applicability

This pattern is appropriate when the use-case instance starts in the upper layer, but will use a service defined in the lower layer. It is not suitable when the use-case instance starts in the lower layer.

Type

Structure pattern.

Layered System: Addition

Model

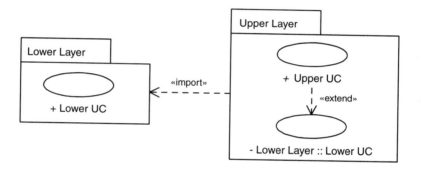

Description

In another *Layered System* pattern, the use case defined in the upper layer extends the use case defined in the lower layer. Here the use-case instance starts in the lower layer, but services defined in the upper layer are inserted into it. The use case in the upper layer is normally abstract; that is, it will usually not be performed as an instance of its own.

The difference between this alternative and the previous one is the relationship between the upper use case and the lower use case.

Applicability

This pattern is applicable when the use-case instance starts in the lower layer, but should not be used if it starts in the upper layer.

Type

Structure pattern.

Layered System: Specialization

Model

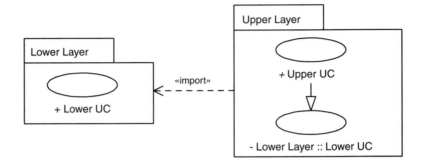

Description

In the Layered System: Specialization pattern, the use case defined in the upper layer is a specialization of the use case defined in the lower layer; that is, the former has a generalization to the latter.

Applicability

This pattern is applicable when the upper use case is of the same kind as the lower use case. (In UML, generalization is a taxonomic relationship; see Chapter 11, "Use-Case Generalization: Classification and Inheritance.") It is not applicable whenever the use-case instance follows a combination of descriptions from the two layers.

Type

Structure pattern.

Layered System: Embedded

Model

Description

In this alternative pattern, no lower-layer use cases are available. Instead, the access of the information inside the lower layer is described inside the descriptions of the use cases in the upper layer.

Applicability

This pattern is used when the upper layer only performs single operations on information in the lower layer or when the lower layer consists of a platform that is not to be modified. The information in the lower layer is considered available in the system when writing use-case descriptions for the upper layer.

Type

Description pattern.

Discussion

Most nontrivial systems are organized in layers, with lower layers containing basic parts and more application-specific parts placed higher up in the layer hierarchy (see Figure 22.1). The latter parts may (as a matter of course) make use of the parts located in the lower layers, although the opposite is not allowed; the general modeling principle when modeling a layered system is that an entity may only be dependent on elements in the same layer or on elements in lower layers, whereas it may not depend on elements higher up in the layer hierarchy. This principle leads to an overall structure having a general direction: *from* application-specific elements *to* elements that are more general. The number of circular or bidirectional dependencies is therefore reduced, because such dependencies are only allowed within layers, not between layers.

When it comes to the question of whether it should be possible to access elements in layers further down in the layering structure—not immediately below the current layer—there are two schools of thought, one stating that this should be prevented, and the other allowing it. Whichever of the alternatives is chosen, it can be imposed by giving imported elements visibility according to the following principle: Giving elements imported into a certain layer from the layer below *public* (+) visibility makes them accessible by elements in the layer above, whereas if they are *private* (–) in the importing layer they are not visible above this layer. In the pattern models presented above, we have applied the conservative approach by making imported elements *private*, but this is obviously easily changed if the other approach is chosen.

We refer you to *Software Architecture in Practice* (Bass, Clements, and Kazman 2003) or *Software Reuse: Architecture, Process, and Organization for Business Success* (Jacobson, Griss, and Jonsson 1997) for a more thorough description of layers.

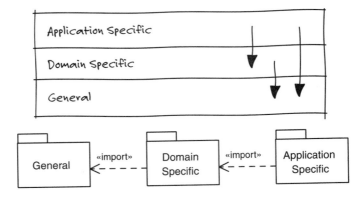

Figure 22.1   Systems are often organized in layers, in which elements in a lower layer may be used by elements in layers above, but not the other way around. It must be decided whether to allow access according to the arrow to the right in the upper part of the figure. In UML, layers can be modeled using packages with package import relationships in the allowed access direction.

This layering technique is also applicable when using a framework or component library where the predefined parts and components are placed in a lower layer and the part of the application to be developed is put in the upper layer.

The structure of a system using layers also affects the use-case model. Although a specific usage of the system—a use-case instance—can span several layers (remember that a use-case instance is a complete usage of the system), the use cases themselves should not do so because the general modeling principles for layered systems say that an element should be located in one layer only. Different use cases will be placed in different, distinct layers based on what information and what services each layer is to contain. This technique implies that separate parts of concrete use cases will be extracted and put into separate, possibly abstract use cases defined in different layers. Relationships are defined between the use cases declared in the different layers to define the complete usages of the layered system. These relationships are of course defined in accordance with the general "downward" direction of the structure.

In the simple case when a usage of the system is localized to one layer—containing and exploiting only information and behavior situated in that layer—it is obviously modeled by a use case that is defined solely within that particular layer.

What then are the implications if the usage spans several layers—if a use-case instance uses information and performs behavior localized in multiple layers? To define one use case containing the complete declaration of such a use-case instance would be impossible, because such a use case would span over multiple layers. Instead, we must split such a use case into several use cases distributed over the layers—each use case to be defined in one layer only.

These use cases are bound to have different kinds of relationships to each other—include, extend, and generalization—so that the use-case instance can be assembled from all these declarations. Again, because of modeling principles, these relationships will always be directed downward in the layer hierarchy.

Simple Access of Lower-Layer Information

When use of a lower layer is limited to applying simple operations on information, defining use cases in the lower layer for this is often overkill. Such use cases would all be very simple and short, and would probably not contribute to the understanding of the lower layer. Instead, we simply consider the information the lower layer contains available in the system when writing use-case descriptions for the upper layer. This makes usage of the lower level embedded in the use-case descriptions instead of explicit in the model, according to the Layered System: Embedded pattern.

This pattern is also suitable in the special case where a lower layer consists of a platform over which we have no influence.

Include Lower-Layer Use Cases

We say that a use case in the upper layer *uses* a service in the lower layer if there is an include relationship from the upper use case to the use case in the lower layer modeling the used service, as in the Layered System: Reuse pattern. In this way, we can reuse the more basic use cases defined in the lower layer when we define the use cases in the upper layer. A use-case instance will follow the flow declared in the upper use case, and in this declaration will be included the flow declared in the lower use case; hence, the use-case instance spans both the upper and the lower layer, as shown in Figure 22.2.

In a bank system, there are two layers. The lower layer contains parts for banking in general, such as handling accounts, managing stock portfolios, and handling loans. Use cases for these parts are defined within this layer. The upper layer contains parts that are specific for this particular bank system, such as financial advice for the customers based on their current situation (age, savings, loans, real estate, and so on). The use cases in this layer describe how they make use of use cases defined in the lower, more general layer.

For example, in the lower layer we will find a use case for buying and selling stocks. This use case includes another use case that retrieves and presents the customer's portfolio so that the Clerk can see the exact number of shares, bonds, liquid assets available, and so forth. In the upper layer, there is a use case to support the Clerk in giving a customer financial advice. During this process, the Clerk has to be able to find out all about the customer's financial situation. Therefore, this use case must also include the View Portfolio use case. An import relationship from the upper layer to the lower one makes it possible to define the include relationship within the upper layer.

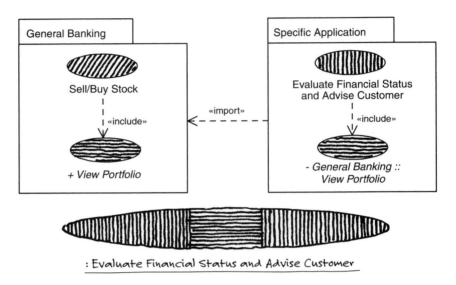

Figure 22.2   A use case in the upper layer may have an include relationship to a use case in the lower layer. A use-case instance will therefore span both the upper and the lower layer, as indicated by the hatching.

To sum up: The portfolio use case is defined in the lower layer, because it models a more general (or basic) service in the system. This makes it possible for other use cases to include it when modeling more specific (or advanced) services defined in the upper layer.

This pattern—*Layered System: Reuse*—proves useful when the flow starts in the upper layer and partly continues in the lower layer (possibly several times in different use cases).

Extend Lower-Layer Use Cases

If the flow instead starts in the lower layer (*Layered System: Addition*), we will use a lower-layer use case describing what happens if an actor of the system performs some action, such as sending some information to the system. This use case describes the system's response to this action, but only that part of the response that takes place in this layer. In the upper layer, we will find a use case that performs the application-specific part of the behavior.

In this case, the include relationship is not applicable to connect the two use cases, because the base use case is in a lower layer, implying that the direction of the include relationship would be upward. Instead, an extend relationship is defined from the upper to the lower use case. Hence, a use-case instance will start by performing the behavior declared in the use case that is defined in the lower layer, and then at the extension point continue by performing the behavior declared in the use case in the upper layer. Again, the use-case instance spans both layers even though each one of the two use cases is defined in only one layer. By using a relationship directed downward in the layering hierarchy, we follow the layer modeling principles (see Figure 22.3).

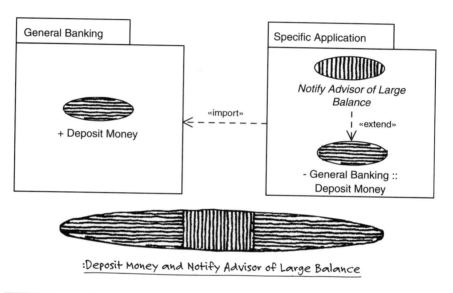

:Deposit Money and Notify Advisor of Large Balance

Figure 22.3   A use case in the upper layer may have an extend relationship to a use case in the lower layer, but not the other way around because of the layer modeling principles. A use-case instance will span both the upper and the lower layer.

In our bank example, the customers can deposit money. If the sum of money in the account is large—that is, if the balance in the account passes a specific threshold value—an advisor of the bank is notified. The advisor will then contact the customer and suggest that they meet to discuss what should be done with this large sum of money. The customer can, of course, always decline that meeting, but the system should at least notify the adviser so that the contact can be made.

In the lower layer, there is a use case modeling how money is to be deposited. This use case is placed in the lower layer because it deals with a general service in the system. The notification use case is placed in the upper layer because it models a specific service for this system and has nothing to do with managing accounts. The use case is abstract because it will never be performed on its own; a notification will not be sent unless there is a use case modifying the balance of an account. To achieve the desired functionality, the notification use case extends the depositing use case; that is, a use-case instance performing the depositing may be extended with the actions described in the use case to notify the advisor.

Combinations of Relationships

These two patterns can be combined, of course. As shown in Figure 22.4, the flow can start as declared by a use case in the lower layer. This use case can be extended by multiple use cases in the upper layer. Once the flow is in the upper layer, it can include flows declared in use cases defined in the lower layer. A similar structure can be obtained if the flow starts in the upper layer.

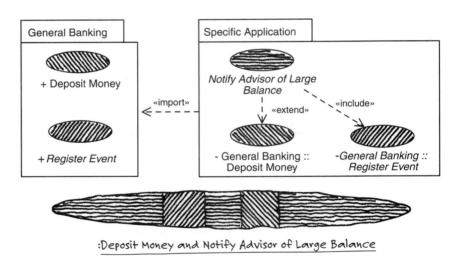

:Deposit Money and Notify Advisor of Large Balance

Figure 22.4   A use-case instance can start following the declaration given by a use case in the lower layer, and then continue according to the declaration in a use case in the upper layer, followed by the flow declared in the use case in the lower layer, and so on.

In the example above, when the advisor is to be notified that the balance of an account exceeds a given threshold level, the system is also to register that this event has occurred so that the advisor can find information about it later. As we already know, this use-case instance starts in the lower layer when the depositing occurs. After the deposit, the balance is seen to exceed the threshold level, and therefore the use-case instance is extended with the actions of the notification use case in the upper layer. These actions include those defined in the use case that registers the event that, in turn, is defined in the lower layer (see Figure 22.4). Therefore, the use-case instance starts in the lower layer, continues in the upper layer, and then it is carried on in the lower layer again before it ends.

Generalization

In some cases, especially where a framework is used, many predefined use cases are included in the system. These use cases exist in the layer modeling the framework. If some of these use cases are to be specialized to capture the exact behavior of the application at hand, the specializations of the use case are put in the application layer (the upper layer) and the generalizations will go from the upper to the lower use cases—once again, in accordance with the modeling principles for modeling layered systems. In this way, complete use cases can be reused, and developers need only provide the specialized parts of those use cases, according to the `Layered System: Specialization` pattern.

In many office systems, there is a part handling the registration and the performance of the work tasks. However, even though the registration service is often useful as it is, the functionality of the performance service must usually be specialized in each installation of the office system.

Assume that there is such an office system in our bank example. This system is included in a layer below `General Banking`, called `General Office`, because it has nothing to do with banking per se. In this layer, there is a use case called `Perform Task` that models that a task is selected from the collection of all the registered tasks, that the task is performed, that the task may have to be rescheduled if it could not be completed, and so on.

However, in the bank system, all tasks having to do with something that affects a customer's money, loans, or securities must always be logged for security reasons. Therefore, the `Perform`

Task use case defined in the office system must be modified to capture this additional requirement. This modification is described in a use case, called `Perform Task in Banking`, defined in the `General Banking` layer, because this modification is specific to the banking business. Because the new use case is of the same kind as the `Perform Task` use case, a generalization is defined between the two, as shown in Figure 22.5.

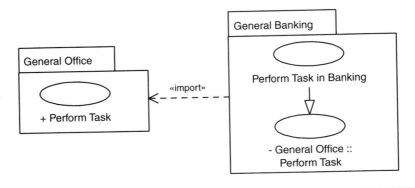

Figure 22.5   A use case defined in a lower layer can be specialized in an upper layer.

Example

This section presents the use-case description of the use cases in the bank example discussed in the previous section and shown in Figure 22.4. Therefore, it uses the first two *Layered System* patterns. The first use case is `Deposit Money`, which models how an amount of money is deposited into a bank account. `Register Event` is the second use case, modeling the registration of an event in a log, so that the information about the event can be retrieved later. The last use case, `Notify Advisor of Large Balance`, informs an advisor that the new balance of an account is above a specific threshold, so that the advisor can contact the customer and discuss what to do with the money. This use case, which is defined in the upper layer, both extends the `Deposit Money` use case and includes the `Register Event` use case. The latter two use cases are defined in the lower layer.

See also the *Message Transfer: Automatic* blueprint.

Example 217

Use Case: Deposit Money

Brief Description

The use case registers the deposition of money into a bank account. The money is handed from a customer to a Clerk, which registers the deposition.

Extension Points

Transaction Completed—After the transaction has been logged.

Basic Flow

The use case starts when the Clerk chooses to deposit some money. The use case requests the account number and the amount to be deposited.

The Clerk enters the number and the amount. The use case checks that there is an account with that number, and that money may be deposited to it. If so, the balance of the account is increased with the deposited amount, as well as the registered balance of the Clerk's cash account.

The use case stores the account number, the Clerk's ID, the date and time, and the amount in the transaction log and retrieves a transaction ID, which is printed on a receipt together with the amount and the date and time of the transaction.

The use case ends.

Alternative Flows

No Account

If there is no account with the given account number, the Clerk is notified with an error message and the use case ends.

Not Enabled for Deposition

If the account must not be used for deposition of money, the Clerk is notified with an error message and the use case ends.

Use Case: Register Event

Brief Description

The use case registers an event in the event log.

The use case is abstract.

Basic Flow

When this use case is included by other use cases, the use-case instance continues by performing the following actions:

The use case stores in the event log all the information about the event as well as the date and time and the identity of the user.

The subflow ends and the use-case instance continues as described in the base use case after the location where this use case was included.

Use Case: Notify Advisor of Large Balance

Brief Description

The use case notifies an Advisor that the balance of an account exceeds a threshold.

The use case is abstract.

Basic Flow

The flow of this use case is inserted into the Deposit Money use-case instance if the balance of the account exceeds the large-balance threshold at the Transaction Completed extension point.

The use case retrieves the name and address of the owner of the account together with the current balance of the account.

The use case identifies the Advisor responsible for the account. This Advisor is notified by the use case that the balance of an account exceeds the large-balance threshold. The use case also sends the retrieved account information to the Advisor.

The use case registers the retrieved account information and by how much the account exceeds the threshold as described in the included Register Event use case.

The subflow ends and the use-case instance continues according to the Deposit Money use case after the Transaction Completed extension point.

Alternative Flows

If no Advisor is assigned to the account, the use case sends the retrieved account information by email to the Head Advisor.

Analysis Model

In principle, the modeling of a layered system will not introduce any specific techniques, as long as the dependency directions between the layers are fulfilled, which is to say that elements in a lower layer must not be dependent on elements in an upper layer. The existing techniques used for realizing use cases and their relationships are sufficient. Following are a few guidelines commonly used when modeling layered systems.

Simple Access of Lower-Layer Information

As mentioned previously, when the only part of a use case that belongs in a lower level is a simple operation on information in the lower layer, this can be modeled entirely within a use case in the upper level (`Layered System: Embedded`).

This implies that classes in the upper layer may have associations to entity classes in the lower layer, as long as these associations are used only for simple operations. These associations are defined in the upper layer, and should be navigable only in the direction toward the lower-layer class. This implies that the lower-layer classes must be imported into the upper layer to become available when defining the associations (see Figure 22.6).

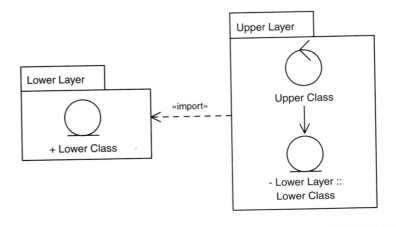

Figure 22.6   A class in the upper layer can have an association to a class imported from the lower layer, so that objects of the upper class can apply operations on objects of the lower class.

Include Lower-Layer Use Cases

When realizing an include relationship from a use case defined in the upper layer to an inclusion use case in the lower layer (*Layered System: Reuse*), we make use of a class defined in the lower layer and use it in the realization of the inclusion use case. This class, usually a control class (see Chapter 15, "Mapping Use Cases onto Classes"), is imported into the upper layer, and an association is defined in the upper layer from a class participating in the realization of the upper use case to this imported class (see Figure 22.7).

This association is used for invoking the realization of the inclusion use case, and when the included flow is completed, the control is transferred back to the realization of the base use case using the same association.

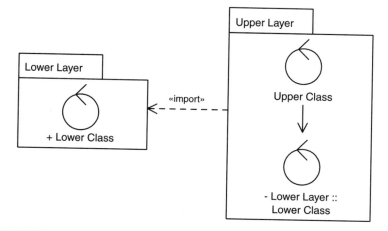

Figure 22.7   The realization of an include relationship from an upper-layer use case to a lower-layer use case is usually done with an association from a control class realizing the upper-layer use case to a control class realizing the lower-layer use case. The latter class must be imported into the upper layer to be available when defining the association.

Extend Lower-Layer Use Cases

When realizing an extend relationship from a use case defined in the upper layer to a base use case in the lower layer (`Layered System: Addition`), we use a technique similar to the one described above; a class defined in the lower layer that is used in the realization of the base use case is imported into the upper layer. Because this class is not to be modified (it is defined in a lower layer and hence must be kept independent of the elements in the upper layer), however, we cannot define a communication from that class to a class defined in the upper layer to invoke the extension flow. Another technique must be used.

We can, for example, define an extend relationship from the class defined in the upper layer to the class defined in the lower layer (Jacobson et al. 1993). Another alternative is to define a subclass of the lower-layer class in the upper layer and let this class send a notification to relevant classes in the upper layer. A third option is to expand the second alternative and use the Observer design pattern (Gamma et al. 1995). However, this alternative requires that the classes in the lower layer have been prepared in advance for this pattern (see Figure 22.8), because we only have read access to the lower layer when developing the upper layer.

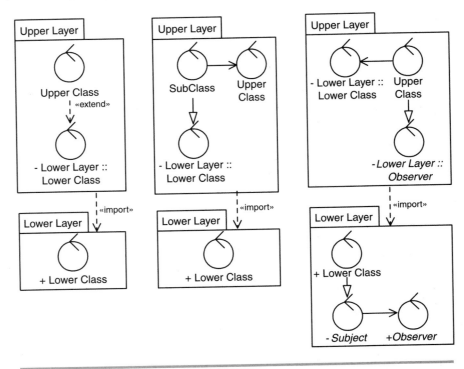

Figure 22.8   The realization of an extend relationship between use cases in different layers can be done in several different ways.

Specialization of a Use Case

If a use case in the lower layer is specialized by a use case defined in the upper layer (`Layered System: Specialization`), two different techniques can be used depending on the situation. In the first case, the upper use case specializes a part of the flow defined in the lower use case. In this case, the class in the lower layer realizing the flow to be specialized is identified. This is usually a control class or a boundary class. This class is imported into the upper layer, and a new class with a generalization to the imported one is introduced in the upper layer. This new class realizes the specialized flow, possibly together with a collection of other classes, also defined in the upper layer (see Figure 22.9).

In the second case, an additional flow is added by the upper use case. Here, the class performing the actions *before* the added ones is specialized in the upper layer. In the specialized version of the class, the new actions are added, possibly including communications to other classes defined in the upper layer (see Figure 22.9).

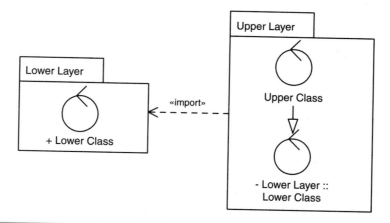

Figure 22.9   Realization of a generalization between use cases in different layers usually involves a specialization of a class defined in the lower layer.

CHAPTER 23

MULTIPLE ACTORS

Intent

Capture commonalities between actors while keeping separate roles apart.

Characteristics: Very common. Basic.

Keywords: Common role, different roles, generalization of actors, overlapping actors, several users of a use case.

Patterns

Multiple Actors: Distinct Roles

Model

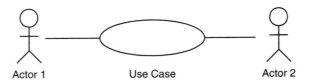

Actor 1   Use Case   Actor 2

Description

The `Multiple Actors: Distinct Roles` pattern consists of one use case and (at least) two actors.

Applicability

This pattern is used when the two actors play different roles toward the use case; that is, they interact differently with the use case.

Type

Structure pattern.

Multiple Actors: Common Role

Model

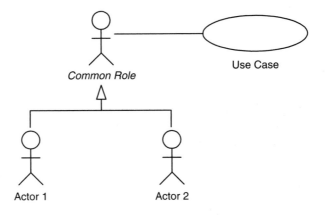

Description

In an alternative pattern, the two actors play the same role toward the use case. This role is represented by another actor, inherited by the actors sharing this role.

Applicability

This pattern is applicable when, from the use case's point of view, there is only one external entity interacting with each instance of the use case.

Type

Structure pattern.

Discussion

When identifying use cases, we often find that two actors become associated with the same use case. Typically, this means that there are multiple external entities interested in using the system in the way modeled by this use case. However, in such situations it is important to find out whether the two actors play identical roles toward the use case or whether the roles differ. We need this information not only to understand the details of the use case, but also to define the interfaces of the system. We need to establish, from the use case's point of view, how many external instances will interact with each instance of the use case.

If two external instances are interacting with an instance of the use case and these external instances act differently, clearly two actors should be associated with the use case, and the `Multiple Actors: Distinct Roles` pattern is to be used.

In the telephone exchange example, two actors are associated with the `Local Call` use case (see Figure 23.1). Clearly, the `Caller` and the `Callee` act differently from the use case's point of view. The `Caller` initiates the use case, dials the digits, and is charged for the call, whereas the `Callee` is the subscriber who just answers the call. Therefore, it is correct to associate two actors with the use case.

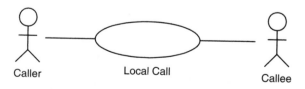

Caller   Local Call   Callee

Figure 23.1   The two external entities play different roles toward the `Local Call` use case.

However, if only one external entity is interacting with each instance of the use case, only one actor should be associated with the use case. Having two actors associated with the use case would give the impression that there will be two external instances interacting with each instance of the use case, which is obviously not correct. Instead, the `Multiple Actors: Common Role` pattern should be applied.

This situation typically occurs when people in different roles within the business use the same use case in the supporting software system. If these act differently toward the system in other contexts than this particular use case—for example, if they use different use cases—they should be modeled as different actors with generalizations to an abstract actor representing the common role. If they always play the same role toward the system, however, only the common role is relevant and the corresponding actor is instead concrete.

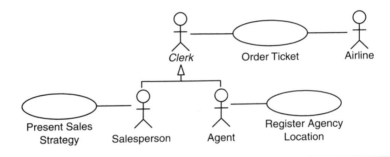

Figure 23.2   There is only one role played by external entities toward the `Order Ticket` use case.

In the Airline ticketing example (see Figure 23.2), both a sales person and an outside agent can order tickets; that is, they can both make use of the `Order Ticket` use case. However, from the use case's point of view, there is only one external entity interacting with each instance of the use case. The salesperson and the agent will play the same role toward the use case, so the use case cannot perceive a difference between them. Therefore, there is only one actor associated with the use case. If we have already identified two actors in the model—`Salesperson` and `Agent`—because of other use cases, we must now introduce a new, abstract actor, called `Clerk`, and define an association between this actor and the `Order Ticket` use case. Because the `Salesperson` and the `Agent` actors are to be associated with that use case, we define a generalization from each of them to the `Clerk` actor. In this way, both the `Salesperson` and the `Agent` have an (inherited) association to the `Order Ticket` use case, and the use case is only associated with one actor.

If `Salesperson` and `Agent` are not needed as actors to other use cases, we just model one actor: the `Clerk`.

Example   229

Example

This section provides two examples of use-case descriptions: Local Call (see Figure 23.1) as an example of the first pattern, and Order Ticket (see Figure 23.2) as an example of the second one. The former is associated with two actors, whereas the latter is associated with one. Obviously, the description of the Order Ticket use case does not indicate whether any actors have generalizations to the Clerk actor.

The *Orthogonal Views* as well as the *Component Hierarchy* patterns are probably useful in the first example, whereas the *CRUD* patterns may be relevant in the second example.

Use Case: Local Call

Brief Description

A Caller makes a call to a Callee connected to the same telephone exchange.

Basic Flow

The use case starts when the Caller lifts the handset. The use case checks that the Caller is allowed to make outgoing calls and, if so, registers that the Caller is busy and sends a connection tone to the Caller.

The Caller dials a digit, and the use case disconnects the connection tone and analyzes whether enough digits have been received for determining the direction of the call.

[. . .]

When the necessary number of digits has been received, the use case identifies the Callee, registers the Callee as busy, and requests that the network connect the call between the Caller and the Callee. Then, a ring tone is sent to the Caller and a ring signal is sent to the Callee.

The Callee answers the call. The use case stops the ring tone and disconnects the ring signal.

When both the Caller and the Callee have hung up, the use case requests the network to disconnect the call. Finally, the use case registers both the Caller and the Callee as idle.

The use case ends.

Alternative Flows

Canceling Call

At any moment in time before the Callee has answered the call, the Caller can hang up. If the network has connected the call, the use case requests that it be disconnected and registers the Callee as idle. Then the Caller is registered as idle, and the use case ends.

Interrupting Call

When the call has been answered, the Caller or the Callee may hang up. Their communication stops, but the network is still connected.

Resuming Interrupted Call

If either the Caller or the Callee has hung up and that party later lifts the handset again, the call will be continued.

Use Case: Order Ticket

Brief Description

The Clerk registers a new ticket in the system and the included flights are booked at the Airlines.

Basic Flow

The use case starts when the Clerk chooses to register a new ticket. The use case asks the Clerk for the name and address of the customer.

The Clerk enters the requested information, and the use case checks whether the customer has been registered earlier. If so, the Clerk is informed how many tickets the customer has bought within the past 12 months, and whether the customer is a VIP customer.

Example   231

The use case asks what flights are to be included in the ticket, their origin and destination, or whether a suitable flight should be found.

- The Clerk enters the selected flight number, the origin and the destination, and the departure date and time.

- If the Clerk instead chooses to ask for a suitable flight, the Look-Up Flight use case is included. If the result consists of several possible flights, the use case asks the Clerk to select one of the flights. The Clerk selects a flight.

For each flight:

The use case sends a booking request to the Airline.

If the Airline returns a confirmation number, the use case includes it in the reservation. If the Airline instead returns a reservation failure, the Clerk is notified and the flight is not included in the reservation.

The use case presents the complete reservation to the Clerk and asks for a confirmation from the Clerk.

The Clerk confirms the reservation. The use case registers a new ticket and stores the name and address of the customer together with the flights and their departure and arrival dates and times. The name of the Clerk is retrieved from the system and stored. Finally, a reservation number is displayed to the Clerk, and the use case asks the Clerk to acknowledge it.

The Clerk acknowledges the reservation number.

The use case ends.

Alternative Flows

No Connection with Airline

If the connection with the Airline cannot be established, the Clerk is notified, and the flight is not included in the ticket.

No Flight

If no flights have been included in the ticket when it is to be registered, the Clerk is notified and no ticket is created. The use case continues by asking what flights are to be included.

RESERVATION CANCELED

If the Clerk chooses not to confirm the reservation, the use case asks for a confirmation of the cancellation.

If the cancellation confirmation is received from the Clerk, the reservation is removed from the system, any booked flight is canceled, and the use case ends. If the cancellation is discarded, the use case continues by asking for confirmation of the reservation.

Analysis Model

There is no analysis model for this chapter, because it is about modeling entities external to the system. However, we have three important comments to make:

- Even if the use case is used by external entities of differing natures, such as a person and a machine, only one actor is associated with the use case if each use-case instance interacts with only one external entity. The difference in communication is handled by having two different boundary classes. In the example in Figure 23.3, the person will use a web page while the computer will interact through a communication protocol.

- For each kind of external entity, there is one use-case realization of the use case. The differences between these use-case realizations are the boundary classes used by the different kinds of external users. However, these boundary classes will share the interfaces toward the interior of the system, such as the control classes. This interaction must be the same, even if the detailed messages sent to the external entities may be quite different.

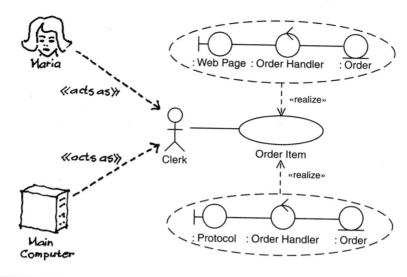

Figure 23.3   One use case can have multiple use-case realizations depending on the external entity playing the role of the actor.

- The different kinds of external users may have different access rights to the system; that is, different levels of information and different functions of the system are available to them. However, this is no reason why we should split the use case into two or to allow two actors to play the same role toward the same use case. Instead, different access rights between the users are handled as is described in Chapter 27, "Access Control."

CHAPTER 24

OPTIONAL SERVICE

Intent

Separate mandatory parts of the use cases from optional parts that can be ordered and delivered separately.

Characteristics: Common. Basic solution.

Keywords: Ordering unit, separating services, system configuration, system version.

Patterns

Optional Service: Addition

Model

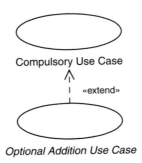

Compulsory Use Case

«extend»

Optional Addition Use Case

Description

The `Optional Service: Addition` pattern contains two use cases and an extend relationship. The first use case models a usage that is compulsory in the system. The second use case models an addition to the first use case that can be added to the system. Because only the additional part is expressed in the second use case, it is abstract; that is, it will not be performed on its own. The complete use case—the compulsory behavior together with the optional behavior—is formed by the aggregation of the two, expressed by the extend relationship.

Applicability

This pattern is preferred when the optional part is a pure addition to the compulsory use case.

Type

Structure pattern.

Optional Service: Specialization

Model

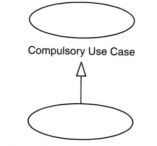

Compulsory Use Case

Optional, More Advanced Use Case

Description

In another `Optional Service` pattern, the compulsory use case is special-ized into a use case including the optional part.

Applicability

We choose this pattern when the compulsory use case includes a simple form of the optional behavior. The child use case will specialize this sim-ple part into the optional, more advanced behavior.

Type

Structure pattern.

Optional Service: Independent

Model

Compulsory Use Case

Optional Use Case

Description

The most straightforward `Optional Service` pattern models the optional parts as separate use cases with no relationships with the compulsory use cases.

Applicability

This pattern is applicable when the optional service is independent of the compulsory services.

Type

Structure pattern.

Discussion

From a configuration point of view, it would be disastrous to mix mandatory and optional parts. The mandatory parts will always be delivered, whereas the optional parts will be delivered only when they have explicitly been ordered. Therefore, these parts must be separated, not only in the code but also in the models, because the models are also deliverables.

More generally speaking, parts with different ordering criteria must be separated because they are not always to be delivered together. Moreover, two parts may both be mandatory, but at the same time also be alternatives to each other, or in other words, be mutually exclusive. For example, a sailing boat may have either a steering wheel or a tiller, but sailing boats with both types of steering equipment are very rare. Still, it is mandatory to have one of the two facilities, each of which will have its own ordering criteria. In the following discussion, we distinguish only between compulsory parts and optional parts, even though the arguments are the same for handling parts with different ordering criteria.

Because one usage of a system often spans over several parts of it, it is quite common that both mandatory and optional parts of the system will be employed. This means that use cases often contain both mandatory and optional parts in the first draft of the use-case model. However, it must be possible to deliver a version of the model that covers only what a particular customer has ordered. The optional parts must therefore be extracted from the mandatory use cases and be put into separate use cases in the final version of the use-case model. In this way, a mandatory use case will contain only actions that every installation of the system must have, and the optional parts can be included upon request.

So, how do we model that the optional parts may be added to the mandatory use cases? Clearly, the most obvious way is to use extend relationships from the optional parts to the mandatory parts as in the `Optional Service: Addition` pattern (see Figure 24.1). This implies that one configuration of the system can contain only the compulsory service, and another configuration has the more advanced one consisting of the compulsory part extended with the optional part. This is one of the original purposes of the extend relationship: It makes it possible to add to an already existing model additional parts having other, less-compulsory ordering criteria, without any changes of the existing parts.

In a typical text editor, there is one use case modeling entering and modification of the text. An optional service that may be included, possibly depending on how much the writer paid for this configuration of the editor, is automatic spell checking. At the same time the writer enters or modifies the text, the editor will look for spelling errors. Because it is not included in all versions of the system, those parts that deal with the spell checking are extracted into a separate use case with an extend relationship to the Edit Text use case (see Figure 24.1).

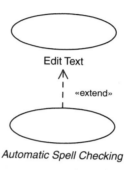

Figure 24.1   The automatic spell checking of a text is treated as an optional part of the system. Hence, it is extracted into a separate, abstract use case with an extend relationship to the Edit Text use case.

There is, of course, more behavior involved in spell checking, such as an administrative use case for defining new words. All these use cases, including the abstract Automatic Spell Checking use case, can be grouped together in a package representing the entire spell checking service.

Another alternative way of handling optional behavior is used when the system always has to include the function: either in a simple or in a more advanced form. In this case, the simple version of the function is modeled with one use case, and the more advanced function as another use case. Because the more advanced version is a specialization of the simple, a generalization is introduced from the advanced use case to the simple use case, according to the *Optional Service: Specialization* pattern. In the basic configuration of the system, the simple use case (the parent), is included and the child use case, which models the advanced form of the function, is included in the more advanced configuration of the system.

Assume that the text editor will always include the automatic spell checking service, but what is done when an error is found may differ. The simplest and most straightforward way is to decorate the erroneous word in some way so that the writer understands that the word is misspelled and can correct it. An optional alternative is to automatically correct the word, if possible (see Figure 24.2).

Each time someone buys a copy of the text editor, he or she has to choose between the `Edit Text with Automatic Decoration of Misspelled Words` use case and the `Edit Text with Automatic Correction of Misspelled Words`. Both of them must not be used in the same installation.

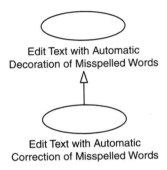

Figure 24.2   The spell checking is mandatory in the system, but it can be performed in two different ways. Therefore, the two use cases are variants of each other, and only one of them should be used in one installation of the system.

In a variant of this model, the function itself is modeled as one use case, the parent use case, and the different versions of it as separate child use cases. This alternative is recommended when there are multiple versions of the functions and there is no one version that can be seen as the parent of all the different versions (see Figure 24.3).

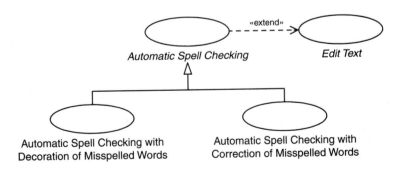

Figure 24.3   The function itself is modeled as a separate, abstract use case (the parent), and the different versions of the function are modeled as children of this use case.

Example 241

In some cases, the optional parts are unrelated to the obligatory ones; that is, they neither extend nor form special cases of the obligatory use cases. An optional part may, for example, compute and present additional statistics, which is unrelated to other usages of the system. In such cases, the `Optional Service: Independent` pattern is applied resulting in the optional usages modeled as separate use cases with no relationships to other use cases in the model.

It is imperative that we do not confuse the term *optional* from a configuration point of view with a conditional usage of a part of the system. The purpose is not to extract all the conditional branches defined in a use case and define them in separate use cases (which would be altogether incorrect). Only those parts that are not to be included in every configuration of the use case should be extracted. Note that these parts are not even necessarily located in conditional branches. Note also that this pattern is applicable when a service is mandatory, but there is a choice between variants of it; that is, each configuration of the system must have the service, but there are different variants of that service.

Example

This section provides an example of the `Optional Service: Addition` pattern and presents two examples of use-case descriptions: `Create Order` and `Restock Item`. A `Clerk` will use the `Create Order` use case to register a new order in the system. The `Restock Item` use case is an example of an optional addition to the `Create Order` use case, adding an automatic check of the number of items remaining in stock, comparing this number with a threshold value, and if needed generating a restock order (see Figure 24.4).

Here, the `Message Transfer` blueprints are useful, and the `CRUD` patterns should also be considered.

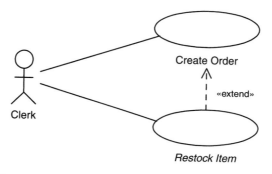

Figure 24.4   The mandatory use case `Create Order` is extended with the optional use case `Restock Item`.

Use Case: Create Order

Brief Description

The use case registers the information about an order to be shipped based on information received from the Clerk.

Extension Points

Order Saved—After the order is saved.

Basic Flow

The use case starts when the Clerk chooses to register a new order. The use case presents a form to the Clerk requesting the shipping address of the order and for each item to be shipped, as well as the ID and the number of the item.

The Clerk fills in the requested information. For each item, the system retrieves its name and description, and the number of instances available and presents the information to the Clerk.

The Clerk asks the system to save the order. The use case checks that the shipping address consists of the name, delivery address, city, zip code, and state of the receiver.

For each ordered item, the use case checks that the number of items in stock is greater than or equal to the number of ordered items.

For each ordered item, the use case reduces the number of items in stock with the number of ordered items.

The use case generates a unique identity and assigns it to the order. Finally, the order is saved and the identity is presented to the Clerk.

The use case ends.

Alternative Flows

CANCELING

The Clerk can, at any time, cancel the order registration. If the Clerk chooses to cancel the operation, the gathered information is discarded and the use case ends.

Example 243

INCORRECT SHIPPING ADDRESS

If the shipping address is incorrect, the Clerk is notified and requested to provide a correct shipping address.

The Clerk enters a new shipping address, and the use case continues where the check of the shipping address is performed.

MISSING ID OR QUANTITY

If the ID or the quantity of an ordered item is missing, the Clerk is notified and requested to enter the missing information.

The Clerk enters the missing information, and the use case continues where the check of the ID and quantity is checked.

TOO FEW ITEMS

If the number of items in stock is less than the number of ordered items, the Clerk is notified and requested to re-enter the ordered number of the item. The use case continues where the items are entered.

Use Case: Restock Item

Brief Description

The use case checks whether the number of items in stock is less than a predefined threshold and, if so, sends a restock message to the Clerk.

The use case is abstract.

Basic Flow

The flow of this use case is always inserted into the Create Order use-case instance at the Order Saved extension point.

For each item in the order, the use case checks whether the number of items in stock is less than the threshold of that item. If so, the use case creates a restock message containing the ID of the responsible purchaser, the item type, and the recommended number of items to buy, and sends the message to the Clerk.

The subflow ends and the use-case instance continues according to the Create Order use case after the Order Saved extension point.

Analysis Model

As pointed out previously, the optional parts should be expressed in separate use cases that have some kind of relationships to the mandatory use cases. This is true in the analysis model as well (and in all other models that follow the analysis model). Operations, attributes, and associations originating in the optional use cases should be captured by optional classes that can be added or removed without affecting the mandatory classes. This should at least be a high-priority requirement when producing the analysis model. As made clear more than 10 years ago (see, for example, the book *Object-Oriented Software Engineering*, Jacobson et al. 1993), it is possible and fruitful to use the same technique with extend relationships between classes as we have done for use cases (see Figure 24.5). The semantics and the pragmatics of the relationship between classes are the same as those of the relationship between use cases.

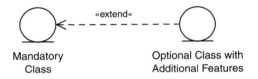

Figure 24.5   Optional features may be added to a mandatory class using an extend relationship.

If you do not want to introduce extend relationships in your model as described above, you can instead use either a generalization or an ordinary association (see Figure 24.6). You will still have localized the optional part mostly to new, optional classes.

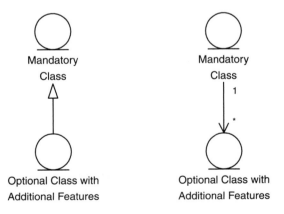

Figure 24.6   Two other techniques for adding additional features to mandatory classes, each with its own drawbacks.

However, there are drawbacks with both alternatives. Replacing the extend relationship with a generalization will force you to replace all the existing instances of the superclass (subclass) with instances of the subclass (superclass) if you add (remove) the optional service to (from) a system that is already in use.

On the other hand, using an association instead implies that you will have to modify the mandatory class to which the association is connected, because it will now have a new association and will have to communicate over this association to initiate the optional class. (This comes for free with the extend relationship because there will still be only one instance.) Moreover, the context, or the namespace, in which the association is defined will also have to be modified.

An extend relationship on the other hand is owned by the client—the optional class—and it extends the already existing instances.

CHAPTER 25

ORTHOGONAL VIEWS

Intent

Provide different views of the flows of a system that are perceived differently by different stakeholders.

Characteristics: Not so common. Advanced solution.

Keywords: Different reader categories, internal structure of use-case model, level of abstraction, multiple descriptions, user view of use-case model.

Patterns

Orthogonal Views: Specialization

Model

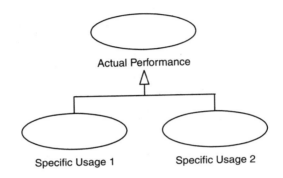

Description
The `Orthogonal Views: Specialization` pattern consists of one use case and a collection of specializations of that use case. The former (the parent use case) models what is actually performed inside the system, whereas each one of the other use cases (each of the children use cases) models one specific usage of the parent use case as it is perceived by the user.

Applicability
This pattern is suitable when the use-case model should make explicit that several different usages of the system are special cases of a general usage of the system and they are all to be performed in the same way internally, although perceived differently by the user.

Type
Structure pattern.

Orthogonal Views: Description

Model

Description

In some situations, a use case includes much more behavior than the users of the system perceive. In this alternative, we model the use case as a single use case with the extra behavior described in separate sections of the use-case description.

Applicability

This alternative is preferable when different stakeholders have different perceptions of a use case; some stakeholders might, for example, be unaware of the magnitude of the use-case performance.

Type

Description pattern.

Discussion

In some systems, such as rule-based systems and meta tools, the external view of the system is quite different from the internal view in the sense that a user of the system might perceive it to be quite different from the actual implementation of it. This causes problems when developing a use-case model of such a system, because different stakeholders will have quite different views on how the system is supposed to work. The users of the system tend to think of the system in terms of what concrete functions can be used, whereas the developers tend to think in terms of what functions will have to be implemented. Other stakeholders, such as the owner of the system, can belong to either of the two groups, depending on their knowledge of the implementation of the system.

In a text editor, there are tools for checking the spelling, for checking the grammar, and for proposing how documents and letters are to be organized and formulated. A user of the text editor would probably model these as three different use cases.

However, assume that this part of the text editor is to be implemented using a rule-matching technique where each rule has a template and a body. The template is used for matching different parts of the written text. If a template matches a part of the text, the body of that rule is executed, so that, for example, the text is highlighted, a certain dialog box is opened, or the text is modified.

A developer of such a system would like the use-case model to contain use cases for defining the rules and for evaluating the rules. This use-case model is quite different from the users' model, even though both of them describe the same system.

The problem arises because of the two main purposes of a use-case model, namely to describe how the system is to be used and to be a basis for developing the realization of the system. There are situations, fortunately not very frequent, when these two goals are more or less impossible to meet in a single description of the system.

From a user's point of view, the use-case model describes how the system is to be used, but such a model does not help the developers who are to implement the requirements using a technique that does not immediately reflect the user's point of view. From a developer's standpoint, the use cases should model how the system is actually used—not how it is per-ceived from the outside—if a proper realization of the system is to be pro-duced (see Figure 25.1). In most projects, there is no significant conflict between the two viewpoints, but using techniques for implementing the system that are not obvious to the user—using techniques that do not reflect how the users normally think—constitutes a problem that must be addressed explicitly. Otherwise, at least one of the groups will not find the use-case model useful.

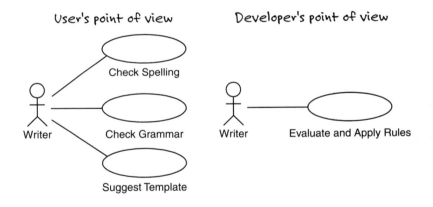

Figure 25.1   A system not implemented with a technique natural to the users
               can be described with two different use-case models, both equally
               correct. The left one is the user's point of view, and the right one is
               the developer's.

The solution to the problem is producing a model that contains the use cases of both sides and establishing firm relationships between them, according to the *Orthogonal Views: Specialization* pattern. Then each group can focus on their subset of use cases, but at the same time also see the constraints placed by the relationships between the use cases that indicate that the other group's use cases cannot be neglected. It must be possible to perform every use case that the users want to use by means of the use cases produced by the developers. Therefore, the users' use cases are specific performances of the use cases presented by the developers. To express this kind of relationship, we use generalization between the use cases. The use cases that the users want to use are specializations of the use cases that are going to be realized by the developers (see Figure 25.2). The realizations of the former use cases will be special cases of the realizations of the latter.

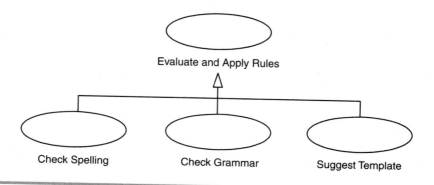

Figure 25.2   The use cases modeling how the system is perceived from the outside are specializations of the use cases modeling how the system is implemented (*Orthogonal Views: Specialization*).

A variant of this situation arises when the number of actions performed inside the system is considerably larger than what is noticed or comprehended by someone on the outside. In most such cases, both sides accept the same use-case model, but the two groups' constraints on the descriptions of the use cases are often in conflict. For example, very few of us know or understand what takes place in a telephone exchange during a telephone call. If the subscribers had to review and agree on what should be included in the descriptions of such a system's use cases, they would no doubt prefer to exclude all the detailed stuff that they do not comprehend. However, the developers of the telephone exchange will insist that the descriptions must include all those details.

In this case, the best solution is to apply the *Orthogonal Views: Description* pattern and develop two descriptions of the use cases, one of them covering how the use case is perceived by the users, and one encompassing all the actions that are actually performed. To minimize the risk of having two descriptions of the same use case that are not compatible, and at the same time reducing the number of documents, the additional descriptions can often be placed in separate subsections of the use-case description (see Figure 25.3). Our experience is that with this approach, both groups of stakeholders will accept the descriptions. One group, the users, will want a stripped version of each description, whereas the other group, including the developers, will use the complete description.

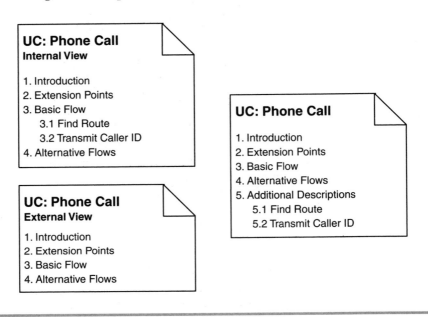

Figure 25.3   A use case can either be described in two documents (to the left), each with its own level of abstraction, or (to the right) in one document, some sections of which are not intended for all of the stakeholders.

Example

This section provides two examples of use cases based on the *Orthogonal Views: Specialization* pattern (see Figure 25.4). The first use case is `Evaluate and Apply Rules`, which models how the system actually behaves, and the second one is `Check Spelling`, which shows how the users perceive one of the usages of the former use case.

The `Large Use Case` patterns might be useful in this example.

Example   253

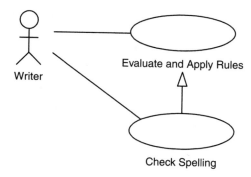

Figure 25.4   The Check Spelling use case models a specific usage of how the rules are evaluated and applied, which is modeled by the Evaluate and Apply Rules use case.

Use Case: Evaluate and Apply Rules

Brief Description

The use case evaluates all the defined rules on the selected text. If one fires, it is presented to the Writer, and if the Writer so chooses, the body of the rule is executed.

Basic Flow

START OF THE FLOW

The use case starts when the Writer chooses to evaluate (a subset of) the rules. If a subset of the rules is to be used, the use case retrieves the selected subset; otherwise, all the rules are used.

EVALUATION AND APPLICATION OF RULES

If one part of the text has been selected by the Writer, the rules will be applied to this part; otherwise, the rules will be applied to the whole text.

The use case starts from the beginning of the text and evaluates each rule. As soon as a rule fires (that is, matches the text starting at the current location), the description of the rule is presented to the Writer together with three options:

- If the Writer chooses to apply the rule, the body of the rule is executed.

- If the Writer chooses to continue, the evaluation continues with the next rule.

- If the Writer chooses to cancel, the evaluation of the rule stops and the use case ends.

When all the rules have been evaluated for the current location in the text, the current location is moved forward one word and all the rules are evaluated again.

END OF THE FLOW

When the end of the text is reached, the evaluation is finished and the use case ends.

Use Case: Check Spelling

Brief Description

The use case checks the spelling and presents any errors to the Writer, who can choose to correct them.

Basic Flow

START OF THE FLOW

The use case starts when the Writer chooses to check the spelling of a text.

EVALUATION AND APPLICATION OF RULES

The use case starts from the beginning and checks for each word whether it is found in the dictionary. The Writer may at any time choose to cancel the checking, in which case the use case ends.

- If the word is found in the dictionary, the use case continues with the next word.

- If the word is not found, the use case presents the erroneous word to the Writer, who is asked to choose one of the following alternatives:

  - If the Writer provides a new word, the misspelled or unsuitable word is replaced by the new word and the checking continues.

  - The Writer can choose to continue the checking without providing a new word, in which case the word is left unchanged.

  - The Writer can select to add the word to the dictionary. The use case adds the selected word to the dictionary and continues the checking with the next word.

END OF THE FLOW

The use case ends as described in the Evaluate and Apply Rules use case.

Analysis Model

There is no analysis model for this chapter because it describes different views of the use-case model. The mapping to the analysis model is done based on the use case that models the actual performance of the flow (in our example, the Evaluate and Apply Rules use case) and not on how the flow is perceived. Moreover, it does not matter how the description of the use case has been organized in the different chapters. Every part of the use case must, of course, be mapped onto the analysis model.

CHAPTER 26

USE-CASE SEQUENCE

Intent

Express the temporal order between a collection of use cases that must be invoked only in a specific order, even though the use cases are functionally unrelated to each other.

Characteristics: Very common. Basic solution.

Keywords: Dependency between use cases, invocation order, order between use cases, precondition, temporal order between use cases.

Patterns

Use-Case Sequence

Model

Description

The Use-Case Sequence pattern affects the descriptions of use cases without any relationships between them, although they should be performed in a certain order. (Of course, some of the use cases might have relationships between them, but such relationships will not be defined because of the temporal order between the use cases.)

Applicability

This pattern is used when there is a temporal order between the use cases but no information retrieved by an instance of one use case is to be included in an instance of another.

Type

Description pattern.

Discussion

In many systems, the user must perform some kind of initiation procedure (for example, log in) before a collection of more or less independent services become available. After using some of these services, the user must execute some finalization procedure (for example, log out). However, although most of these services are unrelated to each other, most likely all of them will not be available at the same time. The user will have to navigate through a menu hierarchy or graph of Web pages to find the desired services and be able to initiate the corresponding use cases (see Figure 26.1).

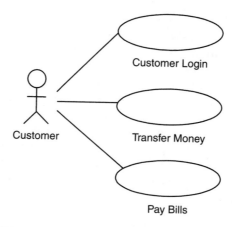

Figure 26.1   The use cases in an Internet bank have no relationships between them, but there is a (partial) order in which they can be performed.

In an Internet bank, the customer starts at a Web page requesting the customer's ID number and password key. After these have been entered, the system checks to see that the entered information is correct and then presents a welcome page with the latest news from the bank and similar information. On this page, the customer can choose between groups of services, such as managing the customer's account, stock portfolio, loans, and so forth. When the customer selects one of these groups, a new Web page will be presented that lists more detailed information, such as the customer's account numbers and the current balance of each account. If the customer requests even more details, the customer will be asked to select one of the accounts and another Web page will be presented with the transactions of the past two months.

In principle, nothing prevents the user from utilizing a particular use case whenever he or she wants to do so, because all the use cases are functionally unrelated. In the preceding example, the Present   Account Transactions use case, which retrieves and presents the details about the past two months' transactions of an account, takes an account number as the input, retrieves the information about the transactions, and presents it to the user. Therefore, from a functional point of view, this use case can be performed at any time, as long as the user provides the account number. It is the user interface that restricts what services can be selected. In this particular example, the user has no possibility to initiate the Present Account Transactions use case and cannot provide the account number as an input, except through specific Web pages.

How do we express that the use cases can be invoked only in a specific order? In principle, there are two ways: by means of preconditions and state machines. A *precondition* of a use case is used for stating which state the system is to be in when the use case is initiated. For example, the precondition of the Present Account Transactions use case includes, at least, the following:

The system must just have presented the number of the account to be selected by the customer.

In this way, the reader of the description of the use case will understand what must have taken place just before this use case is to be executed. Then, GUI specifiers and implementers, among others, will use the precondition as an input to their work, so that the GUI and the system will be specified and implemented accordingly.

A *state machine* can be used to specify what different states the user interface can be in and what transitions can be made between these states. Any use case that can be performed in a certain state is specified on a transition leaving that state and entering the state that the interface will be in after the use case has been performed (see Figure 26.2). Usually, the state machine describes the boundary class implementing the interface toward the user. However, the state machine can be generalized to apply to the whole system.

As a complement to preconditions and state machines, a flow chart or activity diagram may be drawn to show the order in which the use cases are to be invoked.

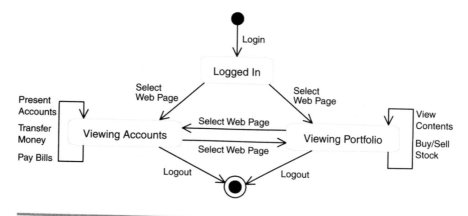

Figure 26.2   A state-machine diagram describing in which order some of the use cases of an Internet bank system can be invoked. The labels on the transitions correspond to the names of the use cases.

Although the use cases can be used only in a certain temporal order, they should not have include or extend relationships to each other to express the order in which they can be invoked. Such relationships are used for describing the addition of actions into another use case's sequence of actions—that is, expanding a use-case instance—and not for expressing temporal order between different use-case instances. If the use cases are complete in themselves, there will be no such additions. The only situations where include and extend relationships are to be used are when a use case initiates the sequence of actions of another use case, and when a use case makes use of a value calculated by another use case. Of course, this defines a temporal order between *the actions* described in different use cases, but these use cases are not independent of each order; they jointly model a complete usage of the system.

To sum up

- We use preconditions or state machines to specify the order in which use cases can be performed.

- We use include and extend relationships to specify that a use case initiates, or makes use of a value produced by, the actions described by another use case.

Smorgasbord

Another name of this pattern could have been *Smorgasbord*. At a (Swedish) smorgasbord, all dishes are present at once, so they are all available all the time to the eater who can choose from any dish that he or she likes. However, the tradition says that one should start with the herring. The next round is a selection of the different kinds of salmon and other cold dishes. Next follows the hot dishes, such as spare ribs, roast beef, and meatballs. Finally, the desserts are chosen. (Here some argue that one should have the cheeses before the sweets, whereas others have it the other way around.) So there is an order between the dishes, even though they are all present all the time.

Example

This section provides an example of the application of the *Use-Case Sequence* pattern and uses preconditions to state the order of the use cases. We provide four use-case descriptions from an Internet bank: Present Navigation Page, Present Accounts, Pay Bills, and Present Account Transactions (see Figure 26.3). The first use case is used for navigating between the different services of the bank, which are presented by different Web pages. The Present Accounts use case can only be performed when the Web page of a service offering to display the accounts is shown. The same procedure is employed in the Pay Bills use case. The last use case presents the transactions that have been performed on an account over the past two months. This use case can be performed only on an account that is presented in the current Web page.

This example could also benefit from one of the *CRUD* patterns, as well as a *Future Task* blueprint.

Example   263

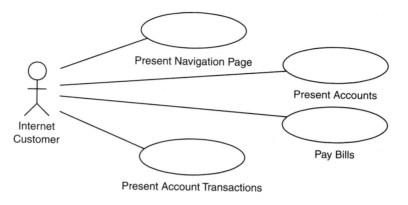

Figure 26.3   The Internet bank offers four different usages to the customer.

Use Case: Present Navigation Page

Brief Description

The Internet Customer selects one of the offered services, and the use case presents the Web page from where the service's use cases can be chosen.

Precondition

A Web page must be presented to the Internet Customer from where the selection of a service can be made.

Basic Flow

The use case starts when the Internet Customer selects one of the services that are presented. The use case retrieves the contents of the selected service—that is, the description of the service and what use cases can be initiated from this service.

The use case presents the retrieved information to the Internet Customer using the Web page connected to the selected service.

The use case ends.

Use Case: Present Accounts

Brief Description

The use case presents the accounts of the Internet Customer.

Precondition

A Web page that includes the option to look at the Internet Customer's accounts must be presented to the Internet Customer.

Basic Flow

The use case starts when the Internet Customer selects to view the accounts registered to the actor. The use case stores the Web page from which the selection was made.

The use case uses the identity of the Internet Customer to retrieve all the accounts available to the customer. For each of these accounts, the use case retrieves the type of the account, the account number, and the balance of the account. The information is presented to the Internet Customer in a new Web page.

When the Internet Customer chooses to end viewing the accounts, the use case restores the previous Web page and presents it to the Internet Customer.

The use case ends.

Use Case: Pay Bills

Brief Description

The use case registers bills entered by the Internet Customer.

Precondition

A Web page that includes the option to register bills must be presented to the Internet Customer.

Example 265

Basic Flow

The use case starts when the Internet Customer selects to pay a collection of bills. The use case stores the Web page from which the selection was made.

The use case uses the identity of the Internet Customer to retrieve the transaction account of the Internet Customer, and continues by performing the following loop until the Internet Customer is done registering bills:

> The use case presents a Web page to the Internet Customer where the account number and the balance of the transaction account are shown. The Internet Customer is prompted to enter the amount of money to be paid, the receiving account, the date the bill is to be paid, and a transaction message.

> The Internet Customer enters the requested information, which is stored by the use case together with the account number of the transaction account of the Internet Customer.

When the Internet Customer chooses to stop registering bills to be paid, the use case retrieves the previous Web page and presents it to the Internet Customer.

The use case ends.

Alternative Flows

If the Internet Customer does not have a transaction account, the use case displays an error message informing the Internet Customer that the service cannot be used, and the use case ends.

Use Case: Present Account Transactions

Brief Description

The use case presents the latest transactions on an account to the Internet Customer.

Precondition

A Web page that includes the account number of the account must be presented to the Internet Customer.

Basic Flow

The use case starts when the Internet Customer selects to view the transactions on an account, at the same time providing the number of the account. The use case stores the Web page from which the selection was made.

The use case uses the account number to retrieve all the transactions that have been performed on the account over the past two months. For each of the transactions, the date, the amount, whether the transaction was a deposit or withdrawal, the number of the other account, and the transaction text are presented to the Internet Customer on a new Web page.

When the Internet Customer chooses to stop viewing the transaction summary, the use case retrieves the previous Web page and presents it to the Internet Customer.

The use case ends.

Analysis Model

There is no analysis model for this chapter because the temporal order between the use cases does not affect the structure of the analysis model. However, the preconditions of the use cases and the state machines are used as inputs when specifying the contents of the classes of the analysis model. Usually, the boundary class associated with the actor to which the use cases should appear in a specific order is to have a state machine allowing different types of input from the actor in different states. As an object of the boundary class changes its state, it offers a different menu alternative or presents another Web page to the user playing the role of an actor.

Part IV

Use-Case Blueprints

This part of the book presents a collection of use-case blueprints of how to model various common usages of systems. We have encountered models of these usages in many different use-case models over the years, and the blueprints in this part of the book are the result of distilling these models into general models of how to express these usages with use cases. The proposed blueprints are not the only ways to model the problems at hand, but they constitute models that we have found useful, understandable, and (last, but not least) correct. All blueprints solving the same modeling problem are grouped into a single chapter where they are presented and discussed.

All chapters in this part are organized in the same way:

- **Name of modeling problem**—A descriptive name of the problem in a few words

- **Problem**—A short description of the modeling problem

- **Characteristics**—States whether the solutions are simple or complex, whether the modeling problem is common or infrequent

- **Keywords**—A list of keywords characterizing the modeling problem

- For each blueprint

  - **Name**—A descriptive name of the blueprint

  - **Model**—A use-case model of the blueprint

  - **Description**—A description of the blueprint model

  - **Applicability**—States when the blueprint should be used

- **Discussion**—A comprehensive discussion on the modeling problem and the different solutions
- **Example**—An example of the modeling problem and one or several of its solutions, including use-case descriptions
- **Analysis model**—A platform-independent class model providing a realization of the use cases in the blueprint use-case models

The chapters containing the use-case blueprints are sorted alphabetically within this part. For each chapter, we list its contained blueprints together with the descriptions of the modeling problems they address.

Chapter 27. Access Control: The system is required to include some kind of access security. Access to the information in the system and to the services of the system is stated by the specific access rights given to the individual user.

- Access Control: Embedded Check
- Access Control: Dynamic Security Rules
- Access Control: Explicit Check
- Access Control: Internal Assignment
- Access Control: Implicit Details

Chapter 28. Future Task: A task is registered in the system at one point of time, although the actual performance of the task is to take place at some later time.

- Future Task: Simple
- Future Task: Specialization
- Future Task: Extraction
- Future Task: Performer Notification

Chapter 29. Item Look-Up: The system is to make it possible for the users to search for items in the system. This look-up procedure can be autonomous, but it can also be used in other use cases.

- Item Look-Up: Standalone
- Item Look-Up: Result Usage
- Item Look-Up: Open Decision

Chapter 30. Legacy System: The system is to include or make use of an already existing system.

- Legacy System: Embedded
- Legacy System: Separate

Chapter 31. Login and Logout: The users must register or identify themselves before using services offered by the system.

- Login and Logout: Standalone

- Login and Logout: Action Addition

- Login and Logout: Reuse

- Login and Logout: Specialization

- Login and Logout: Separate

Chapter 32. Message Transfer: A user uses the system to send a message to another user.

- Message Transfer: Deferred Delivery

- Message Transfer: Immediate Delivery

- Message Transfer: Automatic

Chapter 33. Passive External Medium: The system is to monitor or control an external medium that in itself is passive (for example, the surrounding air or a fluid).

- Passive External Medium

Chapter 34. Report Generation: The system is to contain a collection of templates for generating different kinds of reports that present information in accordance with the definition given in the templates. The templates also define how a report is to be formatted and similar matters.

- Report Generation: Simple

- Report Generation: Specialization

- Report Generation: Dynamic Templates

Chapter 35. Stream Input: An actor provides a stream of input to the system, and the handling of this input is to be described by use cases. The solution to this problem depends on whether the stream consists of discrete values or of continuous values.

- Stream Input: Discrete

- Stream Input: Analog

Chapter 36. Translator: The system is to receive an input stream and produce an output stream based on some translation rules.

- Translator: Static Definition

- Translator: Dynamic Rules

CHAPTER 27

ACCESS CONTROL

Problem

The system is required to include some kind of access security. Access to the information in the system and to the services of the system is stated by the specific access rights given to the individual user.

Characteristics: Common problem. Basic solution.

Keywords: Access rights, checking access rights, data access, information protection, security level, security policy.

Blueprints

Access Control: Embedded Check

Model

System
Administrator

Manage Access
Rights

Description

The first blueprint model consists of one use case, Manage Access Rights, handling registration and deregistration of access rights. The checking of access rights is in this blueprint mentioned in the descriptions of the use cases making use of the restricted resources in the system.

Applicability

This blueprint is preferred when the checking of the access rights should not be explicitly expressed in the model.

Access Control: Dynamic Security Units

Model

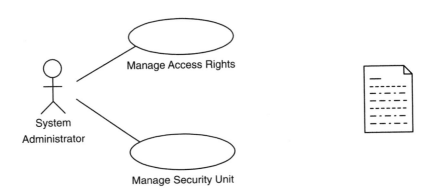

Manage Access Rights

System
Administrator

Manage Security Unit

Description

The second blueprint model consists of two use cases. The new use case compared to the first blueprint, Manage Security Unit, covers the registration and deregistration of the security units (that is, what pieces of information and what services are under access control).

Applicability

This blueprint is preferred when the checking of the access rights should not be explicitly expressed in the model, but the definition of what resources should be checked as well as the management of the access rights are dynamic; that is, they can be modified while the system is up and running.

Access Control: Explicit Check

Model

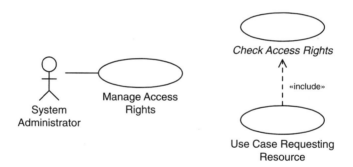

Description

The *Access Control: Explicit Check* blueprint makes checking access rights explicit in the model by adding an abstract use case, Check Access Rights, modeling how the check of the access rights is performed. This use case is to be included in all use cases in which some access right is to be checked.

Applicability

This blueprint is preferred when the checking of the access rights to a resource should be explicit in the model.

Access Control: Internal Assignment

Model

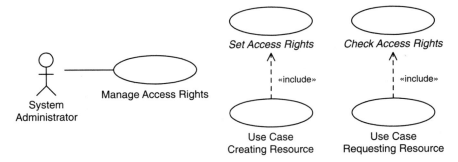

Description

In a blueprint model of a system where pieces of information or functions added dynamically to the system should automatically be assigned their access rights, two additional use cases are needed. The first of them is an abstract use case defining how the access rights are automatically set when a new piece of information is created or a new function is added to the system, without the involvement of the System Administrator. For example, the access rights can be based on default values or can be copied from other security units. The second use case models any usage of the system that creates a new piece of information or adds a new function that should be under access control.

Applicability

This alternative is used when the creation of the resources is dynamic in the system.

Access Control: Implicit Details

Model

Description

Another alternative is to mention the performance of the check of the access rights in the description of the use cases requesting the resources, but all other details on access management are abstracted away from the use-case model. In this alternative, the details of how the checking is performed are captured in the class model realizing the use-case model.

Applicability

This blueprint is applied when the access rights should not be explicit in the model, and no access control details are to be captured in the use-case model.

Discussion

In most systems, no user should be allowed to have access to everything. To protect data, resources, function, and the like from improper as well as from accidental usage, a system must have some sort of access control facility. This protection mechanism can vary from a very simple facility to a highly sophisticated one depending on the needs of security, on how easy it should be to apply, and so forth. In this chapter, we have chosen a rather simple approach where we only focus on reading and updating information and on usage of functions. However, from a use-case perspective, this approach can easily be extended with additional concepts and actions.

At a public library, all visitors may use one of the available computer terminals to search the catalog for information about a book or a magazine, such as the title, the author, the location in the library, and whether it is currently borrowed. However, they are only allowed to read the information about the book; a visitor is not allowed to modify the registered information, only librarians may do that. The system must therefore check whether the user has the right to modify the information about a book before presenting the update option.

In each use case where security is an issue, we must include a check of the access rights as soon as the system is to access a restricted piece of information or is to apply a restricted function. This check can be directly expressed in each relevant use case, as in the *Access Control: Embedded Check* blueprint. However, as soon as several use cases are affected, the main alternative is to apply the *Access Control: Explicit Check* blueprint and extract the check to an abstract use case that is included in all the use cases that need to perform such a check (see Figure 27.1).

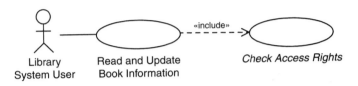

Figure 27.1   The check of the access right is modeled by an abstract use case that is included in all use cases where the access rights must be checked.

The advantage of introducing such an inclusion use case is that the check is made explicit and can be reviewed separately. If the performance of the check needs to be modified, only one use case will be affected.

The disadvantage is that this inclusion use case will often either be very small or expressed at a rather low level of abstraction. If it is considered to be at too low a level of abstraction (see Chapter 42, "Mistake: Mix of Abstraction Levels"), it may be excluded from the model (see the *Access Control: Embedded Check* blueprint again). In this case, the descriptions of the use cases should only state that the access rights are checked but not how, possibly by referring to a business rule describing the security policy (see Chapter 16, "Business Rules"). However, it is always safe to include the abstract inclusion use case in the model.

The management of the access rights of the different users must also be expressed in the use-case model. The use case Manage Access Rights, initiated by the System Administrator, is a typical example of a CRUD use case (see Chapter 20, "CRUD"). It models how access rights are defined, modified, and removed.

A more advanced security solution is achieved by application of the *Access Control: Dynamic Security Units* blueprint. It includes an additional use case, Define Security Unit, which encompasses definition of the different kinds of security units (that is, the units for which access rights can be defined for individual users). In this blueprint, it is possible to dynamically define what function, resource, or piece of information should be included in one access right.

Example 277

The management of the public library noticed that after searching for a book in the computer system, many visitors sent the information about the book to a printer just to have a note where the book was to be found when looking for it. This unnecessary printing of paper cost the library a rather significant sum of money, money that otherwise could have been spent on acquisitions of new books.

Therefore, the system administrator defined the printers as a new kind of security unit that a user must be given the right to use, and then gave each librarian the right to use the printers. Hence, the visitors could no longer use the printers in the library.

In some systems, the System Administrator is not involved when most of the access rights are defined. Instead, the access rights are given default values as soon as a piece of information is created or a new function is added according to the Access Control: Internal Assignment blueprint. For example, when creating a new file in a file system, the access rights to this file are usually given default values automatically, most of the time copied from the folder or directory in which it is created.

The last Access Control blueprint deals with the case where access control management is considered to be at too low a level of abstraction to be captured in the use-case model. Only the fact that appropriate access checks are performed is mentioned in the relevant use-case descriptions, but not how this is done, or any other detail on the matter. Situations where this blueprint is applicable include cases where access control is handled in a lower layer.

Note that the Access Control blueprints almost always have to be combined with a suitable Login and Logout blueprint, because checking of access rights is not possible without some kind of user identification (see Chapter 31, "Login and Logout").

Example

This section provides five use-case descriptions as examples of the blueprints in this chapter (see Figure 27.2). The example is part of an online registration system used at conferences, where the participants can use the system to read about and register to different events, such as presentations, meals, and entertainments. A user must be logged in to the system before using it. Each participant can read the information on public forms or web pages. If access to a form is restricted, only certain participants may read its content, and only a predefined subset of the participants may register to participate in the corresponding event. An administrator is responsible for creating and updating these forms and for defining who is allowed to read and register.

In this example, we have used three of the blueprints. We use the *Access Control: Explicit Check* blueprint for modeling the checking of the participants' rights to see a form and to register for specific events. This blueprint also prescribes a use case for the registration of who is allowed to read and to register through a form: Manage Access Rights of a Form. The Manage Form use case handles the creation of forms, being the security units in this example, and therefore we have also applied the *Access Control: Dynamic Security Units* blueprint. In addition, we use the first blueprint for modeling the Form Administrator's rights to use the Manage Form and the Manage Access Rights of a Form use cases.

See also the *CRUD* and the *Commonality* patterns and the *Item Look-Up* and *Login and Logout* blueprints, which are all useful in this example.

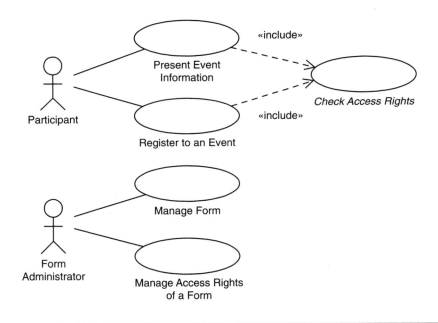

Figure 27.2   The registration of a form and its access rights is modeled by two use cases, and the application of the access rights is modeled by another use case that is included by the use cases where the access rights must be checked.

Example 279

Use Case: Manage Form

Brief Description

The Form Administrator uses the use case to create and update a form.

Basic Flows

The use case starts when the Form Administrator chooses to update an existing form or to create a new form. The use case asks the Form Administrator to enter the user ID and the password.

The Form Administrator provides the requested identification information. The use case checks that the provided user ID and the password are correct and that this user is allowed to modify forms.

The use case retrieves the names of the existing forms, presents them to the Form Administrator, and asks which one is to be modified or whether a new one is to be created.

The Form Administrator selects a form, and the use case retrieves the form and presents it together with its name to the Form Administrator. If the Form Administrator instead requests a new form, the use case presents an empty form.

The Form Administrator enters or modifies the information to be included in the form or the name of the form and chooses to save it. The use case checks that the name is not missing and stores the form under the name provided.

The use case asks the Form Administrator whether the form should be under access control. If the Form Administrator accepts, the form is marked as a security unit. If the Form Administrator rejects, the form is not marked as a security unit. The use case stores the information.

The use case ends.

Alternative Flows

ILLEGAL NAME OR INCORRECT PASSWORD

If no user is registered under the provided name or the provided password does not match the password registered for the user, the use case notifies the Form Administrator that the provided information is incorrect. The use case ends.

INSUFFICIENT AUTHORITY

If the Form Administrator does not have the authority to modify forms, the use case notifies the Form Administrator; then the use case ends.

CANCEL CHANGE

If the Form Administrator chooses to cancel the modification instead of saving it, no modifications are made and the use case ends.

MISSING NAME OF FORM

If the name of the form is missing, the use case asks the Form Administrator to provide a name.

The Form Administrator enters a name. The flow continues where the check of the existence of the name is performed.

Use Case: Manage Access Rights of a Form

Brief Description

The Form Administrator uses the use case to register and deregister the participants' access rights of forms.

Basic Flows

The use case starts when the Form Administrator chooses to assign access rights to a form. The use case asks the Form Administrator to enter the user ID and the password.

Example   281

The Form Administrator provides the requested identification information. The use case checks that the provided user ID and the password are correct and that this user is allowed to modify access rights of forms.

The use case retrieves the names of the existing forms that are marked as security units, presents them to the Form Administrator, and asks which one is to be updated.

The Form Administrator selects a form, and the use case retrieves the form and presents it together with its name to the Form Administrator.

The use case also retrieves the list of participants that have any access rights to the form and present them together with their access rights to the Form Administrator. Then the use case requests the Form Administrator to provide any changes to the list—which participants are to be removed from the list, which participants are to be added or whose access rights are to be changed, and for each of them what access right (*read* or *read and register*) is to be granted.

The Form Administrator provides the requested information, and the use case updates the list.

The use case ends.

Alternative Flows

ILLEGAL NAME OR INCORRECT PASSWORD

If no user is registered under the provided name or the provided password does not match the password registered for the user, the use case notifies the Form Administrator that the provided information is incorrect. The use case ends.

INSUFFICIENT AUTHORITY

If the Form Administrator does not have the authority to modify access rights of forms, the use case notifies the Form Administrator; then the use case ends.

CANCEL CHANGE

If the Form Administrator chooses to cancel the modification, no modifications are made and the use case ends.

Use Case: Check Access Rights

Brief Description

The use case describes how a participant's access rights of a form are checked.

The use case is abstract.

Basic Flow

When this use case is included by another use case, the use-case instance continues by performing the following actions:

The use case checks whether the form is marked as a security unit.

- If the form is marked as a security unit, the use case retrieves the identity of the current user and uses it together with the ID of the current form to check whether this user is allowed to read the information in the form and to register through this form. The results of the two checks constitute the result of the check.

- Otherwise, a positive read result together with a positive registration result constitute the result of the check.

The subflow ends and the use-case instance continues as described in the base use case after the location where this use case was included. The result of the check is available in the base use case.

Use Case: Present Event Information

Brief Description

A form containing information about an event is presented to the Participant.

Precondition

The Participant is logged in.

Example 283

Basic Flow

The use case starts when the Participant chooses to view the event information presented in a form. The use case asks the Participant which form is to be presented.

The Participant enters the name of the form. The included use case Check Access Rights is performed. If the Participant is allowed to read the form, the use case retrieves the form and presents it to the Participant.

After reading the selected form, the Participant notifies the use case and it clears the screen and ends.

Alternative Flows

NOT ALLOWED TO SEE CONTENTS

If the Participant does not have the required access rights to see the contents of the selected form, the Participant is notified, and the use case ends.

Use Case: Register to an Event

Brief Description

A form for registering to an event is presented to the Participant.

Precondition

The Participant is logged in.

Basic Flow

The use case starts when the Participant chooses to register to an event. The use case asks the Participant which form is to be presented.

The Participant enters the name of the form. The included use case Check Access Rights is performed. If the Participant is allowed to read the form, the use case retrieves the form and presents it to the Participant.

If the Participant is allowed to register through the form, the use case enables the registration part of the form.

If the Participant selects to be registered, the use case stores the registration of the user ID together with the event. Otherwise, no registration is made.

The Participant notifies the use case, and it clears the screen and ends.

Alternative Flows

NOT ALLOWED TO SEE CONTENTS

If the Participant does not have the required access rights to see the contents of the selected form, the Participant is notified, and the use case ends.

Analysis Model

Modeling access rights according to the `Access Control: Dynamic Security Units` and the `Access Control: Explicit Check` blueprints requires a collection of classes, as is shown in Figure 27.3. The access right itself is modeled with an entity class called `Capability`. It stores the allowed usage, often a value from the set {*read, write, read and write, applicable*}. The first three values are used for defining the accessibility of a piece of information, and the last for stating if a certain function may be used. A `Capability` also needs to define which piece of information or which function it applies to. In this model, this is expressed with the entity class called `Security Unit`. Therefore, for each combination of user and piece of information/ function, there is a `Capability` instance linking the corresponding instances of `User Information` and `Security Unit`.

A `System Administrator` can request to register new or to modify existing combinations of security units, users, and access rights through the `System Form`. An instance of `Security Handler` is created, which opens a `Registration Form` to the `System Administrator`. The registration, update, or removal of an access right for a user is entered via this form. When a new access right is to be defined for a user, the `Security Handler` instance creates a new instance of the `Capability` class and connects it to the instances representing the user and the security unit. Finally, the `Security Handler` instance is removed. The updating and removal of registered access rights and security units is done in a similar way.

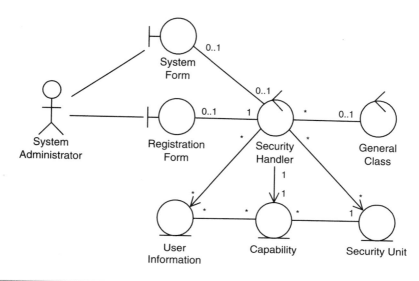

Figure 27.3   An analysis model of a system that has different access rights for different individuals.

The same procedure is used for the `Access Control: Internal Assignment` blueprint, where the access rights are to be registered automatically (that is, without the involvement of the `System Administrator`) when a new function is added or a new piece of information is created. However, the `System Form` and the `Registration Form` will, of course, not be used in this case. Instead, the `Security Handler` will be instantiated by the creator—an instance of the `General Class` class—of this new function or new piece of information.

When an instance in the system—here modeled by the `General Class` class—needs to check whether a user is allowed to access certain information or to use a particular service in the system, that instance creates a `Security Handler` instance and asks it to perform the check. The `Security Handler` retrieves the instance of `User Information` representing the current user, checks whether it has a `Capability` that allows the desired access or application, and returns the response. Finally, the `Security Handler` is removed.

Note that in this description of the model, we have assumed that an instance of the `Security Handler` is created each time a modification or check of access rights is to be performed. As always, it is a design decision whether these instances are to be created and removed as we have described here, or whether a single instance is to be used throughout.

In cases where the checking of access rights is stated explicitly in each relevant use case (the `Access Control: Embedded Check` blueprint), the analysis model presented above can be used as a template to be applied in the use-case realizations of all of these use cases.

If how the checking of the access rights is done is considered to be at too low a level of detail to be modeled even in the analysis model, it may alternatively be defined as a design/implementation issue. Only that the check is performed will then be mentioned in the analysis model.

There is no analysis model for the last blueprint in this section because how the access rights are checked is not modeled within the use-case model in that alternative.

CHAPTER 28

FUTURE TASK

Problem

A task is registered in the system at one point of time, although the actual performance of the task is to take place at some later time.

Characteristics: Very common in some domains. Advanced.

Keywords: Batch job, delayed performance, performance of job, postponed performance, registration of job, scheduling, time-ruled initiation of use case.

Blueprints

Future Task: Simple

Model

Description

The *Future Task: Simple* blueprint consists of two use cases. The first, called `Manage Task`, registers the information received from the `Task Definer` about a task that is to be performed at a later moment in time. The second use case, `Perform Task`, is initiated by the `Task Initiator` at regular intervals. This use case models the selection of the task to be performed as well as the performance of the task. How the different variants of tasks are performed is described as alternative flows of the use case.

Applicability

This blueprint is used when the set of different kinds of tasks is quite small (fewer than four) and is unlikely to be changed, and if their descriptions are short.

Future Task: Specialization

Model

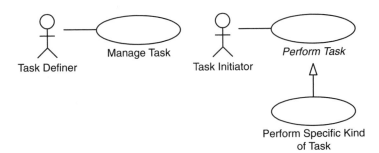

Description

In an alternative blueprint, the `Perform Task` use case models the performance of a task in general. It is an abstract use case. The `Perform Specific Kind of Task` use case is a specialization of `Perform Task`. It describes how a specific kind of task is to be performed while inheriting the selection and initialization procedure of the task from `Perform Task`.

Applicability

This blueprint alternative is preferred when there are several different kinds of performances of tasks and when there is an explicit case for handling unknown task types.

Future Task: Extraction

Model

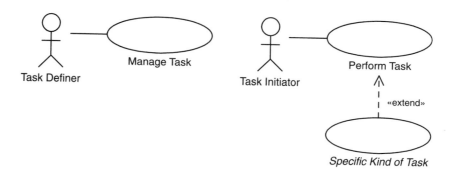

Description

Another alternative is to let `Perform Task` be a concrete use case that selects the next task and then simply removes it. How to perform the chosen task is modeled in an extension use case that is inserted into `Perform Task` after the selection of the task.

Applicability

The advantage of this blueprint is twofold: It is easy to add new types of tasks to the system, and the descriptions of the extension use cases focus on the performance of the task and include nothing about the selection of the task. The disadvantage is that the description of what is to be done if the type of the task is not known has to be modeled in a somewhat awkward way (see the section *Discussion*).

Future Task: Performer Notification

Model

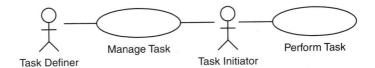

Task Definer   Manage Task   Task Initiator   Perform Task

Description

In this blueprint, the Manage Task use case notifies the Task Initiator each time a new task is registered or an existing task is modified. This means that the Task Initiator can keep track of when the registered tasks are to be performed. The Perform Task use case is initiated only when there are tasks registered in the system and not on just a regular basis.

Applicability

This blueprint is preferable when the tasks are registered or performed at very irregular intervals, or when the Task Initiator is based on an advanced scheduler.

Discussion

When an actor initiates a task in the system, the task is usually to be performed right away. In some situations, however, the task is to be performed at some later point in time. When that moment occurs, the system initiates the task, often after checking that the task is still due to be performed.

A typical example of a task to be performed by the system at a time differing from when it was requested is a wake-up call. Such a call is ordered by a subscriber who dials a given number, enters the time the wake-up call is to be performed, and then hangs up. When the entered wake-up time occurs, the system will call the subscriber and, when the subscriber picks up the phone, it will play a message saying that it is a wake-up call.

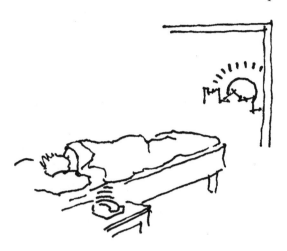

The exact time when the task is to be performed may be given by the Task Definer, but this is not the only way. It can, for example, be calculated by the system, or be guided by some external events. The Task Definer can also enter some constraint on a specific work task (for example, state that it must be performed before a certain time, or after the completion of another work task).

Another example is a work-task scheduling system, where the system calculates when the different work tasks are to be performed according to some algorithm based on the number of tasks to be performed as well as their priority and need of resources. Different individuals, be it persons or other systems, enter the different work tasks into the system, which then schedules them.

In the use-case model, how do we model the performance of a task that is defined at one moment in time and performed at another? A straightforward way would be to model it as one use case including both the definition of the task and the description of its performance. There are, however, some major drawbacks of this approach. The first has to do with the definition of use cases: A use case models a usage of the system. In a business-level model of the organization for which the system is to be modeled, one might say that ordering and performing a wake-up call is one usage of a telephone exchange business, and that scheduling and performing a work task is one usage of a task-oriented business. However, at the system level these are not atomic usages. When reading a use-case model of a telephone exchange, one would expect to find it explicitly stated that a wake-up call can be ordered as well as performed. Similarly, reading a use-case model of a work-task system, one would expect to find that a work task is scheduled at an earlier time than the actual time of performance. Hence, at the system level, the registering of a task is one usage and the performance of the task is another usage.

A second drawback has to do with rescheduling and canceling of tasks. Having ordered a wake-up call, one would certainly like to have the chance to cancel it. It must be possible to change the priority of a previously registered work task, so that another task with higher or lower priority can be performed before or after it, respectively. The rescheduling and canceling of a task is done within the system and it is therefore modeled by a use case. Because use cases do not communicate with each other, it is not possible for the rescheduling/canceling use case to inform the task use case that it is to be performed at another time than what was originally stated, or that it has been canceled.

Another aspect closely related to the rescheduling/canceling problem is that a use case should model the performance of some actions in the system. Now, imagine that the system is shut down for some reason (for example, maintenance purposes). Clearly, the execution of all the use-case instances currently present will then be stopped and the instances will disappear. However, the customers would not like to find that they never had their wake-up calls, or that their paychecks have not been issued, just because the system was shut down because of maintenance between the registration of the wake-up call and when the call is to be performed, or sometime between the registration of the work task to issue a paycheck and the time for the actual issuing.

The solution to the problem is simple. We model the scheduling tasks and their performance by separate use cases. Then there will also be separate use-case instances. This means that a new instance will be initiated when it is time for the wake-up calls and the issue of the paychecks, because at that time the system maintenance will be over and the system will be up and running again.

In other words, we should not model the registration and the performance of a task as one use case—we need two, as in the *Future Task: Simple* blueprint. The first use case will handle the registration of the task. This use case just receives the information about what task is to be performed and any specific constraints on the performance, such as its priority, at what time it must be performed, what tasks must be completed before this task, and so on. Then the use case calculates when the task is to be performed based on some scheduling algorithm and stores the task in a queue based on the calculation.

The use case might also inform a Task Initiator that there is a new task (see Figure 28.1). This notification, captured in the *Future Task: Performer Notification* blueprint, is optional and depends on how the Task Initiator is to be realized in a specific system. Often, the role of the Task Initiator is to be played by a predefined process in the operating system. This situation is often referred to as "use cases initiated by the system clock," or "by the time," and so forth. In other systems, the role of the Task Initiator might be realized by another system or even by a human being. This might be preferable if the tasks are to be initiated once or twice a day (for example, if there are batch jobs to be performed during the night, or if work orders are to be sent out each morning for the duties or tasks to be executed during that day).

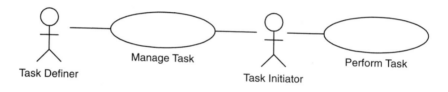

Figure 28.1   The model of a task-handling system consists in principle of two use cases: one for registering tasks and one for performing them. Here, the Task Initiator is informed each time a task is scheduled.

The Perform Task use case models the performance of the tasks. It starts when it receives a notification from the Task Initiator that it should check whether there is a task to be performed at this time. The Task Initiator can do this on a regular basis or based on new information from the registration use case. The performance use case checks the queue for tasks that are ready to be performed and selects one of them based on priorities, available resources, and so on, and removes it from the collection and executes it. How the execution is done can be described by use cases that are specializations of the performance use case, by extension use cases, or by alternative flows in the use case (see Figure 28.2).

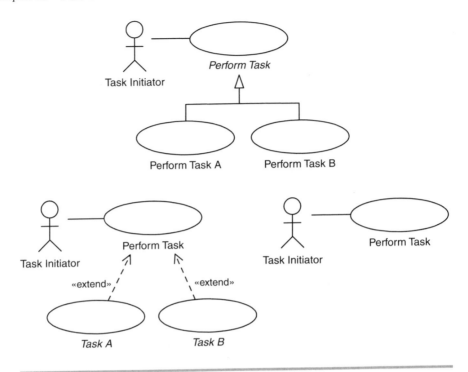

Figure 28.2   The Perform Task use case may either be specialized by or
extended by other use cases that describe the performance of the
specific tasks, or it may itself describe this as alternative flows.

The latter procedure—as in the *Future Task: Simple* blueprint—is preferable if the model is to be kept small and there are only a few, predefined
types of tasks, whereas the first two options are preferable if the model
can be extended with new kinds of tasks.

In general, specialization (*Future Task: Specialization*) is a better alternative than extension (*Future Task: Extraction*) because it is easy to add
an additional specializing use case handling the exceptional case when a
registered task does not belong to one of the predefined kinds. This is
not so easy to capture in the extension alternative, because the base use
case must be independent of the extensions and therefore cannot contain
a description of the exceptional case. The extensions must also be independent of each other, so it is not possible merely to add an extra
extension use case called, for example, "Otherwise." The solution to this

Example   295

problem is to add an extra extension use case, where the condition of the extend relationship captures the negation of the disjunction of all the other conditions. This must be done "by hand" by the modeler, and because the condition must be changed if another extension use case is added to the model, this is a major drawback.

In the generalization blueprint, the performance use case gives a complete description of the flow, although it abstracts away the details of specific task performances. In the extend blueprint, the base use case cannot include any description of the performance of the task; all of the performance is to be found in the extension use cases. In this case, the performance use case will therefore only select the task, remove it from the collection, and delete it. Nothing can be said about performing a task because this is defined in the extension use cases, and the base use case must be independent of these. This makes the base use case quite hollow. However, the advantage with the extend alternative is that it stresses that all cases will always perform exactly the same selection algorithm; it cannot be specialized in a child use case, because only additions are allowed using the extend relationship. Furthermore, this alternative allows the performance use case to select a collection of mixed tasks and then iterate over them. In the generalization case, only tasks of the same kind can be selected if a collection of tasks is to be selected and iterated over. Which one to choose depends on the situation. When in doubt, the best policy is to choose the generalization alternative.

Example

This section provides three examples of use-case descriptions: Manage Task, Perform Task, and Generate Invoicing Basis. The latter is an example of a specialization of Perform Task, and hence this is an application of the *Future Task: Specialization* blueprint. Because Manage Task also informs the Task Initiator about registered tasks, the *Future Task: Performer Notification* blueprint is also applied. Generate Invoicing Basis (see Figure 28.3) models how the information about all noninvoiced orders is compiled and sent to the Financial System actor, which represents an external system that is to receive the information.

See also the *Business Rules*, the *CRUD*, and the *Commonality* patterns, as well as the *Message Transfer* blueprints, which are all relevant to this example.

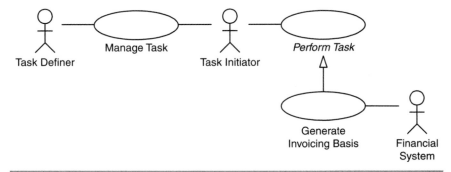

Figure 28.3   The Generate Invoicing Basis use case is a specialization of the Perform Task use case and adds an association to the Financial System actor.

Use Case: Manage Task

Brief Description

The use case registers, modifies, or cancels the information about a task to be performed as stated in information received from the Task Definer. The use case also notifies the Task Initiator.

Basic Flow

The use case has four different basic flows:

- Register Task

- Modify Existing Task

- Cancel Task

- View Tasks That Failed

REGISTER TASK

The use case starts when the Task Definer chooses to register a new task. The use case presents a list of possible kinds of tasks to the Task Definer, and requests what kind of task is to be registered, what name it is to be assigned, and when it is to be performed.

Example   297

The Task Definer enters the required information. The use case checks whether the specified time is in the future, and whether the name of the task is unique.

The use case registers a new task in the system, marks the task as *enabled*, and sends a notification to the Task Initiator that a new task has been registered, together with the time it is to be performed.

The use case ends.

MODIFY EXISTING TASK

The use case starts when the Task Definer chooses to modify an already registered task. The use case retrieves the names of all the tasks not marked as *active* and presents them to the Task Definer.

The Task Definer selects one of the tasks. The use case retrieves the information about the task and presents it to the Task Definer.

The Task Definer modifies any of the presented information except the name of the task.

The Task Definer accepts the information. The use case checks whether the specified time is in the future and, if so, stores the modified information. Finally, the use case checks whether the time the task is to be performed is modified. If so, two notifications are sent to the Task Initiator: one canceling the previous time and one informing about the new time.

The use case ends.

CANCEL TASK

The use case starts when the Task Definer chooses to cancel a task. The use case retrieves all the tasks not marked as *active*.

The Task Definer selects one of the tasks. The use case retrieves the information about the task, presents it to the Task Definer, and asks the Task Definer to confirm the cancellation.

The Task Definer confirms the cancellation, and the use case removes the task and sends a cancellation notification to the Task Initiator; otherwise, no modifications are made.

The use case ends.

VIEW TASKS THAT FAILED

The use case starts when the Task Definer chooses to view a list of all the tasks that have failed. The use case collects all the tasks with the status *failed* and presents their names to the Task Definer.

The use case ends.

Alternative Flows

CANCEL OPERATION

The Task Definer may choose to cancel the operation at any time during the use case, in which case any gathered information is discarded, and the use case ends.

INCORRECT NAME OR TIME

If the name of the task is not unique or the time is not in the future, the Task Definer is notified that the information is incorrect and is requested to re-enter the incorrect information.

The Task Definer re-enters the information. The flow continues from where the check of the information is performed.

Use Case: Perform Task

Brief Description

When initiated by the Task Initiator, the use case retrieves a pre-registered task, and based on the registered information, performs it.

The use case is abstract.

Basic Flow

START OF THE FLOW

The use case starts when the Task Initiator requests it. The use case collects all the tasks that are to be performed at this time and that have not been registered as *active, failed,* or *postponed*. The task with the highest priority is selected and marked as *active*.

PERFORMANCE OF THE TASK

The use case performs the task.

END OF THE FLOW

If the task is performed successfully, it is removed.

The use case ends.

Example 299

Alternative Flows

If the performance of the task fails, the use case changes the status of the task to *failed* and stores it again together with the reason for failure. The use case ends.

Use Case: Generate Invoicing Basis

Brief Description

The Generate Invoicing Basis use case, which is a specialization of the Perform Task use case, generates a basis for invoicing which is sent to the Financial System actor.

Basic Flow

START OF THE FLOW

The use case starts as described in the Perform Task use case.

PERFORMANCE OF THE TASK

The selected task being a *generate invoicing basis* task, the use case collects all the orders that are marked as *shipped*.

For each of these orders, the use case retrieves the customer's name and address, as well as the order number and the ordered value including discounts and tax. The collected information is sent to the Financial System.

The Financial System acknowledges the invoicing information. The use case marks the collected orders as *invoiced*.

END OF THE FLOW

The use case ends as described in the Perform Task use case.

Alternative Flows

NO ORDER

If no orders are marked as *shipped*, no information is sent to the Financial System.

No Acknowledgment

If no acknowledgment is received within two minutes, or if a message stating that something went wrong is received from the Financial System, the status of the orders is left unchanged and the performance of the task fails. The use case continues from where the task has been performed.

Information Not Retrievable

If the required information cannot be retrieved from an order, the status of the order is set to *manual invoicing.* The use case continues with the remaining orders.

Analysis Model

The modeling of a task involves a collection of classes. First, we need to be able to handle information about the task to be performed, such as the name of the task and the time when it is to be carried out. This information is used when the execution of the task is initiated, but the information can also be reviewed and modified before the execution of the task, as well as be removed from the system if the task is canceled. We therefore need an entity class, called Task Information, which is responsible for modeling this kind of information; it represents a task that is to be performed in the future. If different kinds of tasks require different sets of information, this entity class is abstract and subclasses are introduced.

Second, we need a control class, Task Performer, to actually perform the task. This class captures how the execution of a task is to be performed; that is, it models the sequence or sequences of actions that are to be performed by the system. When the performance of a specific task is initiated, the Task Performer is instantiated and initialized with the relevant pieces of information stored in the entity object holding the information of that particular task. Subclasses of the Task Performer are introduced if the different kinds of tasks in our system are performed in different ways.

For each kind of task, there will usually be one entity class, modeling the information required to perform such a task and one control class modeling how such a task is to be performed. However, many kinds of tasks may require the same information about the task but will be executed differently. Similarly, what happens inside the system may be the same for different kinds of tasks, even though they operate on different information. We can therefore not presume that each kind of task will have its own pair of entity class and control class.

In cases where multiple subclasses of Task Performer could be used to execute a certain task registered in an instance of (a subclass of) Task Information, it must also be registered in the instance what subclass of Task Performer is to be used when executing it. Therefore, in the general case, when there is no one-to-one relationship between the subclasses of Task Information and the subclasses of Task Performer, there must be an association from Task Information to Task Performer referencing the class to be instantiated when the task registered in the (subclass of) Task Information is to be performed.

This leads us to the model presented in Figure 28.4. The Register Task flow of the Manage Task use case starts in the System Form where the Task Definer chooses to register a task. An instance of the Task Handler is created that retrieves a list of all possible performances—that is, what Task Performers are defined in the system. Then it presents the list to the Task Definer using a Task Registration Form. The actor enters the necessary information and chooses one of the Task Performers, which is then instantiated to request any additional information required for its performance. When the information is received from the Task Definer, a new instance of Task Information or one of its subclasses is created. Optionally, if the *Future Task: Performer Notification* blueprint is applied, the Task Handler then informs the Task Initiator via the Task Initiator Interface that a new task has been registered. Obviously, the registration can be done in the opposite order in the sense that the kind of Task Information is selected first. Finally, the registration use case ends.

The Perform Task use case starts on the Task Initiator's request. The request can be made on a regular basis or when needed as is the case when the time is sent to the Task Initiator from the Manage Task use case (*Future Task: Performer Notification*). An instance of Task Handler is created that checks whether there is a task to be performed and, if so, selects the task with the highest priority.

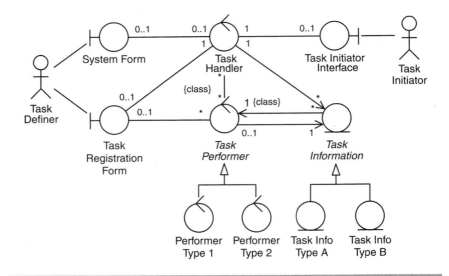

Figure 28.4   An analysis model of a system for registering and performing
tasks. The string {class} denotes that it is the associated class or a
subclass of it that is to be attached to that end of a link; the absence
of the string denotes the default case where instances are attached.

The Task Handler changes the state of the Task Information instance to
active and requests which Task Performer subclass is to be instantiated
from that Task Information instance. Then, the Task Handler creates an
instance of that subclass of Task Performer. If it is required that all the
tasks to be performed at this time are to be performed in parallel, no selection is made based on priority. Instead, the Task Handler iterates over the
identified collection of Task Information instances and instantiates the
appropriate Task Performer for each of them.

The instance of Task Performer is initialized with the instance of the Task
Information, retrieves the required information from it, and starts performing the task in accordance with its own definition combined with the
information retrieved from its Task Information.

If the task is successfully completed, the Task Information is removed,
and the Task Performer removes itself. If not, the Task Performer registers
the reason why the task failed in the Task Information instance and then
it removes itself.

The model presented above is an example of control classes participating
in the realization of more than one use case. Both the Task Handler and the
Task Performer are involved in the performance of the two use cases
Manage Task and Perform Task.

CHAPTER 29

ITEM LOOK-UP

Problem

The system is to make it possible for the users to search for items in the system. This look-up procedure can be autonomous, but it can also be used in other use cases.

Characteristics: Very common in most domains. Basic solution.

Keywords: Find information, functional dependency between use cases, invocation order, order between use cases, reuse of search result, search.

Blueprints

Item Look-Up: Standalone

Model

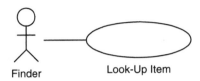

Description

The *Item Look-Up: Standalone* blueprint consists of one use case, called Look-Up Item. It receives search criteria from the Finder actor and uses the criteria to identify the correct item in the system.

Applicability

This blueprint is preferred when the search of an item is a usage of its own and is not performed as part of another usage of the system.

Item Look-Up: Result Usage

Model

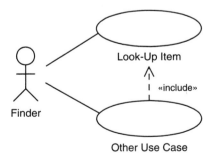

Description

In an alternative blueprint, the procedure modeled by the Look-Up Item use case is included by the Other Use Case use case. In this case, the item (or items) resulting from the look-up is to be reused in the other use case after the look-up is performed. Often, the `Look-Up   Item` use case is abstract; that is, it is only performed as part of other use cases, although it is not required. The execution starts in an instance of the `Other  Use  Case` use case and the look-up procedure is included in that instance.

Applicability

This alternative is preferable when the result of the look-up procedure needs to be reused within other use cases. Otherwise, the *Item Look-Up: Standalone* blueprint is the recommended one.

Item Look-Up: Open Decision

Model

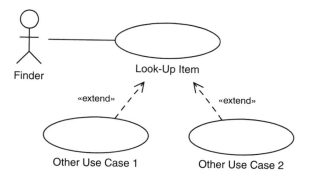

Description

A third alternative is to extend the `Look-Up Item` use case with other use cases. In this case, the decision on what to do with the search result is left open until after the search. When the search procedure is completed, any of the extension use cases may be inserted, the condition either being computed by the system based on the search result, or that the `Finder` chooses to perform a certain function using the search result as an input.

Applicability

This blueprint should be used when what to do with the result of the looking-up procedure is not known until after the result is presented.

This alternative should not be used if the result of the looking-up procedure is not to be used in other use cases, nor when it is known from the beginning what service to use when the looking up is completed.

Discussion

Many systems include functions for searching or looking up items stored in the system. The user will enter some search criteria to find the desired item, and the use case will look up all the items matching the entered conditions. This kind of function can be performed as a standalone usage of the system as well as be part of another usage that requires the look-up procedure. In the former case, corresponding to the *Item Look-Up: Standalone* blueprint, the usage will be modeled as a use case in a standard way, whereas in the latter case there must be some kind of relationship between the look-up use case and the use case in which the result is to be used. If this relationship is missing, the two use cases will be independent of each other. Therefore, no information about which item has been looked-up in an instance of Look-Up Item will be available in any other use-case instance (see Chapter 26, "Use-Case Sequence," and Chapter 7, "Include: Reusing Existing Use Cases").

To be able to use the information about which item has been looked up, the look-up procedure must be performed by the same use-case instance as is to use that item. Furthermore, if the look-up procedure is to be general so that it can be reused in multiple use cases, the look-up use case must not be dependent on the use cases in which its behavior is to be reused. Therefore, the relationship must be directed *from* the use case in which the looked-up item is to be used *to* the look-up use case (see Figure 29.1). This situation is captured in the second blueprint (*Item Look-Up: Result Usage*). The flow then starts in an instance of the other use case, and the look-up procedure is included in that instance.

> In a warehouse management system, it must be possible to look up the information about an item stored in the warehouse to be able to find its location as well as to see whether it is available when a customer calls the warehouse. The use-case model of the warehouse management system will therefore include a Look-Up Item use case.
>
> Furthermore, when a customer places an order, the clerk may not always remember the item number to be entered. The system must therefore allow the clerk to look up the item in the system when performing the Create Order use case. When the item is found, its item number will be entered into the order by the system.
>
> Both the Look-Up Item use case and the Create Order use case are concrete, because it should be possible to use the system in both these two ways independently. Furthermore, because the Look-Up Item use case models a general look-up procedure, the use case must not be dependent on any other use cases.

Therefore, because information about the looked-up item is to be used in the Create Order use case, there must be an include relationship from the Create Order use case to the Look-Up Item use case.

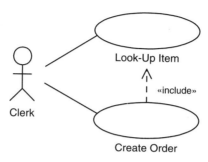

Figure 29.1   Both the Look-Up Item use case and the Create Order use case are concrete as they can be performed on their own. Furthermore, because the looked-up item may be used in the Create Order use case, there is an include relationship from the Create Order use case to the Look-Up Item use case.

In some situations, the decision about what to do with the search result cannot be made until the result is there. In this case, the execution must start with the Look-Up Item use case. When the search is done, it can be decided which service to use next. Because this service will use the search result as an input, it has to be performed as part of the same instance as the looking-up procedure. In this case, extend is the preferred relationship, according to the *Future Task: Open Decision* blueprint, directed from the use cases that will need the search result to the Look-Up Item use case (see Figure 29.2).

> In a task management system, the Task Manager can start by looking up tasks by giving certain search criteria to the system. When the result of the search is presented, the Task Manager may decide for each of the found tasks to initiate its immediate performance, or to update the task by, for example, rescheduling it or changing its priority. Depending on what the Task Manager chooses to do, the current use-case instance is extended with the behavior defined in the appropriate use case.
>
> Both Update Task and Perform Task are concrete, so that they can be individually initiated as well.

In case the result of the look-up is not to be used in other use cases and no additional actions are to be performed depending on the result of the look-up, the look-up is modeled as a separate use case without relationships to other use cases, as in the first blueprint.

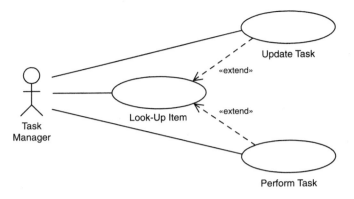

Figure 29.2   In a task management system, the Task Manager can choose to update the definition of a task or to initiate the performance of a task. It is also possible to start by looking up the task, and then decide what to do with it.

Example

This section provides an example of the *Item Look-Up: Result Usage* blueprint and examines two examples of use-case descriptions: Look-Up Flight and Order Ticket from an airline ticketing system (see Figure 29.3). The first one looks up information about flights based on search criteria provided by the clerk, whereas the second one models the ordering of a ticket. In this example, the Look-Up Flight use case is abstract, because we have assumed that it will never be performed on its own; for information about how it can be described if it is concrete, see Chapter 19, "Concrete Extension or Inclusion."

Apart from the *Concrete Inclusion* or *Extension* patterns, the *CRUD* and the *Commonality* patterns may be useful in this example.

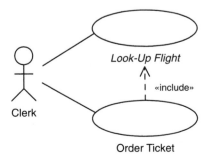

Figure 29.3   The Order Ticket use case includes the Look-Up Flight use case.

Example   309

Use Case: Look-Up Flight

Brief Description

The use case looks for a flight that matches a search criterion given by the Clerk.

The use case is abstract.

Basic Flow

When this use case is included by other use cases, the use-case instance continues by performing the following actions:

The use case requests the origin and the destination of the flight as well as the preferred time for take off and landing from the Clerk. If a flight has been selected in the base use case, the use case presents its destination as a suggestion for the origin of the flight to be looked for, and suggests its arrival time plus one hour as departure time. If no flight has been selected, no suggestions are made.

The Clerk enters the values, and the use case retrieves all the flights between the origin and the destination that leave within a three-hour time difference from the given departure time.

The use case presents the flight number, the departure time, and the arrival time for each retrieved flight to the Clerk.

The subflow ends and the use-case instance continues as described in the base use case after the location where this use case was included. Information about the retrieved flights is available in the base use case. If no flight is found matching the search criterion, no information is available in the base use case.

Alternative Flows

If the origin, the destination, or the departure time is missing when the Clerk has entered the requested information, the use case asks the Clerk to enter search values again. The use case continues from where the Clerk enters the requested values.

Use Case: Order Ticket

Brief Description

The Clerk registers a new ticket in the system and the included flights are booked at the Airlines.

Basic Flow

The use case starts when the Clerk chooses to register a new ticket. The use case asks the Clerk for the name and address of the customer.

The Clerk enters the requested information and the use case checks whether it is a registered customer. If so, the Clerk is notified whether the customer is a VIP customer and how many tickets the customer has bought in the past 12 months.

The use case asks what flights are to be included in the ticket, their origin and destination, or whether a suitable flight should be found.

> The Clerk enters the selected flight number, the origin and the destination, and the departure date and time.

> If the Clerk instead chooses to ask for a suitable flight, the Look-Up Flight use case is included. If the result consists of several possible flights, the use case asks the Clerk to select one of the flights. The Clerk selects a flight.

For each flight:

> The use case sends a booking request to the Airline.

> If the Airline returns a confirmation number, the use case includes it in the reservation. If the Airline instead returns a reservation failure, the Clerk is notified and the flight is not included in the reservation.

The use case presents the complete reservation to the Clerk and asks for a confirmation from the Clerk.

The Clerk confirms the reservation. The use case registers a new ticket and stores the name and address of the customer together with the flights and their departure and arrival dates and times. The name of the Clerk is retrieved from the system and stored. Finally, a reservation number is displayed to the Clerk, and the use case asks the Clerk to acknowledge it.

The Clerk acknowledges the reservation number.

The use case ends.

Alternative Flows

No Connection with Airline

If the connection with the airline cannot be established, the Clerk is notified and the flight is not included in the ticket.

No Flight

If no flights have been included in the ticket when it is to be registered, the Clerk is notified and no reservation is created. The use case continues by asking what flights are to be included.

Reservation Canceled

If the Clerk chooses not to confirm the reservation, the use case asks for a confirmation of the cancellation.

If the cancellation confirmation is received from the Clerk, the reservation is removed from the system, any booked flight is canceled, and the use case ends. If the cancellation is discarded, the use case continues by asking for confirmation of the reservation.

Analysis Model

Most of the analysis model in this section is based on the usual mapping of use cases onto classes. What is additional is the realization of the include and the extend relationships, respectively (see Figure 29.4).

The Look-Up Item use case maps onto one boundary class, Look-Up Form, where the search criteria is to be entered and the result will be presented. A control class, Information Finder, is responsible for performing the search among the (collection of) entities.

If the Look-Up Item use case is included in or extended by other use cases, objects of classes in the realizations of these use cases will interact with objects of the control class (Information Finder) in the realization of the Look-Up Item use case to request the search and to receive the resulting item(s).

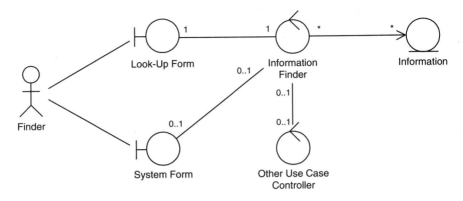

Figure 29.4   An analysis model of the *Item Look-Up* blueprints. The Other
Use Case Controller is a control class from another use case
that includes or extends the Look-Up Item use case.

If the Look-Up Item use case is concrete, the flow starts when the Finder via
the System Form requests the system to search for an item. The request is
sent to an Information Finder, which will ask for the search criteria using
a Look-Up Form. After the Finder has entered the search criteria, the
Information Finder will search the relevant entity objects, here modeled
by the Information entity class, for objects fulfilling the criteria, and present the result in the Look-Up Form.

If the Look-Up Item use case is extended by another use case (*Item Look-Up:
Open Decision*), the flow will start as described above. When the result is
found, the Information Finder will start interacting with the appropriate
Other Use Case Controller.

If the Look-Up Item is included by another use case (*Item Look-Up: Result
Usage*), the flow will start in that use case and the Information Finder will
be called from a control object of the realization of that use case (*Other Use
Case Controller*). The flow continues as described above, but after the
result has been retrieved and presented to the Finder (or if no presentation
is made of the result), the result is returned back to the Other Use Case
Controller object.

CHAPTER 30

LEGACY SYSTEM

Problem

The system is to include or make use of an already existing system.

Characteristics: Common. Basic solution.

Keywords: Embedding existing system, existing system, incorporating existing system, old system, using existing system.

Blueprints

Legacy System: Embedded

Model

Description

This blueprint captures the situation where the system includes a legacy system as a part of it, which implies that the legacy system is not structurally visible in the use-case model. However, it appears in the description of the use cases.

Applicability

This blueprint is preferred when there should be no explicit interaction with the legacy system in the use-case model. Instead, the parts of the use cases that are performed in the legacy system are described briefly in the use-case descriptions; that is, the behavior and the information of the legacy system are described at a higher level of abstraction than are the other parts of the system.

Legacy System: Separate

Model

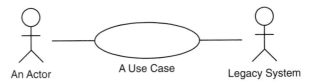

Description

An alternative way is to keep the legacy system outside the new system. In this model, the legacy system appears as an actor to the new system.

Applicability

This alternative is the one to use when other systems must have direct access to the legacy system. If the other systems are to access the behavior and information of the legacy system through the new system, the first blueprint described above is better.

Discussion

When a new system is to be developed, there is often already an older system that partly covers the needs of the new system. If the old system is to be replaced by the new one after it has been developed, this causes no problem. However, the situation is more complicated if the transition from the old to the new system will take place over a sequence of versions of the new system—that is to say, if the two systems will live in parallel for a while.

How can we incorporate the old system in the new system, or, from our point of view, how can we incorporate it in the use-case model? In principle, there are two ways to handle the old system: Either we keep it outside the new system or we wrap it up inside the new system where, hopefully, it will eventually be replaced by a new, possibly better implementation.

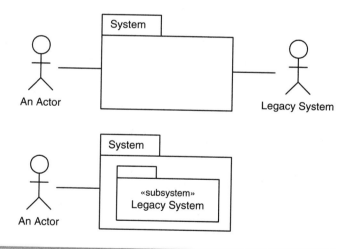

Figure 30.1   A legacy system can either be modeled as an actor to the new system or as a subsystem inside the new system.

In the former case, we treat the existing system as an actor to the new system, and in the latter, we treat it as a subsystem (see Figure 30.1). Several factors have to be considered when deciding which alternative is preferable, some of which are discussed here.

One important factor is whether other systems and users are to continue to use the old system as is, or whether it is to be replaced by the new system altogether. If others are to continue to use the old system, it must be treated as an actor to the new system because it must be possible to continue using its functionality independently of the new system. In this case, the Legacy System: Separate blueprint is applied and the old system is modeled as an actor that is given the same name as the old system, as is shown in the upper part of Figure 30.1. If the old system consists of clearly distinguishable parts that are used independently, the old system might even be modeled as a collection of actors, each of them given the name of the part it represents.

When it is not necessary to access the old system directly, it is better to apply the Legacy System: Embedded blueprint and treat the old system as a subsystem in the new system. One advantage of this approach is that it enables gradual replacement of the old system. This means that when developing new versions of the new system we can move functionality from the old subsystem (that is, stop using that functionality) to other subsystems that will implement the corresponding functionality. Eventually the subsystem modeling the old system can be removed completely as all its functionality and information are covered by other parts of the new system (see Figure 30.2).

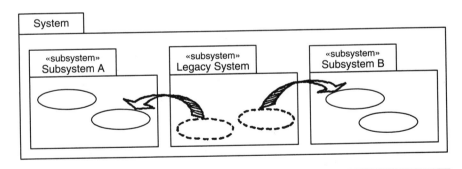

Figure 30.2   In each new version of the new system, functionality is moved from the subsystem modeling the legacy system (Legacy System: Embedded) into other subsystems, so that it can finally be removed.

In both cases, it is important that a well-defined interface be defined for the old system, where we define how it is to be accessed by the new system. Failure to do so will imply that the boundaries of the two systems will be undefined, that it will be difficult to access the old system in a homogeneous way, and that the systems might eventually blend together into one cemented blur.

When the legacy system is represented by an actor, this interface is often realized by a separate component between the actor and the other parts of the new system. All interaction with the actor must go through this interface component, which transforms the interaction and transferred information to suitable formats and signals.

In the encapsulation case, we instead create a subsystem enclosing the legacy system, acting as a wrapper and defining all the operations that can be applied to the legacy system.

How, then, do we express the use cases when we are dealing with a legacy system? In the actor alternative (the `Legacy System: Separate` blueprint), the use cases must include the sending and the receiving of messages to and from the actor modeling the old system. The interaction with the old system must be explicitly stated; that is, it must not be hidden or abstracted away because a reader would then easily misunderstand the use case, thinking that the functionality of the old system is captured by the new system. It is imperative to use phrases like this:

The use case sends the information about X to the OldSystem where Y is to be calculated and then sent back to the use case.

Or, in the other direction:

The use case requests information about P from the OldSystem. When the use case receives information from OldSystem, it is used for Q.

We need not mention that the information or the requests must be transformed into other formats. This transformation is handled by the interface and will not add to the understanding of the use case. Furthermore, how the old system performs an operation, or stores or retrieves relevant information, should not be described in the use case because this is handled outside the system that is modeled by the use cases.

This means that in general the use cases of the new system are modeled and described as ordinary use cases. However, it might be useful to give a slightly more thorough description of what the actor modeling the legacy system does in the interaction with the use cases than is normally done for actors. If this information is left out, the user might find it difficult to understand the service modeled by the use case because several important parts are performed by an actor and not by the use case.

When the old system is wrapped inside a subsystem of the new system (the `Legacy System: Embedded` blueprint), the use cases of the new system should be described as normal use cases. The only difference is that the description of the parts of the use cases that take place inside the legacy subsystem can be expressed at a more abstract level than usual because these parts have already been implemented and are not to be developed. The description of these parts should cover only what is needed for a reader to understand what they accomplish, and exclude other details.

This is different from an ordinary use-case description where the whole use case should be described at a uniform level of abstraction. It is advisable to explicitly mention in the use-case descriptions that a certain part of the behavior is performed in the legacy subsystem, because this explains the difference in level of detail and abstraction in the description. How the transformation of information inside the legacy subsystem is to be performed should not be captured in the description of the use cases, nor how the interaction with the legacy subsystem is to be performed. This is design information, and should be described within the wrapper.

When a part of the legacy subsystem is to be enhanced and therefore moved to and implemented by another subsystem, the corresponding parts of the use cases must also be enhanced so that they capture the new requirements. These parts must then be expressed at a more detailed level—that is, at the same level as the rest of the use cases—because the modified parts are now to be used for developing new realizations (see the following example).

Example

This section provides an example of wrapping a legacy system inside a subsystem defined in the new system—that is, the `Legacy System: Embedded` blueprint. (Handling the legacy system as an actor as in the `Legacy System: Separate` blueprint does not imply anything specific to the use-case descriptions. All interactions are described as usual interactions with actors.)

Two versions of the flow description of one use case are provided. The first one uses the existing functionality of the legacy system. In the second version, some of this functionality has been replaced by an enhanced procedure to be implemented in a new subsystem.

The example is a warehouse system for registering orders to be shipped to customers. The warehouse has a legacy system for scheduling deliveries at a first-come, first-served basis. The first version of the new system is to use the old scheduling system (the legacy system) for scheduling new orders. In the second version of the system, the scheduling of deliveries will be more intelligent (for example, so that deliveries to addresses close to each other will be handled in one shipping).

Example   319

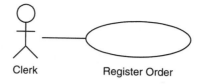

Clerk   Register Order

Figure 30.3   The Clerk registers new orders in the system. In the first version of
the system, the scheduling of the deliveries of the orders is done
using the functionality of the legacy system. In the second version
of the system, a new algorithm is used.

The following section presents the two versions of the use case `Register
Order` (see Figure 30.3). In the first one, the legacy system is used, which
implies that the planning of the deliveries is described at a high level of
abstraction. The second version includes an enhanced planning procedure
of the shipment, so the corresponding part of the flow in this version is
given at the same level of abstraction as the rest of the flow.

The *Business Rules* and the *CRUD* patterns might also be useful in this
example, as might the *Future Task* blueprints.

Use Case: Register Order, Version 1

Brief Description

The use case registers an order based on the information received
from the Clerk and schedules its shipping.

Basic Flow

The use case starts when the Clerk chooses to register an order. The
use case requests the name and the address of the customer.

The Clerk enters the required data, also stating whether it is a rush
delivery or a normal delivery. The use case creates a new order and
initializes it with the entered information.

The use case requests the identities of the ordered items together
with the number of each ordered item.

The Clerk enters the required information. The use case checks that
the items exist and that the ordered number of each item is available.

The following paragraph will be replaced in the new version of the use case. In this version, the legacy system is used.

When the Clerk states that all items have been entered, the use case schedules the order in the Shipping Scheduling subsystem. The use case displays the shipping ID to the Clerk and requests an acknowledgment.

The Clerk acknowledges the ID, and the use case ends.

Alternative Flows

MISSING NAME OR ADDRESS

If the Clerk has not entered the name or the address of the customer, the use case asks the Clerk for the missing information. When the information is entered, the use case continues as if the information had been entered from the beginning.

CANCEL THE REGISTRATION

If the Clerk selects to cancel the order when the use case is waiting for an input, all entered information is discarded and the use case ends.

MISSING ITEM

If one of the items is not registered in the system, the use case notifies the Clerk and that item is discarded from the order.

NOT ENOUGH NUMBER OF ITEMS AVAILABLE

If the number of available items is fewer than the ordered number of that item, the Clerk is notified and the number of available items is presented.

- If the Clerk enters another number of items to be ordered, the entered number is used, and the use case continues as if that number had been given from the beginning.

- If the Clerk chooses to cancel the item from the order, the item is discarded from the order. The use case continues with the next item.

Example 321

Use Case: Register Order, Version 2

Brief Description

The use case registers an order based on the information received from the Clerk and schedules its shipping.

Basic Flow

The use case starts when the Clerk chooses to register an order. The use case requests the name and the address of the customer.

The Clerk enters the required data, also stating whether it is a rush delivery or a normal delivery. The use case creates a new order and initializes it with the entered information.

The use case requests the identities of the ordered items together with the number of each ordered item.

The Clerk enters the required information. The use case checks that the items exist and that the ordered number of each item is available.

So far, the description is the same as in version 1 of the use case. The following paragraphs take the place of the one in the old version where the legacy system was used.

When the Clerk states that all items have been entered, the use case schedules the order for shipment.

- If it is a rush order, a new delivery is created and the order is added to it. The time for the delivery is stated in Business Rule BR24.

- If a normal delivery is requested, the use case checks whether there is a delivery registered in the neighborhood of the customer (see Business Rule BR68). If this is so and there is room for the current order (see Business Rule BR10), it is added to the delivery registered previously. Otherwise, a new delivery is created with the current order added to it.

The use case displays the shipping ID to the Clerk and requests acknowledgement.

The Clerk acknowledges the ID, and the use case ends.

Alternative Flows

These flows are the same as in version 1 of the use case.

Analysis Model

The analysis model for a system using a legacy system depends on how the legacy system is modeled. In the *Legacy System: Embedded* blueprint (see Figure 30.4), the legacy system is wrapped inside a subsystem in the system. Therefore, all interaction with the legacy system is expressed as interactions with that subsystem. Here the content of the new system is represented by a control class, but it can, of course, be any kind of class in the new system.

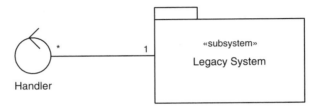

Figure 30.4   In the analysis model of the *Legacy System: Embedded* blueprint, the interaction with the legacy system is expressed as interaction with the subsystem enclosing the legacy system.

In the *Legacy System: Separate* blueprint, where the legacy system is modeled as an actor, a boundary class, `Legacy Interface`, is introduced, which is to transform the different data formats and signals between the new system and the legacy system (see Figure 30.5). This boundary class will often correspond to a large chunk of code, but there is no reason to model it in detail during the analysis because its responsibility is quite obvious. The details are left to be worked out during design.

Figure 30.5   In the *Legacy System: Separate* case, the interaction with the legacy system goes through a boundary object.

CHAPTER 31

LOGIN AND LOGOUT

Problem

The users must register or identify themselves before using services offered by the system.

Characteristics: Common. Some blueprints are basic, whereas others are advanced.

Keywords: Password, PIN code, user authorization, user identification, user identity.

Blueprints

Login and Logout: Standalone

Model

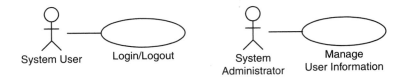

Description

The *Login and Logout: Standalone* blueprint consists of two use cases. The first use case, Login/Logout, models the login and the logout procedures; that is, it models how a user is to register as well as deregister as a current user. The utilization of the other use cases in the system is independent of the actual procedures for registering and deregistering. Those use cases in the system that require the user to be logged in before using the service state this as a precondition. The second use case, Manage User Information, registers and deregisters user identities and their passwords.

Applicability

This alternative is used when the login and logout procedures change the state of the system, but are independent of the actions in the other use cases of the system.

Login and Logout: Action Addition

Model

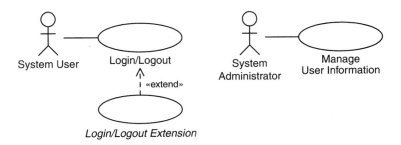

Description

This blueprint captures the case where the general login (and/or logout) procedure is extended with system-specific actions to be performed when a user logs in or logs out. These actions are described by a separate use case that extends the `Login/Logout` use case.

Applicability

The `Login and Logout: Action Addition` blueprint is preferred when there are some additional actions that should be performed when the user logs in to or logs out from the system, but these actions are independent of the actual login or logout procedure.

Login and Logout: Reuse

Model

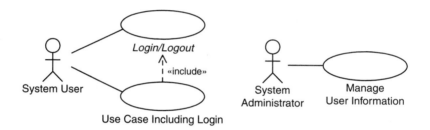

Description

In the `Login and Logout: Reuse` blueprint, the login and logout procedures are modeled by a separate use case that is included by all other use cases requiring user identification.

Applicability

This alternative is preferable when each usage of the system must include a verification of who the user is.

Login and Logout: Specialization

Model

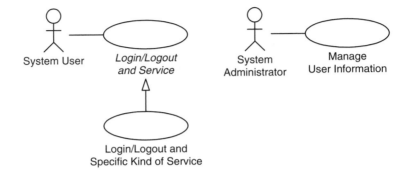

Description

Another variant is to model the login procedure, followed by a general service performed by the system, and then the logout procedure, together in an abstract use case. Then, all use cases modeling services of the same kind can be expressed as specializations of that use case.

Applicability

When every usage of the system is a specialization of a generic use case that includes the login and logout procedures, this is the preferred blueprint. The advantage of this alternative is that the login and logout procedures are described once in the parent use case and that the similarity of the child use cases becomes explicit in the model.

Login and Logout: Separate

Model

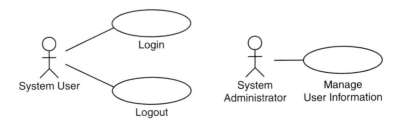

Description

This blueprint is a variant of the `Login and Logout: Standalone` blueprint but with the `Login/Logout` use case split into two separate use cases.

Applicability

This blueprint should only be used either if the descriptions of the two procedures are quite large or if there is an explicit request from the stakeholders that the two procedures should be distinct in the model.

Discussion

In several systems, it is a requirement that the user is logged in before any of the services of the system can be used; that is, the users must identify themselves by providing some kind of identity and secret key. A few different models of the login procedure to a system are available; in some of them, a relationship is modeled between the login use case and the other use cases of the system, whereas in others the use cases are kept independent. Sometimes it is not necessary to model a login use case, but often an explicit login use case is required. How dependent the other use cases in the system are on the login procedure determines which of the blueprints to apply.

Independent Use Cases

The first question to ask is whether the system's services—the other use cases—are independent of the actual login procedure. If they are independent, there is no include or extend relationship between the login use case and the other use cases (see Figure 31.1), and the `Login and Logout: Standalone` blueprint is applicable. Here the performance of a login procedure is modeled as a separate use case, which, after verifying the correctness of the password, enables the set of services the user can choose between (usually they are also presented to the user) and then the use case ends. If the allowed set of services depends on the user's access rights, the corresponding selection must also be included in the login use case.

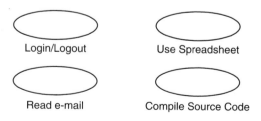

Figure 31.1   If the use cases are independent of how the login procedure is performed, there are no relationships between those use cases and the `Login` use case.

To state that a user must be logged in before a use case can be used, we can provide a precondition of the other use cases stating that the user must be logged in. However, remember that if the system is to check whether the user is logged in each time a use case is performed, this check must be included as an explicit part of the flow in that use case. If such a check is not to be performed, the GUI designer (or similar) must ensure that the precondition is fulfilled by making it impossible for a user that is not logged in to initiate the use cases (see also Chapter 26, "Use-Case Sequence").

Include or extend relationships between the other use cases and the login use case are not to be used because they would state that the other use cases are dependent on the login use case or vice versa. Furthermore, they would then be performed as one flow, but in this case the login procedure is not considered part of the other use cases, and the other use cases are not considered parts of the login use case.

Addition to Normal Login Procedure

In some cases the login procedure is to be extended with additional actions. For example, in some systems all failures of login are logged, so that the system administrator can analyze possible attempts to break in to the system.

If there are any such application-specific actions to be performed when the user logs in to the system, these actions should be expressed in a separate use case that has an extend relationship to the login use case, as is shown in Figure 31.2. We define an extension point in the login use case where the extension is to be made. In this way, the login procedure can be realized in different ways depending, for example, on the security management system of the computer the application is running on, while the application-specific part can be handled separately. This is the case modeled in the `Login and Logout: Action Addition` blueprint.

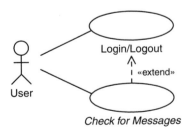

Figure 31.2   When a user logs in to a system, the standard login procedure is performed. During the login, the system checks whether there are any unread messages for the user and, if so, sends a notification to the user. This check is modeled in a separate use case extending the Login/Logout use case. See also Chapter 32, "Message Transfer."

The application-specific parts must not be modeled as a concrete use case because it will not be initiated by an actor. It is the performance of the login procedure that causes the extension to be performed. Moreover, do not include the application-specific parts in the description of the login use case, because this would dilute the description of the application-specific behavior with the description of the login procedure, which most stakeholders are not interested in.

Verification Before Each Usage

If each usage of the system must verify the identity of the user, the login procedure will have to be included in every use case, as in the `Login and Logout: Reuse` blueprint. A typical example is an ATM machine where the user must be identified each time the machine is used. In this case, we describe the login procedure as a separate use case to which all the other use cases have include relationships (see Figure 31.3). In this way, the login procedure is described only once, and each time a new service is added to the system (or removed), this new use case states that it will use the login procedure by including it, without having to change the login use case.

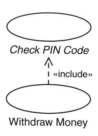

Figure 31.3   Here the login procedure is modeled with an inclusion use case.

Another possibility, which is preferable when all the application use cases are of the same kind, is to define a transaction use case that includes a general description of how a transaction is performed together with the login and the logout procedures (`Login and Logout: Specialization`). Each application use case will have a generalization to the transaction use case and only specify how its specific transaction is performed (see Figure 31.4). The other parts of the transaction use case, including the login procedure, are inherited. The advantages of this structure are that all application use cases will automatically include the login procedure as soon as it is stated that they are transaction use cases, and that the similarity of the application use cases becomes explicit in the model. However, as stated previously, this requires that all the application use cases be of the same kind as this is a universal requirement for using a generalization in UML.

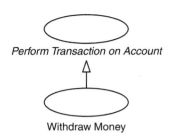

Figure 31.4   When several system usages are of the same kind, the login procedure can be modeled as part of a parent use case.

Neither of these two techniques should be used unless the login procedure
is to be performed each time the application-specific use case is performed.
Otherwise, even if it would be possible to enclose the login procedure
within a condition (a guard) in the application-specific use case, every
reader of the model would misunderstand such a model. Furthermore, the
use cases would be more difficult to realize and implement.

You can find examples of these two techniques in the Chapter 7, "Include:
Reusing Existing Use Cases," and Chapter 11, "Use-Case Generalization:
Classification and Inheritance." Chapter 13, "Describing Use Cases," cov-
ers how they are to be documented.

No Login Use Case

Many applications do not specifically require a login procedure. It is just
assumed that after you have logged in to a computer where the application
is installed, the application will be available. In this case, we do not include
a login use case in the application. We need not even describe it in a precondition of each use case. Because the application itself does not need the
information about the user, it should not be included in the model.

Obviously, we must include the login use case in the model if some of the
use cases of the application have to know the identity of the user because
it might confuse a reader of the model if the user identity is found in the
system while the identity is never established in any of the use cases.
However, the realization of this use case is often quite simple: It is already
provided by the operating system on which the application is to run, and
the user's identity can be requested from the operating system. In the use
cases needing the user's identity, we simply state the following:

The user's identity is retrieved . . .

Because it is a design matter, we need not say from where it is retrieved.

Example   *331*

Logout

Most systems require not only that a user log in to them but also that the user log out from them when finished. Therefore, if there is some kind of login use case, a logout use case will also be necessary. Both of the login and the logout procedures can be modeled within the same use case. This use case, called, for example, Login/Logout, will have two basic flows, because neither procedure is an alternative of the other.

We should not model login and logout as two separate use cases, as in the *Login and Logout: Separate* blueprint, unless the descriptions of the two procedures are quite large (or if a stakeholder insists on separating them). Both procedures will use the security mechanisms of the system. Moreover, separating them would increase the size of the model and make it more difficult to understand without really adding anything of value to the model. The two procedures form one conceptual unit: It is very seldom that one of them, but not the other, will be needed in our model.

Manage User Information

In a system utilizing a login process, it must be possible to register and deregister user identities and passwords. This information is used when checking the information provided by the user when trying to log in to the system. The management of the user identities and passwords must also be expressed in the use-case model. The use case Manage User Information, which is found in all the *Login and Logout* blueprints, initiated by the System Administrator, is a typical example of a CRUD use case (see Chapter 20, "CRUD"). It models how a user identity is registered, modified, and removed from the system, together with the associated password.

Example

The example in this section illustrates two of the blueprints. The first case describes a situation when the system's services are independent of the login procedure, as in the Login and Logout: Standalone blueprint. The model includes the Login/Logout use case, the Manage User Information use case, and fractions of an example use case, called Order Ticket (see the left part of Figure 31.5). The latter has been included to show how we can state that the user must be logged in to the system without having to define a relationship to the Login/Logout use case.

The second case describes addition of actions to the login procedure, which is described in the *Login and Logout: Action Addition* blueprint. Here the model contains a use case called Check for Messages. This use case will present any notifications that arrived while the System User was not logged in to the system. The use case has an extend relationship to the Login/Logout use case so that its actions will be executed whenever a login procedure is performed (see the right side of Figure 31.5).

Note that the same use-case description of Login/Logout is used in both examples.

Here, the *CRUD* and the *Use-Case Sequence* patterns as well as the *Message Transfer* blueprints might also be useful.

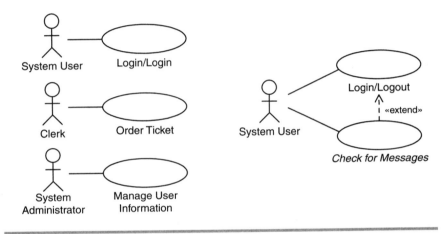

Figure 31.5   The example captures two of the alternatives: independent use cases and additions to login procedure.

Use Case: Login/Logout

Brief Description

The System User uses the use case to sign on to and to sign out from the system.

Extension Points

Logged In—After the registration that the System User has logged in.

Example   333

Basic Flow

The use case has two different basic flows:

- Login

- Logout

LOGIN

The use case starts when the System User chooses to log in to the system. The use case requests the name and the password of the System User.

The System User provides the name and the password. The use case checks whether there is a user registered with the provided name and, if so, whether the password equals the one stored for that user. If the name and the password are correct, the use case registers that the System User has logged in together with the current date and time.

The use case presents the available system services to the System User.

The use case ends.

LOGOUT

The use case starts when the System User chooses to log out from the system. The use case asks the System User for a confirmation.

- If the System User cancels the logout, the use case ends.

- If the System User confirms the logout, the use case removes the possibility to use the system services from the System User. The use case registers, together with the current date and time, that the System User has logged out. The use case ends.

Alternative Flows

ILLEGAL NAME OR INCORRECT PASSWORD

If no user is registered under the provided name or the provided password does not match the password registered for the user, the use case notifies the System User that the provided information is incorrect. The use case ends.

Use Case: Order Ticket

Only a sketch of this use-case description is provided, so that the reader can see how the precondition is expressed. You can find a complete description of the use case in Chapter 13, "Describing Use Cases."

Brief Description

The Clerk registers a new ticket in the system.

Precondition

The Clerk must be logged in to the system.

Basic Flow

The use case starts when the Clerk chooses to register a new ticket.

[. . .]

Use Case: Check for Messages

Brief Description

The System User is informed if there are any unread messages.

The use case is abstract.

Basic Flow

The flow of this use case is always inserted into the Login/Logout use-case instance at the Logged In extension point.

The use case retrieves the identity of the User and checks whether there are any messages sent to that identity with the status *unread*. If so, the use case sends a notification to the System User informing that there are unread messages.

The subflow ends and the use-case instance continues according to the base use case after the Logged In extension point.

Example   335

Use Case: Manage User Information

Brief Description

The System Administrator registers or deregisters a user identity together with a password.

Basic Flow

The use case has three different basic flows:

- Register User

- Modify User Information

- Remove User Information

REGISTER USER

The use case starts when the System Administrator chooses to register a new user. The use case asks the System Administrator for the first name, the last name, the employee number, the login identity, and the password.

The System Administrator enters the requested information. The use case checks that all the information is provided.

The use case checks that the chosen login identity is unique and that the password consists of at least 10 characters.

The use case stores an encrypted version of the password together with the other user information.

The use case ends.

MODIFY USER INFORMATION

The use case starts when the System Administrator chooses to modify a user. The use case asks the System Administrator for the employee number or the login identity of the user.

The System Administrator enters the requested information. The use case retrieves the information about the user except the password and presents it to the System Administrator.

The System Administrator enters the new information. If a new login identity is given, the use case checks that it is unique. If a new password is given, the use case checks that the password consists of at least 10 characters. The use case stores the entered information and leaves all the other information unchanged.

The use case ends.

REMOVE USER INFORMATION

The use case starts when the System Administrator chooses to remove a user. The use case asks the System Administrator for the employee number or the login identity of the user.

The System Administrator enters the requested information. The use case removes the stored information.

The use case ends.

Alternative Flows

MISSING INFORMATION

If one or more of the first name, the last name, the employee number, the login identity, and the password is missing, the use case notifies the System Administrator that the information is missing. The use case continues where the information was requested.

NOT UNIQUE IDENTITY

If the given login identity is already registered, the use case notifies the System Administrator that the login identity is not unique. The use case continues where the login identity was requested.

TOO SHORT PASSWORD

If the given password consists of fewer than 10 characters, the use case notifies the System Administrator that the password is too short. The use case continues where the password was requested.

IDENTITY NOT FOUND

If the given login identity or the given employee number is not found, the use case notifies the System Administrator that the provided information is not found. The use case continues where the information was requested.

CANCEL OPERATION

If the System Administrator chooses to cancel the operation, no information is modified and the use case ends.

Analysis Model

The model presented in Figure 31.6 is quite straightforward. The System User requests to be allowed to log in to the system using the Start Form. An instance of Login Handler is created to manage the login procedure. It opens a Login Form to the System User where the user information, such as the name and the password, PIN code, or similar, is to be entered. When the Login Handler receives this information from the Login Form, it verifies the correctness of the entered information using information stored in the instance of User Information identified based on the given information. The Login Handler handles all error cases such as invalid password or PIN code, nonregistered user, and the procedure to be followed when too many invalid attempts have been made.

Finally, when the System User has successfully entered the login information, the Login Handler registers that the System User has logged in, and an instance of the System Form is presented to the System User. This instance will, possibly depending on who the System User is, display welcome messages and open up different services to be used by the System User.

If any additional actions are to be performed (*Login and Logout: Action Addition, Login and Logout: Reuse,* and *Login and Logout: Specialization*), the Login Handler creates instances of appropriate Other Handler classes. After creating the System Form for the System User, the Login Handler and the Start Form cease to exist.

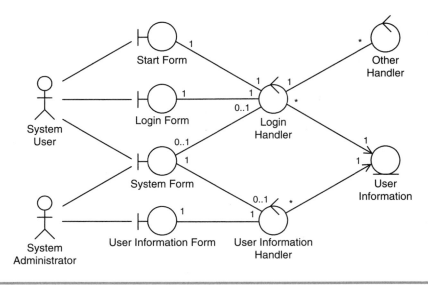

Figure 31.6   An analysis model of a system for registering in and deregistering from the system.

When the System User requests to log out from the system, the System Form creates a Login Handler to manage the logout procedure. It registers that the System User exits, removes the System Form, and presents the Start Form. Finally, the Login Handler ceases to exist.

To register or deregister user information, the System Administrator initiates the Manage User Information use case via the System Form, which creates an instance of the User Information Handler. It opens a User Information Form, where the System Administrator can enter and modify the information. Finally, the information is stored in an instance of the User Information class.

CHAPTER 32

MESSAGE TRANSFER

Problem

A user uses the system to send a message to another user.

Characteristics: Very common in some domains. Simple.

Keywords: Batch job, communication, email, SMS, system alert.

Blueprints

Message Transfer: Deferred Delivery

Model

Description

The *Message Transfer: Deferred Delivery* blueprint consists of two use cases. The first, called `Register Message`, receives a message from the `Sender` and stores it to be delivered at a later moment in time. When requested by the `Receiver`, the second use case, `Deliver Message`, checks whether there are any stored messages to be delivered to the actor. If there are, these messages are delivered to the actor and then, possibly, eliminated from the system.

Applicability

This blueprint is preferred when the messages are created by a user of the system and are to be delivered to the receiver upon request.

Message Transfer: Immediate Delivery

Model

Description

The `Message Transfer: Immediate Delivery` blueprint captures the situation when messages are delivered right away, and are not to be stored in the system. If no receiver is available when a message arrives, the message is just discarded and is not delivered to that receiver. No use case retrieving messages is therefore needed in this blueprint.

Applicability

This blueprint is applicable when the message will not be relevant if it is not received immediately.

Message Transfer: Automatic

Model

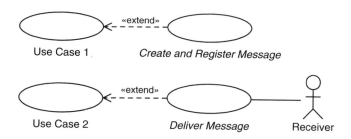

Description

Another `Message Transfer` blueprint describes the situation when it is not an actor that initiates the sending of the message, but an action performed inside the system. In this case, the `Create and Register Message` use case models the creation and the storage of the message in the system. This use case will have an extend relationship to the use case comprising the initiating action, so the creating and storing actions will be added when a use-case instance executes the initiating action. Similarly, the delivery of the message is initiated by the performance of a use case, instead of by request of an actor.

Applicability

This alternative is to be used when messages are created and delivered because of actions inside the system and not because of the actions of actors.

Discussion

When an actor sends a message to the system to be delivered to another actor (or to a collection of actors), the system looks up the receiver of the message and checks where it should be delivered so that it will reach its receiver. After the delivery location has been identified, the system delivers the message (*Message Transfer: Immediate Delivery*).

> There is a huge number of examples where a system is used for transferring a message from one user to another user (or users). Two obvious examples are sending emails and sending SMS (Short Message Service), where the sender enters a message together with the address of the receiver. The system translates the address to a location where the message is to be delivered, and finally the system transfers the message to that location where it will reach its receiver.
>
> Another kind of system emitting messages to its users is a warehouse system that will notify the purchaser when the number of items of a specific type falls below a threshold.
>
> A third example of such a system is a surveillance system transferring alarms, such as burglary alarms, fire alarms, and flooding alarms, to an operator to take proper actions.

However, in some cases, the delivery of the message may be deferred. For example, the system may be overloaded; the message, its sender, or its receiver may have a low priority; the message can have a later delivery time; or the receiver may be disconnected from the system. In all these cases, the message must be stored in the system to be delivered later, as in the *Message Transfer: Deferred Delivery* blueprint.

> If the receiver of an SMS has switched off the mobile phone, the system cannot deliver the SMS instantly. Instead, it is stored in the system until the receiver switches on the mobile phone. When the system detects that the receiver is again connected to the system, it delivers the SMS.

In some applications, there will not be a user of the system who initiates the sending of the message: It will be the system itself. In these cases, an action inside the system causes the creation and the transmission of the message. As discussed in Chapter 8, "Extend: Expanding Existing Use Cases," the addition of extra actions is preferably modeled by a separate use case with an extend relationship to the original (the base) use case. Therefore, creating and transmitting the message is expressed in an extension use case with an extend relationship to the use case comprising the action causing the message to be sent. This situation is captured in the *Message Transfer: Automatic* blueprint.

People often have badges or cards granting them access to buildings and rooms. To enter through a locked door, they slide their cards through a card reader, which allows the system to check whether the cardholder is allowed to enter through that door. If so, the system unlocks the door. Otherwise, the door remains locked.

In such a system, a guard is notified, depending on the level of security, if an unauthorized person is trying to enter into a restricted area. The use case sending the message to the security guard is extending the use case checking whether the person is allowed to enter through the door and, if so, sends an unlock signal to the locking device of that door. In this example, we have used a degenerated form of the `Message Transfer: Automatic` blueprint, where the use cases for creating and for delivering the message are merged (see Figure 32.1).

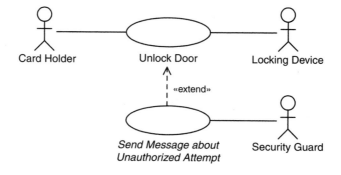

Figure 32.1   The system creates and sends a notification to the Security Guard when an unauthorized person tries to open a door.

Example

This section provides an example of the *Message Transfer: Automatic* blueprint, and presents four examples of use-case descriptions from a warehouse system (see Figure 32.2).

A Clerk will use the Create Order use case to register a new order in the system. The Restock Item use case extends the Create Order use case to check for each ordered item whether the number of items in stock falls below a given threshold. If so, a restock message to the purchaser is created in the system. Each time a System User, among them the purchaser, logs in to the system, the Deliver Message use case extends the login procedure and checks whether there are any messages to that user. If so, these messages are presented.

See also the *CRUD* and the *Optional Service* patterns and the *Login and Logout* blueprints, which are all relevant to this example.

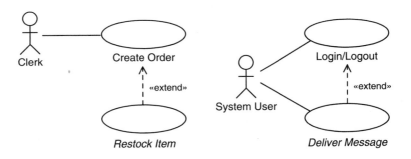

Figure 32.2   The messages created in the Restock Item use case are delivered by the Deliver Message use case.

Use Case: Create Order

Brief Description

The use case registers the information about an order to be shipped based on information received from the Clerk.

Example   345

Extension Points

Order Saved—After the order is saved.

Basic Flow

The use case starts when the Clerk chooses to register a new order. The use case presents a form to the Clerk requesting the shipping address of the order and for each item to be shipped, also the ID and the quantity of the item.

The Clerk fills in the requested information. For each item, the system retrieves its name and description, and the number of instances available and presents the information to the Clerk.

The Clerk asks the system to save the order. The use case checks that the shipping address consists of the name, delivery address, city, zip code, and state of the receiver.

For each ordered item, the use case checks that the number of items in stock is greater than or equal to the number of ordered items.

For each ordered item, the use case reduces the number of items in stock with the number of ordered items.

The use case generates a unique identity and assigns it to the order. Finally, the order is saved and the identity is presented to the Clerk.

The use case ends.

Alternative Flows

CANCELING

The Clerk can, at any time, cancel the order registration. If the Clerk chooses to cancel the operation, the gathered information is discarded, and the use case ends.

INCORRECT SHIPPING ADDRESS

If the shipping address is incorrect, the Clerk is notified and requested to provide a correct shipping address.

The Clerk enters a new shipping address, and the use case continues where the check of the shipping address is performed.

Missing ID or Quantity

If the ID or the quantity of an ordered item is missing, the Clerk is notified and requested to enter the missing information.

The use case continues where the items are entered.

Too Few Items

If the number of items in stock is fewer than the number of ordered items, the Clerk is notified and requested to re-enter the ordered number of the item. The use case continues where the items are entered.

Use Case: Restock Item

Brief Description

The use case checks whether the number of items in stock is less than a predefined threshold and, if so, creates a restock message.

The use case is abstract.

Basic Flow

The flow of this use case is always inserted into the Create Order use-case instance at the Order Saved extension point.

For each item in the order, the use case checks whether the number of items in stock is less than the threshold of that item. If so, the use case creates a restock message for the responsible purchaser stating the item type and the recommended number of items to buy, and stores the message in the system.

The subflow ends and the use-case instance continues according to the Create Order use case after the Order Saved extension point.

Example 347

Use Case: Login/Logout

Brief Description

The System User uses the use case to sign on to and to sign out from the system.

Extension Points

Logged In—After the registration that the System User has logged in.

Basic Flow

The use case has two different basic flows:

- Login

- Logout

LOGIN

The use case starts when the System User chooses to log in to the system. The use case requests the name and the password of the System User.

The System User provides the name and the password. The use case checks whether there is a user registered with the provided name and, if so, whether the password equals the one stored for that user. If the name and the password are correct, the use case registers that the System User has logged in together with the current date and time.

The use case presents the available system services to the System User.

The use case ends.

LOGOUT

The use case starts when the System User chooses to log out from the system. The use case asks the System User for a confirmation.

- If the System User cancels the logout, the use case ends.

- If the System User confirms the logout, the use case removes the possibility to use the system services from the System User. The use case registers, together with the current date and time, that the System User has logged out. The use case ends.

Alternative Flows

ILLEGAL NAME OR INCORRECT PASSWORD

If no user is registered under the provided name or the provided password does not match the password registered for the user, the use case notifies the System User that the provided information is incorrect. The use case ends.

Use Case: Deliver Message

Brief Description

Any unread messages are presented to the System User.

The use case is abstract.

Basic Flow

The flow of this use case is always inserted into the Login/Logout use-case instance at the Logged In extension point.

The use case retrieves the identity of the User and checks whether there are any messages with the status *unread* for that identity. If so, the use case retrieves these messages and presents them to the System User.

For each message, the use case asks the System User what to do with the message. If the System User responds that it should be removed, the use case removes the message. Otherwise, the message is kept in the system.

The subflow ends, and the use-case instance continues according to the Login/Logout use case after the Logged In extension point.

Analysis Model

The analysis model realizing the *Message Transfer* blueprints involves a collection of classes. First, we need to be able to handle information about the message to be transmitted, such as who is the receiver and what is the message. Second, to be able to check whether the receiver is connected to the system, and if so where the message is to be delivered, the model must capture information about the receivers. The model therefore contains two entity classes, called Message and User Information. Furthermore, the model contains one control class, called Message Handler, which performs the checks and stores, retrieves, and delivers the messages.

Finally, there must be a collection of boundary classes for the interactions with the two actors. For the Sender, we need a boundary class, called Message Definition UI, for preparation of the message. If the Sender can transmit messages directly to the system, this boundary class acts as a communication protocol. If the Sender is a human being who can select to send messages among a collection of tasks, however, this selection must be made through a separate, basic interface. Therefore, we introduce the System Form boundary class. In this case, the Message Definition UI will most likely be a kind of editor, like an email editor.

The situation is similar for the Receiver. There is one boundary class for presenting the message, called Message Presenting UI, which will be a communication protocol if the Receiver is a kind of machine or system. Otherwise, if the Receiver is a human being, the boundary class will be a window, a form, or similar. The System Form boundary class is used when the Receiver must request the system to deliver the stored messages. This leads us to the model presented in Figure 32.3.

The flow of the Transfer Message use case will start when the Sender chooses to send a message. This is either done in the System Form, where the Sender chooses to send a message that will cause the Message Definition UI to be presented where the Sender enters the message, or, for nonhuman senders, the Sender can immediately send the message through the Message Definition UI without initiating the use case through the System Form.

An instance of Message Handler is created that receives the message and checks where to find the receivers using the information in the User Information instances together with the information in the message. If the message is to be delivered immediately (*Message Transfer: Immediate Delivery*), the Message Handler transmits the message to the Receivers through the Message Presenting UI, whereas for a message to be stored in the system and delivered later (*Message Transfer: Deferred Delivery*) the Message Handler creates an instance of the Message entity class that will be stored in the system.

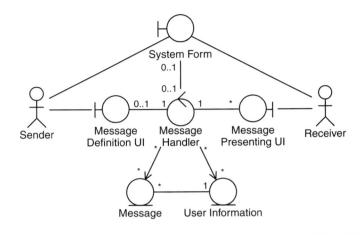

Figure 32.3   An analysis model of a system for transferring messages.

The next time a Receiver requests the stored messages, an instance of Message Handler is created to check whether there are any messages to that Receiver. If so, the Message Handler retrieves these messages, removes those instances of the Message entity class, and presents the messages to the receiver.

In those cases where the creation and the delivery of the messages are modeled in extension use cases (*Message Transfer: Automatic*), control classes of the base use cases replace the Message Definition UI and the System Form, respectively.

CHAPTER 33

PASSIVE EXTERNAL MEDIUM

Problem

The system is to monitor or control an external medium that in itself is passive (for example, the surrounding air or a fluid).

Characteristics: Common in some domains. Advanced blueprint.

Keywords: Measuring, sensor, unbound external medium.

Blueprints

Passive External Medium

Model

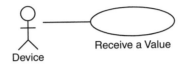

Device   Receive a Value

Description

This blueprint consists of one actor and one use case. The use case receives a value from a medium external to the system, but the medium itself is passive; that is, it does not actively send any information to the system. That is why the device measuring the value from the medium rather than the medium itself is modeled as the actor.

Applicability

This blueprint is used when there is no obvious user sending the input to the system. Instead, a device is examining the environment and sending input to the system.

Discussion

In some problem domains, it is quite common that a device in the system's surroundings provides input to the system. It can, for example, be a thermometer that transmits information about the current temperature of a liquid, or an altimeter that continuously transfers information about the present altitude above sea level.

In situations such as these, we measure some property of a medium outside the system: the liquid or the air, respectively. In neither case does the medium itself send a stimulus to the system, nor does it make use of the system; the medium is passive relative to the system. It would therefore be unnatural to say that the medium is an actor to the system and that the medium sends information to the system. Likewise, it would be wrong to say that the system sends information to the medium. Therefore, when the external entity is a passive, possibly unbound medium, such as a liquid or

Example 353

a gas, we usually model the measuring device as the actor to the system. The device can be said to interrogate the medium and inform the system about the current state of the medium; that is, the device actually does something to the system whereas the passive medium does not (see Figure 33.1).

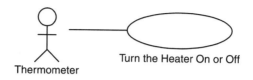

Turn the Heater On or Off

Thermometer

Figure 33.1   If the external entity affecting the system is a passive medium, we model the device interrogating the medium as the actor, whereas in all other cases, we do not model the device but the user of the system as an actor.

It is important to emphasize that we normally do not model devices as actors but rather the individuals behind the devices, and that this situation with the passive medium is an exception. Usually it is the individual using the device for communication with the system that will benefit from using the system, whereas the device will not. The latter will just transform the input or the output into something that the system and the user can understand. For example, we do not model the receipt printer device or card reader device as actors to an ATM, because we do not see them as users of the ATM—they gain nothing from interacting with the ATM. The printer and the reader are just pieces of machinery transforming communications. It is the customer who takes an interest in using the ATM, and therefore the customer is modeled as the actor.

Example

The example provided in this section consists of a heating control system. The model consists of two use cases guiding a heater (see Figure 33.2). The first use case reads the input values, and if they differ more than 2 degrees from the normal value, it will turn on or turn off the heater so that it will run or stop running at half capacity. If the input value is more than 5 degrees below the normal value, the second use case will start, and the heater will run at full power for 1 minute. Then the heater is turned off, and the use case ends. Because the heater is allowed to run on full power only for a short period and then it must be turned off, we have chosen to model this usage as one use case instead of applying a *Future Task* blueprint.

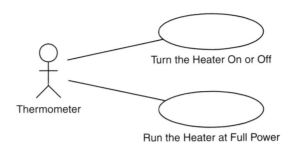

Figure 33.2   The thermometer, which is an external device, gives input to two use cases.

In this example, the heater is considered part of the system, and therefore it is not modeled as an actor. If it were not part of the system, we would just model the heater as an actor, and then have the two use cases associated with it.

Note that this is an example of a situation where the two use cases start in the same way, so it will not be possible to determine which of the two use cases a use-case instance will follow from the start (see the section *Use-Case Instance: A Specific Utilization* in Chapter 4, "Use Cases"). This cannot be determined until the use-case instance has calculated the temperature difference.

New use cases can be added to the model if other alternative responses to the value received from the thermometer are to be provided.

The `CRUD` and the `Optional Service` patterns and the `Stream Input` blueprints are also useful in this example.

Use Case: Turn the Heater On or Off

Brief Description

The use case receives an input value from the Thermometer and depending on the value it may turn on or turn off the heater.

Basic Flow

The use case has two different basic flows:

- Turn on the heater

- Turn off the heater

Example   355

TURN ON THE HEATER

The use case starts when the Thermometer enters a value. If the value is more than 2 degrees lower than the desired value and the heater is not running, the use case turns on the heater at half power.

The use case ends.

TURN OFF THE HEATER

The use case starts when the Thermometer enters a value. If the value is more than 2 degrees higher than the desired value and the heater is running, the use case turns off the heater.

The use case ends.

Use Case: Run the Heater at Full Power

Brief Description

When the use case receives a very low input value from the Thermometer, the use case turns on the heater at full power for one minute.

Basic Flow

The use case starts when the Thermometer enters a value. If the value is 5 or more degrees lower than the desired value, the use case turns on the heater at full power.

After 1 minute, the use case turns off the heater.

The use case ends.

Analysis Model

Figure 33.3   The analysis model of a system interacting with a passive external medium.

The analysis model of a system with a passive external medium is modeled as an ordinary analysis model. The only thing specific with such a model is that the actor is a mediating device, but this is no different from any analysis model with a nonhuman actor. In Figure 33.3, the `External Device` actor interacts with an object of a boundary class, `Device Interface`, that models the interaction protocol between the system and the device. The boundary object transforms the received input to internal messages and sends them to objects of the `Device Input Handler` control class, which handles them as is formulated in the use-case descriptions. This may involve interaction with other control objects and entity objects as well as other boundary objects for communication with other actors.

CHAPTER 34

REPORT GENERATION

Problem

The system is to contain a collection of templates for generating different kinds of reports that present information in accordance with the definition given in the templates. The templates also define how a report is to be formatted and similar matters.

Characteristics: Very common in some domains. Advanced.

Keywords: Formatting, printing template, printout, report, report template, template.

Blueprints

Report Generation: Simple

Model

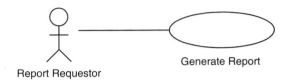

Report Requestor

Generate Report

Description

The `Report Generation: Simple` blueprint consists of one use case, modeling how to generate all kinds of reports. Actions that are specific for the various kinds of reports (for example, different checks) are described as alternative flows of the use case.

Applicability

This blueprint is used if there are only a few (fewer than four) different alternatives of how to generate a report, in terms of what kinds of checks and so on to perform, and these variants are not likely to change. Moreover, these alternatives should be rather similar.

Report Generation: Specialization

Model

Report Requestor

Generate Report

Generate Specific Kind of Report

Description

An alternative is to model the generic procedure on how to generate a report in an abstract use case `Generate Report`. The details of how specific kinds of reports are generated are modeled in separate use cases that are specializations of the `Generate Report` use case.

Applicability

This blueprint is chosen if there are several significantly different procedures on how to generate reports.

Report Generation: Dynamic Templates

Model

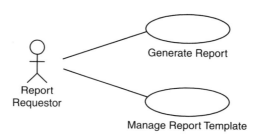

Description

In the `Report Generation: Dynamic Templates` blueprint, a use case `Manage Report Template` is added. It enables the system to support dynamic creation, modification, and deletion of report templates. It is used to modify the templates while the system is up and running.

Applicability

This alternative is preferred when the set of templates is to be dynamically changed.

Discussion

A system can usually present information stored in or calculated by the system. In a use-case description, it is often enough to describe these actions with statements such as this:

The User selects to print the information presented on the screen, and the use case prints it.

Or perhaps:

The use case retrieves the price of each item, calculates the total cost, and prints the name and the price of each item and the total cost.

After generating the postscript code, the use case might send the information to a printing device, which prints it.

However, in some business systems, defining what information is to be printed and how it is to be formatted is a more complex matter, which calls for definition of report templates. A report template states which information is to be printed when a report is generated based on the selected template. The layout of the report is often included in the definition of the template. Clearly, this printing procedure must be modeled explicitly in use cases because it is too complex to be described in a sentence or two.

We start by defining one use case for managing the templates and another for generating the reports, as in the `Report Generation: Dynamic Templates` blueprint. As you will see later, it is quite possible that we will need more use cases to handle differences between the reports.

Let us begin with the use case modeling the generation of a report: the `Generate Report` use case. After the actor has decided which report is to be generated, the use case looks up the template that is to be used for the selected report. Then based on what information the actor has chosen to have printed, the use case uses the definitions given in the template to retrieve all the information to be printed. Finally, the use case sends the information to a printing device together with the layout information also retrieved from the selected template.

> One of the sales managers, using the warehouse system in the role of `Salesperson`, selects to print the order with the ID ZYX-321 based on the template named Order Template. Using this template, the use case finds that the following information is to be printed: the order ID, the name, ID, price, quantity of each ordered item, and the total cost. The use case retrieves all this information and then uses the layout defined in the template to generate the report, and finally sends it to the `Salesperson`.

Using this technique, we need only one use case for modeling the generation and printing of the reports. The definitions of what kind of information is to be printed are stored together with the report layout in the system and can be retrieved as well as modified by different use cases. If there are different groups of templates requiring different kinds of checks, confirmations, validations, and so on, however, the model will often be easier to understand if there is one use case for each of these categories of reports. Because all of these use cases will share the same structure and behavior, this general procedure is preferably expressed in a separate abstract use case. This abstract use case is specialized by the use cases that generate the different categories of reports (`Report Generation: Specialization`). The general procedure is described only once, and the variants such as checks and validations are added in specializations of that use case.

In the warehouse system, there are three categories of reports: one category containing different kinds of reports about orders, one covering financial reports, and one about the contents in the warehouse. As shown in Figure 34.1, the generation of these groups of reports is modeled with three use cases: `Generate Order Report`, `Generate Financial Report`, and `Generate Stock List`. All three of them are specializations of the abstract use case `Generate Report`. This use case describes how the generation of a report is done in general—that is, the looking up of the template, the retrieval of the information to be printed, and so on, as described previously.

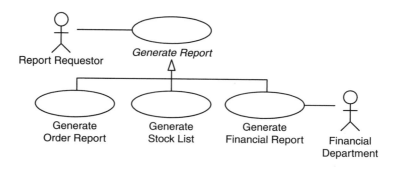

Report Requestor

Generate Report

Generate Order Report

Generate Stock List

Generate Financial Report

Financial Department

Figure 34.1   In the warehouse system, there are three groups of reports, each represented by a specialization of the general `Generate Report` use case.

However, before the generation of an order report, it must be checked whether all the items mentioned in the order are available or whether they are sold out and must be delivered later. Therefore, the `Generate Order Report` use case includes this check; because this use case is a specialization of `Generate Report`, however, it also consists of the generating and printing procedure.

Generating a financial report will include, in addition to the general procedure, interactions with the `Financial System` actor to retrieve some of the information to be printed.

Finally, when generating different kinds of stock lists, we must differentiate between items that are available, items that are sold but not yet delivered to the customer, and items that have been sold out and will have to be restocked before they can be delivered.

How a template is defined is modeled by another use case: `Manage Report Template`. This use case is not present in the first *Report Generation* blueprint. Strictly speaking, it is superfluous when the templates are hard-coded into the system, but it is required if it is to be possible to add new templates during runtime, or to modify or remove existing ones. We treat this use case as an ordinary administrative use case (see Chapter 20, "CRUD"). The use case receives text, layout, and scripts from the actor. The latter state what information is to be retrieved from the database or how it is to be calculated. These scripts are stored in the system under the proper template name. The definition of the layout is defined in a similar way.

Example

This section provides an example consisting of a combination of the second and the third *Report Generation* blueprints. The example consists of three use-case descriptions: Generate Report, Manage Report Template, and Generate Order Report. The latter is an example of a specialization of Generate Report to be used for generating order reports (see Figure 34.2).

Patterns useful in this example include the *Commonality*, the *CRUD*, and the *Optional Service* patterns.

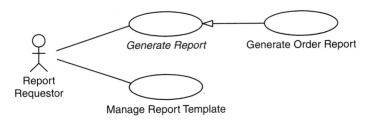

Figure 34.2   The Generate Order Report is a specialization of the Generate Report use case.

Use Case: Generate Report

Brief Description

The use case generates a report to the Report Requestor.

The use case is abstract.

Example   363

Basic Flow

START OF THE FLOW

The use case starts when the Report Requestor chooses to generate a report. The use case presents the available templates to the Report Requestor.

SELECTION OF REPORT TEMPLATE

The Report Requestor selects one of the templates. The use case looks up what information must be provided to use this template, and requests that information from the Report Requestor.

The Report Requestor provides the prompted information. The use case checks that the information is provided.

GENERATION AND PRESENTATION OF THE REPORT

The use case retrieves the layout for the template and starts generating the report based on the layout. Scripts that are found in the description of the template are evaluated.

When the complete report is generated, the use case presents the generated report to the Report Requestor together with an offer to print the report.

If the Report Requestor chooses to print the report, the use case sends the generated report to the printer.

END OF THE FLOW

The Report Requestor chooses to stop viewing the report, and the use case ends.

Alternative Flows

MISSING INFORMATION

If the prompted information is missing, the use case asks the Report Requestor to re-enter the missing information.

The Report Requestor provides the missing information. Then the use case continues where the use case checks that the information is provided.

OPERATION CANCELED

If the Report Requestor chooses to cancel the operation, which can be done at any time during the flow, the gathered information is discarded and the use case ends.

SCRIPT EXECUTION FAILURE

If the evaluation of a script fails, the error text "Information could not be retrieved" is inserted at the location in the generated report where the information resulting from the script evaluation was to be presented. The use case continues with the next script.

Use Case: Manage Report Template

Brief Description

The Report Requestor uses the use case to create a template that can be used for generating reports.

Basic Flow

The use case starts when the Report Requestor chooses to create a template. The use case presents the layout parameters to be supplied by the Report Requestor. For each field, the Report Requestor is asked to supply name, type, position, and script.

The Report Requestor enters the requested information together with the name of the template and the input parameters required by the scripts.

When this information is received by the use case, it checks that the name of the template is unique and, if so, creates a new template and stores the provided information.

The use case ends.

Example 365

Alternative Flows

OPERATION CANCELED

If the Report Requestor chooses to cancel the operation, which may be done at any time during the flow, no template is created and the use case ends.

ILLEGAL TEMPLATE NAME

If an already existing template has the same name as the one provided for the new template by the Report Requestor, the use case informs the Report Requestor and asks for another name. The Report Requestor either gives a new name or cancels the operation.

Use Case: Generate Order Report

Brief Description

The use case, which is a specialization of the Generate Report use case, generates a report of an order to the Report Requestor.

Basic Flow

START OF THE FLOW

The use case starts as described in the Generate Report use case.

SELECTION OF REPORT TEMPLATE

The Report Requestor selects an order template. The use case looks up what information must be provided to use this template—that is, the identity of the order—and requests that the Report Requestor provide this information.

The Report Requestor enters the order identity. The use case checks that there is an order with the provided ID, that all items referenced in the order are available, and that the order is not locked due to modification.

GENERATION AND PRESENTATION OF THE REPORT

The use case generates and presents the report as described in the Generate Report use case.

END OF THE FLOW

The use case ends as described in the Generate Report use case.

Alternative Flows

UNDEFINED ORDER

If no order is registered with the provided identity, the use case notifies the Report Requestor and asks for another identity. The use case continues as described in the basic flow from where the Report Requestor provides the order identity.

UNDEFINED ITEM

If the order references items that are currently not available, this is stated at the beginning of the report. The use case continues as described in the basic flow from where the report is generated.

ORDER LOCKED

If the order is locked, the Report Requestor is notified and the use case ends.

Analysis Model

There are two ways to model the templates: one that allows dynamic modifications of the templates (*Report Generation: Dynamic Templates*) and one where the templates are statically defined. In the first model, there is an entity class called Template whose instances model the actual templates. Each of these instances contains the definition of a template. The specific values for one template are expressed as attribute values of the instance. This model allows dynamic modifications both of the collection of templates and of the definition of the individual templates (see Figure 34.3).

The flows start in the System Form, where the actor selects which operation is to be performed. Depending on the choice, there will be created either a Report Generator or a Template Handler. Either produces a specific form to be used in the communication with the actor, as well as performs the checks and so on stipulated in the use case.

Instances of the `Template` entity store the definitions of the templates, whereas instances of the `Generated Report` entity keep the information that is to be presented in the reports that are currently generated. Unless the generated reports are to be saved, these instances are transient; that is, they exist only during the performance of the use-case instances. `General Class` is any class in the system whose instances store information that the scripts need to access.

If specializations of the use case `Generate Report` are used (*Report Generation: Specialization*), it is quite natural to introduce specializations of the `Report Generator` class as well, to capture the specific parts defined in the specialized use cases. If the `Report Requestor` chooses to print the report, it is sent to the `Printer Device`.

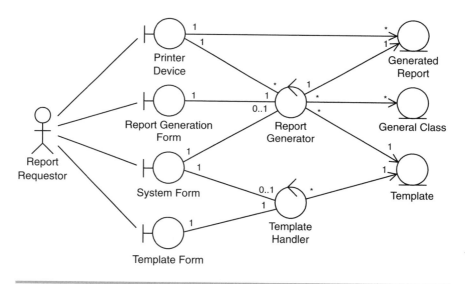

Figure 34.3   An analysis model of a system for generating reports. The model allows dynamic modifications of the templates.

In the second model, the templates are fixed; that is, neither the collection of templates nor the definition of a template can be modified during the execution of the system. In this model, each template is modeled as a separate class containing the definition of the layout as well as of the content of a report that is based on the template. The class is modeled as a boundary class because it is to be used for communication from the system to the actor (see Figure 34.4).

Once again, the flows start in the `System Form`, where the actor selects to generate a report. A `Report Generator` is created handling the creation of a `Report Generation Form` from which the actor selects the report to be generated. The `Report Generator` also performs the checks and the executions of scripts and so on. The different kinds of reports, with their specific content and layouts, are modeled as subclasses of the `Report` class, such as the `Specific Report` class. This class contains the general definitions of how a report is to be produced, whether the report can be printed, and how the report will be presented to the actor.

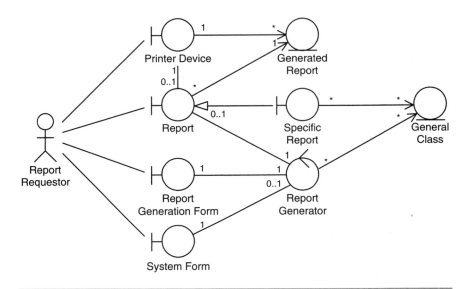

Figure 34.4   Another analysis model of a system for generating reports. This model does not support dynamic modifications of the templates; all the templates in the model are expressed explicitly.

CHAPTER 35

STREAM INPUT

Problem

An actor provides a stream of input to the system, and the handling of this input is to be described by use cases. The solution to this problem depends on whether the stream consists of discrete values or of continuous values.

Characteristics: Common in some domains. Advanced.

Keywords: Analog device, analog system, continuous system, discrete stream, input signal, input stream.

Blueprints

Stream Input: Discrete

Model

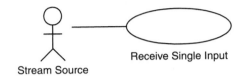

Description

The `Stream Input: Discrete` blueprint contains one actor producing an input stream of discrete values and one use case. The use case models the reception of a single value in the stream.

Applicability

This blueprint is applicable when the stream consists of discrete values.

Stream Input: Analog

Model

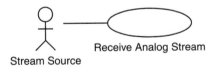

Description

In the `Stream Input: Analog` blueprint, there is one actor producing a continuous stream of values. In this case, the use case models the reception of the whole, analog stream.

Applicability

This blueprint is used when the input stream is analog.

Discussion

Some systems continuously receive a stream of values to be handled in some way. We differentiate between two kinds of streams: streams consisting of discrete values and analog streams with analog values.

Discrete Values

Typical examples of systems with input streams of discrete values are surveillance systems reading the distinct values produced by other systems, and production systems producing output values based on the received input. In cases such as these, we apply the first *Stream Input* blueprint and let the use case model how one value from the stream is consumed and handled by the system. Instances of these use cases will run very quickly, and there is, practically all the time, an instance of this type running in the system.

One advantage of modeling the consumption of only *one* value in a use case rather than including a loop in the use case consuming *all* the values in the stream is that we can have multiple use cases each of which describes how a subset of the possible input values are to be handled (see Figure 35.1). Therefore, we do not have to cover all the possible values in one use case. New types of values can be added in later versions of the model by just adding new use cases; we will not have to modify the existing ones.

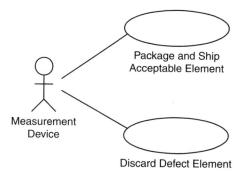

Figure 35.1   If the system receives a discrete stream of input values of different kinds, we describe the handling of the different kinds of values in different use cases.

Another reason why we model only one input to the use case and not the complete sequence is that inserting a loop around the description of how the input is to be handled by the use case will not add any extra meaning to the model—it already captures what the system will do with the input. The only effect is that we reduce the number of instances of that use case. This may be tempting, especially for programmers who are used to thinking in terms of effectiveness and saving resources, but keep in mind that a use-case model does not capture such aspects. The number of use-case instances has no impact on the performance of the final implemented system!

Furthermore, we must not confuse the use case with a probable implementation of the system, which may contain a loop retrieving all input values and dispatching them to different routines handling different kinds of values. The use case describes one usage of the system, which, in this case, is the reception and handling of one value. If we insert the loop into the use case, we must also describe when and how we exit the loop, what is to be done when an unrecognized value is received (this can be captured by a separate use case if no loop is used), and so on.

Obviously, if the input stream consists of sub-sequences of discrete values forming a whole, the use case should consume a whole sub-sequence.

Analog Stream

What, then, is to be done when the input can be characterized as a continuous function? A typical example of such a system is an analog electric amplifier. Unfortunately, use cases do not handle continuous values too well. In fact, languages based on Turing machines deal only with discrete, not continuous, values. We have found that such cases are best captured if the input and the checking of values are described using ordinary use-case description techniques, whereas the output function can be given in a separate chapter in the use-case description. The chapter on the output can of course be structured with subsections if the output function is complex with, for example, different behavior at different intervals of input.

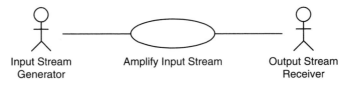

Input Stream   Amplify Input Stream   Output Stream
Generator   Receiver

Figure 35.2   The system acts partly as an analog system, and this part of the system is described in one use case.

According to the `Stream Input: Analog` blueprint, we have one use-case instance running as long as the input stream keeps coming (see Figure 35.2). This would seem to contradict what we said above about discrete input streams, where a use-case instance handles only one entity in the stream.

Example 373

However, in a continuous analog signal, it is not possible to identify separate entities of the input, by definition.

The description of a use case operating an analog input stream looks quite like the description of an ordinary use case. However, there is one difference: What is performed on the input stream (the transformation) is here described by means of a mathematical function and not in the form of an operational description, like as a sequence of actions.

Example

As stated previously, a use case receiving one value in a stream of discrete values is described as any other use case receiving a single input value, so there is no point in giving an example of such a situation.

The following example is an application of the *Stream Input: Analog* blueprint, describing a use case which models an amplifier that receives input in the form of an analog electrical current and outputs the amplified current (see Figure 35.2).

Other useful patterns in this example are the *Business Rules* and the *Multiple Actors* patterns.

Use Case: Amplify Input Stream

Brief Description

The use case amplifies an analog electric current received from the Input Stream Generator, and outputs it to the Output Stream Receiver.

Basic Flow

The use case starts when it receives an analog electric current from the Input Stream Generator.

As long as the current is received, the use case outputs an amplified analog output stream to the Output Stream Receiver according to the amplification function described in the section *Function*.

The use case ends when no input stream is received.

Function

The amplification is modeled by the following function:

$$\frac{V_{out}}{V_{in}} = -\frac{\beta R_C}{r + (\beta + 1)R_E}$$

where

    V_{out} : voltage on the collector

    V_{in} : voltage on the base

    β : base–collector current amplification

    R_C : resistance connected to the collector

    R_E : resistance connected to the emitter

    r   : base–emitter resistance

For a more thorough description, see *Microelectronic Circuits and Devices* (Horenstein 1996).

Analysis Model

The model of a system receiving a stream input will look like an ordinary analysis model (see Figure 35.3).

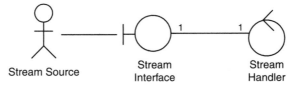

Figure 35.3   The analysis model of a system receiving a stream of input values.

However, our experience is that if the system models the reception of an analog stream, it is unlikely that the model will contain an entity class, because no information is stored, and the number of control classes will also be small, as there will be only a few different tasks. The descriptions of the boundary classes and the control classes will mostly reference specifications found in other documents, like information about which amplification function is to be used.

CHAPTER 36

TRANSLATOR

Problem

The system is to receive an input stream and produce an output stream based on some translation rules.

Characteristics: Common in some domains. Advanced.

Keywords: Compiler, encryption, import, parser, transformation, XML.

Blueprints

Translator: Static Definition

Model

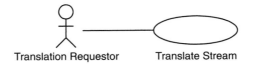

Translation Requestor   Translate Stream

Description

The *Translator: Static Definition* blueprint consists of one use case, called Translate Stream. It receives an input stream consisting of different kinds of tokens that together form a structure, and produces an output stream based on the input stream and a collection of translation rules.

Applicability
This blueprint is used when the translation procedure will not be changed dynamically.

Translator: Dynamic Rules

Model

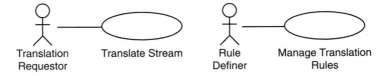

Translation   Translate Stream   Rule   Manage Translation
Requestor   Definer   Rules

Description

An alternative blueprint also includes a use case for management of the translation rules. With this use case, it is possible to define and modify the translation rules dynamically. The rules are not statically defined in the system; they can be enhanced without recompiling and restarting the system.

Applicability
This alternative is preferable when the translation rules may be modified frequently.

Discussion

A translator, such as a compiler or an XML parser, is a system producing an output stream based on an input stream and on a collection of translation rules. In principle, such a system is modeled by one primary use case and possibly a small collection of supporting use cases (see Figure 36.1). The primary use case models the translation process while the supporting use cases describe, among other things, displaying the version number of the translator, and modification of translation rules (if it is to be possible to modify them dynamically, as in the *Translator: Dynamic Rules* blueprint). The definitions of these latter use cases follow ordinary techniques (see Chapter 20, "CRUD"). We therefore concentrate on the translation use case.

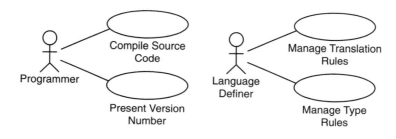

Figure 36.1   A compiler is usually described with one translation use case (the primary use case) and possibly a collection of supporting use cases.

A software compilation is usually performed in a few steps, such as checking that the received elements appear in the right order (the syntax check), building up an internal representation of the received input, and checking that the elements together produce well-formed expressions (the well-formedness rules check). It may also be necessary to check whether the received elements are of the right types (the type checking). After all these actions have been carried out, the output stream is produced according to the production rules. Because the translation of an input stream to an output stream will include all of these steps, they are modeled by one use case. However, it might be that by providing different parameters as input, the use case may perform only a few of the steps described, but these are variants (alternative flows) of the normal flow of the use case. The whole compilation is one usage of the system, and it is therefore described as one use case.

The reason why we must not model the different steps as separate use cases is that they will always be performed together in a predefined sequence. Therefore, there is just one use case.

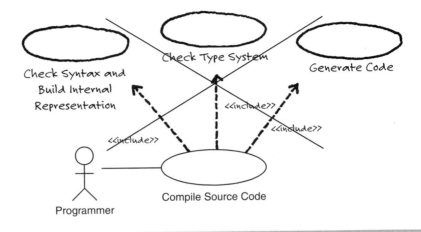

Figure 36.2   A common mistake when modeling a translator is to model the steps as separate use cases, possibly with include relationships from the translation use case.

It would also be a mistake to model the different steps as separate use cases that are included by the "main" use case, as in Figure 36.2, where the "main" use case has include relationships to the use cases denoting the different checks and code generation. This is best described as functional decomposition of the Translate Stream use case, which clearly is a misuse of the use-case construct (see Chapter 40, "Mistake: Functional Decomposition"). It is crucial to always keep in mind that a use case models a usage of the system and that inclusion use cases, apart from expressing common parts, are to be used only when they are important enough to be promoted into use cases in their own right. There is always a price to be paid for introducing inclusion use cases such as these "step" use cases, which do not even add to the understanding of the system. Actually, functional decomposition often reflects the internal structuring of the system and this is not to be mirrored in the use-case model.

Accordingly, we model the translation procedure as one use case as the complete procedure is one usage of the system. However, the description of this use case may very well be organized with several subsections (for example, one for each step). Note, however, that the best way of describing the flow of this use case is to focus on the ordering of the steps, on alternatives that are allowed, on additional input parameters and their meaning, and on general issues regarding the algorithms. The specific syntax rules, well-formedness rules, type rules, and translation rules are much better expressed using ordinary production rules (see, for example, the book *Compilers: Principles, Techniques, and Tools* [Aho, Sethi, and Ullman 1986]), and then treated as business rules—that is, be placed in a separate chapter or appendix on the description of the use case (see Chapter 16, "Business Rules").

Example 379

Example

This section provides an example of the *Translator: Static Definition* blueprint. The additional rule-management use case included in the second blueprint is described as an ordinary CRUD use case (see Chapter 20).

The example describes the translation of source code into machine code. We have excluded the translation rules and the type rules from the text, as these are specific for the language to be compiled.

See also the *Business Rules* and the *CRUD* patterns. The *Stream Input* blueprints are also relevant to this example.

Use Case: Compile Source Code

Brief Description

The use case reads a stream of source code provided by the Programmer and produces a stream containing an executable module.

Basic Flow

The use case starts when the Programmer requests compilation of the provided stream containing the source code of a program.

The use case reads the stream, checks the syntax according to the description in the section *Syntax*, and builds an internal representation (a parse tree) of the program.

If the program is syntactically correct and the internal representation of the program is created, the use case checks if the program is type correct according to the type system in the section *Type System*.

If the program is type correct, the use case produces a stream of executable code according to the production rules in the section *Code Production Rules* and sends it to the Programmer. Finally, the internal representation of the program is discarded.

The use case ends.

Alternative Flows

ONLY SYNTAX CHECK

If the flag stating that only the syntax check is to be performed is set, the use case ends after the production of the internal representation of the program.

ONLY TYPE CHECK

If the flag stating that only the type check is to be performed is set, the use case ends after checking the type correctness of the program.

INCORRECT SYNTAX

If the syntax is incorrect, the use case displays the unacceptable structure to the Programmer. After identifying the incorrect phrase, the use case tries to recover from the error by discarding the subsequent tokens in the input stream until it can identify the next expression, and then the syntax check continues from there. No type checking or code generation is performed.

INCORRECT TYPING

If a type error is found, the use case displays the misconstructed statement to the Programmer together with the type information. No code is generated.

UNABLE TO BUILD INTERNAL REPRESENTATION

If the use case fails to build an internal representation of the program, it presents an error message to the Programmer, and the use case ends.

Syntax

[. . .]

Type System

[. . .]

Code Production Rules

[. . .]

Analysis Model

The realization of the Translate Stream use case includes two principal classes: a control class called Translator and an entity class called Rule. The latter models the information about a single rule and can check whether the rule is applicable to the current input and, if so, it can generate output based on the input. The Translator class is responsible for identifying and choosing between the applicable rules, for requesting generation of the output, and for handling error cases. Often, subclasses of these two classes are introduced to handle specific kinds of procedures and rules.

In addition to these classes, other classes might also be required, such as classes for representing intermediate results. For example, when reading the input stream and checking whether the syntax is correct, a compiler often builds up a parse tree that represents the source code that is received in the input stream. This tree is used internally by the compiler when performing the other steps in the translation, such as the type checking and the production of the output stream (the code). The nodes in the tree are instances of subclasses of the Node class. The different kinds of language elements in the source code are represented by subclasses of the Node class. This leads us to the model presented in Figure 36.3.

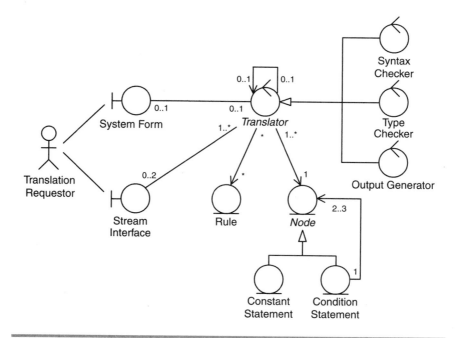

Figure 36.3   An analysis model for the *Translator: Static Definition* blueprint.

The use case `Translate Stream` is initiated through the `System Form`, where the `Translation Requestor` enters the input parameters (for example, compilation flags). An instance of (a subclass of) the `Translator` class is created that reads the input stream through a `Stream Interface`. For each of the tokens read, the `Translator` tries to find rules that match the input token. If multiple rules match, the `Translator` chooses one of them based on some information in each rule, such as its priority. The `Translator` asks the selected rule to perform its action on the input token, which for example may be to create a new `Node` instance, or create tokens to be added to the output stream, depending on the rule. Finally, when the input stream ends, the `Translator` performs its final task, which may be to create another instance of a `Translator` dedicated to type checking or generation of the output stream. When the last `Translator` has performed its task, and if all the steps in the translation were successful, an output stream has been produced and presented via a `Stream Interface`.

The realization of the *Translator: Dynamic Rules* blueprint will use two additional classes: one boundary class, `Rule Interface`, and one control class, `Rule Handler` (see Figure 36.4). The `Rule Definer` will define and modify rules through the `Rule Interface`, which sends the information to the `Rule Handler`, which checks that the right information is provided and stores the information in instances of the `Rule` class.

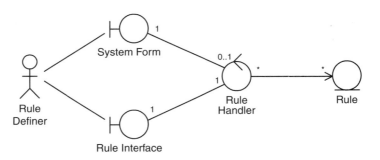

Figure 36.4   The *Translator: Dynamic Rules* blueprint requires two additional analysis classes.

Part V

Common Mistakes

This part of the book covers a collection of mistakes often found in use-case models. This collection should be used to detect that something may be wrong in the model. Although rare, there may be a good reason why a model matches one of these erroneous models and still be correct.

All chapters in this part are organized in the same way:

- **Name of mistake**—A descriptive name of the error in a few words

- **Fault**—A short description of the mistake

- **Incorrect model**—A use-case model illustrating the mistake

- **Discussion**—A discussion on why this is an incorrect model

- **Way out**—Hints on what to do to correct the incorrect model

The chapters presenting the mistakes are sorted alphabetically within this part.

Chapter 37. Alternative Flow as Extension: Modeling an alternative flow of a use case as an extension of that use case.

Chapter 38. Business Use Case: Modeling a business process as a system use case.

Chapter 39. Communicating Use Cases: Modeling two use cases with an association between them, implying that the use cases communicate with each other.

Chapter 40. Functional Decomposition: One large use case with include relationships to a set of inclusion use cases, each modeling a subfunction of the large use case.

Chapter 41. Micro Use Cases: Modeling single operations performed by the users as separate use cases, resulting in a use-case model consisting of a large number of very small use cases.

Chapter 42. Mix of Abstraction Levels: A use-case model containing use cases defined at different levels of abstraction.

Chapter 43. Multiple Business Values: Incorporating too much in a single use case by capturing several goals or business values in one use case.

Chapter 44. Security Levels with Actors: Capturing the security levels restricting who may use the different services of the system only by defining actors corresponding to the security levels.

CHAPTER 37

MISTAKE: ALTERNATIVE FLOW AS EXTENSION

Fault

Modeling an alternative flow of a use case as an extension of that use case.

Keywords: Addition to flow, alternative flow, extend relationship, extracting flow.

Incorrect Model

Model

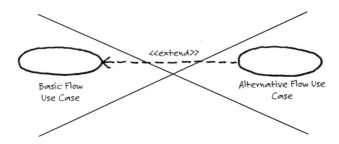

Detection

A clear sign of this modeling mistake is when the flow of an extension use case is supposed to replace a part of the base use case flow. Another indicator is, of course, that the base use case is not complete without the extension, because it lacks an alternative flow.

Discussion

A use case has one flow, or sometimes multiple flows, considered to be the normal or basic flow of that use case. This flow will be performed when everything goes according to plan in the use case; this is the flow a reader of the model will associate with the use case.

However, a use case also includes variants of that flow to be used if a condition is not fulfilled, if something goes wrong, if the actor gives an unexpected input, and so forth. All of these are different paths through the use case, and from a user's perspective, all of them are important. Remove one of them and the system will not function properly—it might even crash. Similarly, adding one of these alternative flows to another flow or appending it to another flow will also result in strange and unwanted behavior of the system. Unfortunately, this is what often happens when an alternative flow is extracted from a use case into an extending use case.

The reason for this is to be found in the definition: The meaning of an extend relationship is that the extension may be *added* to the flow of the base use case (see Chapter 8, "Extend: Expanding Existing Use Cases"). This implies that behavior of the base use case cannot be *replaced* by behavior defined in the extension use case. Therefore, it is not possible to extract an alternative flow into an extension use case, because this extracted behavior will be performed only in *addition to* and not *instead of* what is described in the base use case.

To overcome this problem, we might erroneously believe we could use the condition of the extend relationship to be able to extract the alternative behavior. For example, we might consider describing the *true*-path in the base use case together with the statement that this path is only to be taken if the condition is evaluated to *true*, and extracting the *false*-path into an extension use case. The extend relationship will state that the addition is to be made at the location of the condition in the base use case, and the condition of the relationship will be the negation of the condition in the base use case. The problem with this scenario is that the base use case becomes dependent on the extension use case; the base use case is not complete without the extension use case as it is lacking what is to happen if the condition is not fulfilled.

Way Out

Obviously, we must correct the ill-formed model by merging the base use case and the extension use case. The flow captured in the extension use case is moved into the base use case, where it will be an alternative flow, and then the extend relationship together with the extension use case is removed from the model. Note that it is not necessary to also remove the extension point from the (former) base use case, because having an extension point does not change the behavior of a use case in itself. In fact, it must not be removed without making absolutely certain that it is not used by another extension use case or planned to be used in a future version of the model.

If it is still desirable to model the alternative flow as a separate use case, you can do so by using an include relationship between the two use cases. This works because in an include relationship, there is no problem with the base use case being dependent on the inclusion use case (see Figure 37.1). However, before choosing this way out, it is important to make sure that the inclusion use case has a business value of its own. In this case, only the extension relationship and possibly the extension point is removed from the model, and an include relationship is added instead.

Figure 37.1   An alternative flow may be extracted from a use case if an include relationship is defined from the remaining base use case to the new use case.

CHAPTER 38

MISTAKE: BUSINESS USE CASE

Fault

Modeling a business process as a system use case.

Keywords: Business process, large use case, level of abstraction, long use case, multiple initiating actors, pause in use case.

Incorrect Model

Model

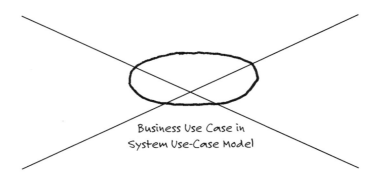

Detection

In some cases, business use cases might be hidden in a system use-case model without making their presence noticeable in diagrams; it is only in the description of these use cases the mistake can be detected. However, the name of such a use case typically starts with `Handle`, `Manage`, or `Perform`, followed by the name of a concept in the business domain. Furthermore, it is not uncommon that more than one actor is involved in use cases of this kind. Obviously, these are both very weak indications since both situations may well occur in a correct model.

To verify that this modeling mistake has not been made in a model, it is necessary to check the descriptions of suspected use cases. When a use case consists of two or more parts that are disconnected in the sense that they are performed at different points in time, it describes how the business acts and not how the system is used; therefore, it should be split.

Discussion

Use cases are normally used for modeling how a system is used. However, the same technique is applicable when modeling how an organization is used by its environment. In this case, the use cases will model different processes starting from someone outside the organization, such as a customer, and model what actions are performed inside the organization as a response to the interaction from the entity outside the organization. We call the use cases modeling an organization rather than a software system *business use cases*. Fragments of the business use cases can be realized by the software systems supporting the organization; that is, they can be traced to traditional system use cases.

When a business flow should be more or less completely implemented in a supporting software system, it is sometimes not obvious whether the flow should be represented by a single use case in the system's use-case model or if it should be split into several use cases.

An example of a business use case that will be supported to a high degree by a software system is Manage Order in a warehouse business. The flow comprises among other things the registration of an order, the generation of a pick-list for the assembly of the shipment, the generation of an invoice when the order has been shipped, and finally the registration of the payment from the customer. It should also comprise the possibility to change or to delete a registered order.

Why not capture this as a single use case in the system use-case model? The problem is that this use case does not model one usage of the *software*; it models one usage of the *business*. The flow consists of several subflows that will be performed at different points in time, at irregular time intervals, and possibly initiated by different persons. Furthermore, each of these subflows provides a value to someone inside the warehouse. Hence, every subflow constitutes a use case in the *software*; that is, they are complete usages of the software. If we change focus and study the entire warehouse, however, none of them constitutes a use case on its own; they are only fragments in the usage of the warehouse *business*. The key here is the subject of the model: Is it the software system or is it the business?

One problem of including business use cases in the use-case model of the software system is that their purposes and stakeholders are different from those of the system. Furthermore, business use cases are normally described at a higher level of abstraction. If they were to be described at a suitable level for a model of a software system, they would become very long and complex.

In general, if a use case requires an actor to do something at some point during its performance, such as provide additional input or to acknowledge the reception of information, this implies an interrupt in the execution of the use case. If the required input is most likely to arrive at a significant later moment in time, it is no longer a continuation of the current use case. We are not even sure that this input will ever happen. Therefore, we say that the use case will end here and another use case will be initiated when the input arrives.

In situations where the input from the actor is expected to normally arrive more or less immediately, such as a confirmation from another system to which our use case sends information, it is usually best to model the complete flow in one use case. The situation where the input does not arrive as expected can then be handled in an alternative flow by introducing a timeout interrupt.

Note that it is possible for a business use case to be a suitable use case in the system use-case model as well, so a one-to-one mapping from the business model to the system model is not wrong per se. Again, the key is to keep in mind what the subject of the model is—it models a supporting software and not the business.

Pauses in Use Cases

A somewhat related situation is when the performance of a use case includes a scheduled pause. A typical example is the telephone exchange system supporting a hotel, where one important service to the customers is to offer automatic wake-up calls. From the business perspective, the complete flow starts when a customer requests a wake-up call at some future point in time and ends when the wake-up call has been performed the next morning.

It is tempting to model this flow as one use case, but this is not the best way to do it. First, there is a long period of time during this process when nothing happens, and it is generally considered bad practice to model use cases whose execution largely consists of doing nothing. Second, it may be the case that the wake-up call is never performed at all (for example, if the customer cancels the request or decides to check out before the wake-up time). In this case, the use case has been waiting for a long time for nothing (see also Chapter 28, "Future Task").

Way Out

When a business use case, which is not also a suitable system use case, is detected in the use-case model, the model is corrected by splitting the use case. For each separate task in the original use case to be performed in the system at hand and with a specific business value, a new use case should be defined. The corresponding part of the original use case's flow is extracted into the new use case, where it probably will be described more thoroughly. Like this, the original use case should eventually be empty; that is, it will not contain any system behavior not captured by the new use cases, and it can be removed from the model.

One criterion on when to introduce a new use case is when there is an actor sending an input to the system without being requested by the system to do so. In such a case, there is no ongoing usage of the system waiting for an input from the actor. Therefore, a new use case should be initiated.

Another criterion is that each situation in the flow where there will be a major delay (for example, because of the necessity to wait for input that will be supplied at another occasion), a new use case should be prepared having that actor as the initiator and comprising what happens as a result of the input.

Because the original use case was actually a business use case, it was probably described in less detail than software use cases need to be. This implies that after copying the relevant part of the original use-case description into each new use case, more detail must probably be added to the description.

The fact that the use cases have to be performed in a certain order, as required by the business flow, can be captured by defining preconditions in each of the new use cases (except of course the first one in the sequence; see Chapter 26, "Use-Case Sequence").

The same solution is applicable to use cases with a more or less lengthy pause in their execution (see Chapter 28).

CHAPTER 39

MISTAKE: COMMUNICATING USE CASES

Fault

Modeling two use cases with an association between them, implying that the use cases communicate with each other.

Keywords: Dependency between use cases, combination of use cases, interacting use cases, messages between use cases, split a use case.

Incorrect Model

Model

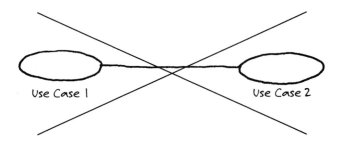

Detection

As soon as there is an association between two use cases, this mistake has been made, which makes it very easy to detect.

Discussion

Each use case models a complete usage of the system. This means that an instance of the use case comprises the performance of the complete usage—that is, the execution of the actions inside the system as well as its interactions with specific persons and systems outside the system that is being modeled.

However, the use-case instance will never send messages to other use-case instances inside the same system. If it did, the use-case instance would not perform the complete usage, because it would request additional actions to be performed by another use-case instance. Clearly, if the actions executed by the other use-case instance must be performed for the usage to be complete, they must be included in the first use-case instance. Otherwise, the first use-case instance is incomplete.

Interacting use cases will occur when developers wrongly try to express the internal structure of the system in the use-case model by modeling the behavior of one part of the system in one use case and the behavior of another part in another use case. As you know, the use cases model the usages of the system as a whole and not usages of parts (see also Chapter 18, "Component Hierarchy"). Furthermore, the use-case model should not reveal anything about the internal structure of the system.

Way Out

A model that is ill-formed because it contains use cases with associations between them can easily be corrected. The two use cases that seem to communicate should be merged and the original two use cases and their association be eliminated.

In practice this is best done by defining a new use case representing the whole flow expressed by the two use cases together. The flow of the new use case should consist of a merge of the two original flows, where all communication between them is eliminated.

Start by making sure where the combined flow starts (that is, which of the two use cases receives the initiating input from an actor). This actor will be the initiating actor of the new use case. Then, the first part of the new flow should be identical to the first part of that use case of the original two where the combined flow starts. When that original flow reaches a call to the other use case, this is ignored in the new flow, which instead should continue like the first part of the other use case's flow. The complete new flow is then constructed by interleaving parts of the original flows between internal calls like this.

When all parts of the original two flows have been captured in the new use case, the original two use cases and the association between them can safely be eliminated.

If it is still necessary to keep the two use cases separate, merging them is not appropriate. Instead, another kind of relationship has to be defined between them, the goal being that when performed, there should be just one use-case instance. This means that either an include or an extend relationship should be used between them:

- If one of the use cases is complete without the other one, an extend relationship can be defined to that use case from the other one.

- If one of them consists of a coherent subflow of the entire flow— that is, in the erroneous model it is called only once from the other use case—it can be an inclusion use case of the other one.

Most likely, neither of these two alternatives can be used immediately. Adjust the two use cases terms of moving subflows between them until either of the two conditions is met and an include or an extend relationship can be defined.

CHAPTER 40

MISTAKE: FUNCTIONAL DECOMPOSITION

Fault

One large use case with include relationships to a set of inclusion use cases, each modeling a subfunction of the large use case.

Keywords: Large use case, level of abstraction, levels of use cases, long use case, split a use case.

Incorrect Model

Model

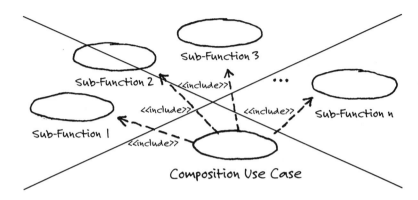

Detection

The presence of the *Functional Decomposition* modeling mistake can often be detected by a disproportionately large number of include relationships in the model. Other things to look out for are base use cases that basically do not contain anything apart from what they include, and inclusion use cases included by only one base use case.

Discussion

Traditional techniques for decomposing a function into smaller subfunctions are sometimes mistakenly used for extracting subflows of a use case into separate, inclusion use cases. The base use case can then be seen as an assembly of, or a composition of, the included use cases. Consider, for example, the functional decomposition of a compiler into the subfunctions Parse Stream, Perform Semantic Check, Perform Type Check, and Generate Output. Defining separate use cases for each of these functions and an aggregate use case called Compile Stream with include relationships to them results in a typical example of this mistake. Basically, the Compile Stream use case will contain no additional actions except what is included from the other use cases.

Use cases model usages of a system. Each such usage provides a value to a stakeholder of the system; that is, there is someone, usually a user of the system, who has an interest in that use case. To make the use-case model easier to maintain, it is possible to extract subflows into separate, abstract use cases that are to be included by or to extend the original base use case. This should be done, for example, when we want to model commonalities between use cases (a subflow is to appear in multiple use cases), when there are to be different system configurations (a subflow should appear only in some configurations), when the subflows are defined in different layers, or when a stakeholder requires that a subflow be explicitly stated in the use-case model.

However, extracting subflows into separate use cases just to make them explicit to the *developers* is not an acceptable reason! The size of the model will increase, there will be more documents to maintain, no other stakeholder will be interested in and defend the existence of those use cases, and, perhaps most importantly from a modeling perspective, the overview of the complete usage of the system will be lost.

To sum up, a use case should not be functionally decomposed as the overview of the complete usage will be lost and the cost for maintaining the model will be increased.

Way Out

The way out from the decomposition trap is to take a few steps back: We must return to basics; that is, first we have to verify that all the base use cases really represent complete usages of the system initiated by actors. Then we must eliminate all inclusion use cases with no clear value to a stakeholder other than the developers and merge them with their base use cases.

Doing this merge is quite straightforward: In each place where the use-case description of the base use case says that another use case is to be included, determine whether that use case is among those that should remain in the model, or whether it is to be merged with the base use case. In the latter case, replace the statement to include the other use case with the flow of the inclusion use case. Then the include relationship and the inclusion use case can be eliminated from the use-case model.

When we are tempted to make use of functional decomposition, it is often an indication that we are dealing with a system that is so large and complex that it is hard to create an overview of it and at the same time provide enough details. Such situations should be handled using a *Component Hierarchy* pattern (see Chapter 18, "Component Hierarchy") or a *Large Use Case* blueprint (see Chapter 21, "Large Use Case").

CHAPTER 41

MISTAKE: MICRO USE CASES

Fault

Modeling single operations performed by the users as separate use cases, resulting in a use-case model consisting of a large number of very small use cases.

Keywords: Functional decomposition, large number of use cases, level of abstraction, order between use cases, simple operation, small use case.

Incorrect Model

Model

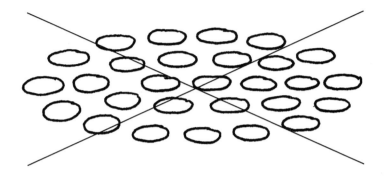

Detection

A good indicator that this mistake has been made in a use-case model is the large number of use cases. Furthermore, studying the names of the use cases will reveal that the use cases model single operations. If not before, this will become obvious when the description documents for use cases are prepared and it becomes evident that the flows are very short. In other words, each document will contain extremely little substance, and no one will be interested in them individually but only in what sequences the use cases can be performed.

Therefore, an additional indication of this modeling mistake is that there will be a need to express the order in which this huge collection of use cases is to be performed. It may even be tempting to introduce communication between use cases to make the sequences explicit, which of course is a clear indicator that something is wrong (see also Chapter 39, "Mistake: Communicating Use Cases").

Discussion

When modeling a system, especially when it is an already existing system, it is sometimes tempting to focus on the different actions a user can perform and express these as use cases. The cause of this error is often focusing on how to interact with the system or on its user interface, instead of on what the user wants to do with the system.

An example of micro use cases is a model where each single menu alternative in the GUI is modeled by a separate use case. In such a case, the flow of each use case will consist of the user selecting one alternative from a menu, and the system's response to this selection.

In general, a single user-provided input together with the corresponding system response will seldom provide a business value to any stakeholder— no user will use the system just to provide this single input. For this reason, it is not a complete usage. Of course, such use cases do exist, but most use cases consist of several user actions in a sequence.

Way Out

Obviously, we must consider how the users would like to use the system. We also have to define a use case for each set of micro use cases that are to be performed together, that is, the sequences that make up the complete usages.

Merging a set of small use cases into larger ones according to the sequence in which they are to be performed is done by first defining a new use case to capture the complete usage. Then the small use cases should be taken one by one, starting with the one that is performed first. The flow of this use case makes up the first part of the new use case's flow. The next part of the flow consists of the flow of the second micro use case, and so on. As soon as the flow of a micro use case is appended to the new use-case flow, it should be removed from the use-case model.

Note that the resulting, merged use cases will contain the actions of the micro use cases as part of their flows. However, it is important not to fall into the trap of composing the new, proper use cases by defining include relationships to the micro use cases! This would result in another ill-formed use-case model where the model would still contain use cases without business value (see Chapter 40, "Mistake: Functional Decomposition").

CHAPTER 42

MISTAKE: MIX OF ABSTRACTION LEVELS

Fault

A use-case model containing use cases defined at different levels of abstraction.

Keywords: Business use case, different reader categories, level of abstraction, level of detail, levels of use cases.

Incorrect Model

Model

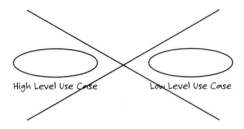

Detection

It is often apparent already from the use-case names when a model comprises use cases at different levels of abstraction. Some will be describing general actions and abstract concepts, whereas others will describe detailed actions and concrete concepts.

Otherwise, a litmus test for this modeling mistake is to let a designer perform a review of the use-case model, checking whether the model is detailed enough to be used as a basis for use-case realization and design. The designer may then point out use cases that are described at too high a level of abstraction, asking for more details, and complain about use cases described at too low a level of abstraction, because they go into detail on design issues.

The same kind of review can be done by a business stakeholder, such as a system user, who will most likely make the opposite complaints.

Discussion

Use cases that are to be realized and implemented by the development team and not by existing products must be detailed enough to make it possible to identify the internal structure of the system based on the use cases, as well as to describe these components' behaviors.

An example of mixing use cases at different levels of abstraction from the telecom world is a model containing both the use case `Make Telephone Call` and the use case `Check Background Noise on a Call Using a Trunk of Type X`. The former use case models a general flow at a high level of abstraction, whereas the latter is defined at a very detailed level of abstraction.

Models with use cases at different abstraction levels are difficult to read and understand, as well as to realize and implement. Furthermore, some parts of the system's services will be emphasized just because they are much elaborated, whereas other parts will seem less important as they are modeled briefly.

System owners and users will probably appreciate the high-level use cases, whereas they will have difficulties understanding the low-level use cases. On the other hand, the developers of the system will consider the high-level use cases as insufficient input to the design work.

Way Out

Usually the final use-case model will have to be refined into quite a low level of abstraction to provide sufficient input to the realization, design, and implementation work. Therefore, the way to resolve the problem is to elaborate on those parts of the model that are defined at a high level of abstraction to make them harmonize with the low-level parts. Rewrite (the parts of) the descriptions that are defined at a too abstract level. The descriptions of the use cases must contain all details needed to design the system based on them; that is, they must describe all platform-independent actions as well as all actions independent of the internal structure of the system performed by the system when it is used. However, make sure not to define the model at too low level of abstraction! The model should still model the usages of the system and be understandable by the different stakeholders. Furthermore, writing extremely detailed use-case descriptions is a task very much subjected to the temptation to unconsciously make design or implementation decisions and include them in the flow descriptions. Even if this pitfall is avoided, many of the details will still have to be changed as a result of design decisions.

Probably, elaborating the high-level parts of the use-case model implies not only detailing the descriptions, but also defining new sets of use cases instead of the high-level ones.

If it is desirable to keep the original high-level use cases in the model, we define generalizations from the new low-level concretizations to the high-level use cases (see Figure 42.1).

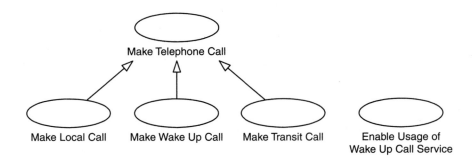

Figure 42.1   If high-level use cases are to be kept in the final use-case model, you can do so by showing how they are concretized by low-level use cases.

CHAPTER 43

MISTAKE: MULTIPLE BUSINESS VALUES

Fault

Incorporating too much in a single use case by capturing several goals or business values in one use case.

Keywords: Alternative flow, business value of a use case, large use case, long use case.

Incorrect Model

Model

Detection

When a use-case model has very few use cases, this modeling mistake may be the cause. The developers should then look for single use cases with lots of alternative flows with disparate goals that offer different values to stakeholders.

Discussion

It is sometimes tempting to identify use cases that are oversized, that is, use cases including too many alternative flows. In an attempt to reduce the size of the model, the developers might have merged certain use cases that ought to have been kept separate. Each use case should have only one goal. This makes it easier for a reader to understand the purpose and the value of the use case. Furthermore, when a use case encompasses too many goals, there are usually many stakeholders interested in that use case, making it complicated to make decisions regarding that use case. Many people will want to have their say, incorrect assumptions might be made, and various compromises might have to be made before the stakeholders will settle on a definition of the flow of the use case. Different readers might also misinterpret a use case whose definition is very general, and therefore they are likely to assume that it captures things that it really does not offer.

Furthermore, it is bad use of resources to have reviewers read what they neither need nor opted for, which will be the case if a certain stakeholder is interested in only a small part of a large use case.

Splitting a use case does not increase the amount of development work, although it increases the number of use cases and the documents describing them, but it clearly increases the understandability of the model. If too much is expressed with a single use case, the use-case modeling effort has not added much to the understanding of how the system is to be used.

In a sense, this modeling mistake can be seen as the counterpart of the *Micro Use Cases* modeling mistake.

Way Out

The way forward when trapped by this modeling mistake is of course to split the "Do Everything" use case into several use cases, one for each business value or goal.

As a first step, the actors involved in the use case should be reviewed. Sometimes, perhaps as a consequence of this modeling mistake, there are also actors capturing too much. Make sure that all the different roles played by the system surroundings interacting with the use case that need to be split are represented by a separate actor and, if not, identify additional actors for individual roles.

The next step is to focus on one of the actors at a time. For each of the actors, the parts of the large use case that this actor will want to make use of all constitute candidates for new use cases. When such use-case candidates are identified from the original, large use case for all the actors, it may be apparent that some of them should be combined into CRUD use cases (see Chapter 20, "CRUD"). The other candidate use cases will be new use cases of their own.

After the relevant parts of the original use-case description have been moved into the descriptions of the new use cases, you can remove the original use case from the model.

CHAPTER 44

MISTAKE: SECURITY LEVELS WITH ACTORS ·

Fault

Capturing the security levels restricting who may use the different services of the system only by defining actors corresponding to the security levels.

Keywords: Access rights, business role.

Incorrect Model

Model

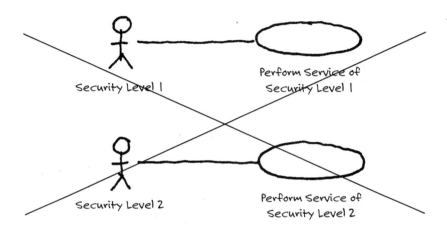

Detection

A use-case model lacking an explicit use case for checking access rights is a warning sign when the usage of the system is to be restricted. However, it is necessary to check the details in the use-case descriptions to be sure this modeling mistake has been made, because the check of the access rights might be hidden inside the use cases (see Chapter 27, "Access Control").

Discussion

The actors of a system are often very close to roles in the business, all of them having their own security levels within the business, and consequently also in relation to the services of the system. Therefore, it might be tempting to express the security levels of the system by attaching them directly to the actors.

However, an actor models a role played by an external user of the system *as seen from the system's point of view*. This role cannot be chosen by an external user. This implies that as soon as a person, or any other entity external to the system, initiates a certain use case, this person or entity will automatically play the role modeled by the initiating actor of that use case. It is not as if a security check were performed by magic as soon as someone plays the role defined by a certain actor. In other words, if we were to capture the security requirements in the use-case model by just connecting the security levels to the actors, anyone using a use case associated with a certain actor would have the security level of that actor from the system's point of view. This is obviously *not* what we want!

Of course, there is nothing wrong per se to have actors corresponding to the different roles in the business. Often these roles have different responsibilities in the organization and hence they use the system differently. Modeling these roles as actors often makes the use-case model easy to understand and verify for system owners and users. However, we must not assume that actors equal business roles and, above all, we must not forget to express security within the use cases!

Way Out

The way to resolve the situation is to apply one of the `Access Control` blueprints so that the access rights are explicitly modeled. These blueprints capture checking of access rights, as well as setting of access rights for individual users. You can find details about how to select the appropriate `Access Control` blueprint, and how to apply it, in Chapter 27.

In most cases, the actors can remain the same even after applying the blueprint, and therefore correcting a use-case model with this kind of error implies addition of information rather than restructuring it (and is thus a rather straightforward procedure).

GLOSSARY

Abstract—An abstract classifier is not a complete declaration and cannot be instantiated. It is used in definitions of other classifiers, like in generalizations, and in extend and include relationships.

Activity diagram—A diagram presenting a control flow or a data flow. It focuses on sequences of actions and not on the instances performing the actions.

Actor—A role played by an entity outside a system, as perceived from the system's point of view, when it uses the system.

Analysis class—A class used in analysis models, usually less detailed than a class in a design model. Often, three kinds of analysis classes are used: Boundary class, Control class, and Entity class.

Analysis model—A model of a system that is independent of the implementation technology. It is usually expressed in terms of (analysis) classes, components, and subsystems.

Association—A declaration of a semantic relationship between classifiers. In a use-case model, it usually indicates that instances of the classifiers communicate.

Attribute—A named piece of the declared state of an instance. The attribute is declared in a classifier and each instance of that classifier will have a slot corresponding to the attribute holding one value or a collection of values.

Base use case—The target use case of an extend relationship or the origin use case of an include relationship.

Boundary class—A class that transforms communication from the inside of a system to something understandable for the outside of the system and vice versa. The class usually appears in an analysis model.

Class—A classifier describing a set of objects. It declares the attributes and the operations of the objects.

Classifier—Classifier is a generic term for all kinds of elements that can have instances. A classifier declares the structural and behavioral features, usually attributes and operations, of its instances.

Component—A classifier that encapsulates its contents. It has a collection of provided interfaces defining how to interact with it as well as a collection of required interfaces defining how it interacts with its environment. A component may also have a collection of ports, modeling connection points between its interior and its environment.

Concrete—A concrete classifier can be instantiated. It is the opposite of abstract. The term is often used when stressing that the classifier is not abstract; otherwise, it is usually omitted.

Control class—A class modeling a task to be performed in the system. The class usually appears in an analysis model.

Design model—An implementation technology–specific model of a system. It is usually expressed in terms of classes, components, and subsystems.

Entity class—A class handling a piece of information. The class usually appears in an analysis model.

Extend—A relationship between use cases, causing an instance of the target use case to be extended with the features, typically behavior, declared in the origin use case of the relationship. The relationship is conditional.

Extension use case—The origin of an extend relationship.

Generalization—A taxonomic relationship between classifiers. It states that the origin of the relationship is of the same kind as the target. An instance of the origin classifier, the child, will have all the features declared in the target, the parent, although possibly refined in the origin.

Include—A relationship between use cases, causing an instance of the origin use case of the relationship to include the features, typically behavior, of the target use case.

Inclusion use case—The target of an include relationship.

Instance—An element with a unique identity following the declaration in a classifier. It has slots corresponding to the attributes of the classifier and all the operations declared in the classifier can be applied to the instance. If a kind of behavior specification other than

operations has been used in the classifier, like a state machine or an activity diagram, the instance will follow that specification.

Link—An instance of an association. It connects instances of the classifiers at the ends of the association.

Logical model—See *analysis model*.

Object—An instance of a class.

Operation—A declaration of a behavioral feature. When an operation is applied to an instance, the behavior specified for the operation (for example, as informal text or by an associated state machine or activity diagram) is performed.

Package—A package is an element that can own other elements. It is often used for grouping purposes. A package defines a namespace, so each element in the namespace can be identified by its name.

Package import—A relationship between namespaces, such as packages, which makes all the public elements in the target namespace available inside the importing namespace; that is, no qualification of the imported element's name is needed.

State machine—A specification of behavior using nodes (states) and directed arcs (transitions). An instance following a state machine will wait for a triggering event at a state. When the event occurs, the instance will perform the actions associated with the transition matching the event. When these actions are performed, the instance will wait for a new event at the state where the transition ends.

Stereotype—A specialization of a construct to which it is applied. It may extend the construct with additional semantics as well as provide a notation. If no new notation is used, the name of the stereotype is shown within guillemets (« ») above or before the name of the element to which it is applied.

Subsystem—A part in a decomposed system. The definition varies between domains, but it often has both a black-box specification and a realization.

Use case—A use case models a complete usage, including variants, of a system. It provides a business value to one of the stakeholders of the system. A concrete use case is always initiated by an actor.

Use-case instance—An actual usage of a system.

Use-case model—A model of all the different kinds of usages of a system. It contains use cases, actors, and their relationships, and makes up a complete description of the behavior of a system.

References

Adolph, S., and P. Bramble. 2002. *Patterns for effective use cases.* Addison-Wesley.

Aho, A. V., R. Sethi, and J. D. Ullman. 1986. *Compilers: principles, techniques, and tools.* Addison-Wesley.

Alexander, C., S. Ishikawa, and M. Silverstein. 1977. *A pattern language: towns, buildings, construction.* Oxford University Press.

Alur, D., D. Malks, and J. Crupi. 2003. *Core J2EE patterns: best practices and design strategies.* Addison-Wesley.

Bass, L., P. Clements, and R. Kazman. 2003. *Software architecture in practice.* Addison-Wesley.

Bittner, K., and I. Spence. 2002. *Use case modeling.* Addison-Wesley.

Brown, W., R. Malveay, H. McCormick, T. Mowbray. 1998. *AntiPatterns: refactoring software, architectures, and projects in crisis.* John Wiley and Sons.

Buschmann, F., R. Meunier, H. Rohnert, P. Sommerlad, and M. Stal. 1996. *Pattern-oriented software architecture, volume 1: a system of patterns.* John Wiley and Sons.

Cockburn, A. 2000. *Writing effective use cases.* Addison-Wesley.

Fowler, M. 2002. *Patterns of enterprise application architecture.* Addison-Wesley.

Frankel, D. 2003. *Model driven architecture: applying MDA to enterprise computing.* John Wiley and Sons.

Gamma, E., R. Helm, R. Johnson, and J. Vlissides. 1995. *Design patterns: elements of reusable object-oriented software.* Addison-Wesley.

Grand, M. 2002. *Patterns in Java: a catalog of reusable design patterns illustrated with UML.* John Wiley and Sons.

von Halle, B. 2001. *Business rules applied: building better systems using a business rules approach.* John Wiley and Sons.

Horenstein, M. 1996. *Microelectronic circuits and devices.* Prentice-Hall.

Jacobson, I. 1985. *Concepts for modeling large real time systems.* Ph.D. thesis, Royal Institute of Technology, Stockholm, Sweden.

Jacobson, I. 1987. "Object-oriented development in an industrial environment." Proceedings of OOPSLA'87. Sigplan Notices 22(12):183–191.

Jacobson, I. 2003 (March). "Use cases—yesterday, today, and tomorrow." *The Rational Edge.*

Jacobson, I., G. Booch, and J. Rumbaugh. 1999. *The unified software development process.* Addison-Wesley.

Jacobson, I., M. Christerson, P. Jonsson, and G. Övergaard. 1993. *Object-oriented software engineering: a use-case driven approach.* Addison-Wesley.

Jacobson, I., M. Ericsson, and A. Jacobson. 1994. *The object advantage.* ACM Press Books.

Jacobson, I., M. Griss, and P. Jonsson. 1997. *Software reuse: architecture, process, and organization for business success.* Addison-Wesley.

Kroll, P., and P. Kruchten. 2003. *The Rational Unified Process made easy: a practitioner's guide to the RUP.* Addison-Wesley.

Marinescu, F. 2002. *EJB Design patterns: advanced patterns, processes, and idioms.* John Wiley and Sons.

Object Management Group, Framingham, MA, USA. 1997. UML proposal to the Object Management Group, version 1.1.

Object Management Group, Framingham, MA, USA. 2003. UML 2.0 superstructure specification, ptc/03-08-02.

The Open Group. 2004. *Security design patterns.* Catalog number G031.

Övergaard, G. 2000. *Formal specification of object-oriented modelling concepts.* Ph.D. thesis, Royal Institute of Technology, Stockholm, Sweden.

Rational Software Corporation. 2003. Rational Unified Process, version 2003.06.00.65, 2003.

Rumbaugh, J., I. Jacobson, and G. Booch. 1999. *The Unified Modeling Language reference manual.* Addison-Wesley.

Rosenberg, D., and K. Scott. 1999. *Use case driven object modeling with UML.* Addison-Wesley.

Schneider, G., and J. Winters. 2001. *Applying use cases: a practical guide.* Addison-Wesley.

Taylor, D. 1998. *Object technology: a manager's guide.* Addison-Wesley.

Index

Register
Your Book

at www.awprofessional.com/register

You may be eligible to receive:

- Advance notice of forthcoming editions of the book
- Related book recommendations
- Chapter excerpts and supplements of forthcoming titles
- Information about special contests and promotions throughout the year
- Notices and reminders about author appearances, tradeshows, and online chats with special guests

Contact us

If you are interested in writing a book or reviewing manuscripts prior to publication, please write to us at:

Editorial Department
Addison-Wesley Professional
75 Arlington Street, Suite 300
Boston, MA 02116 USA
Email: AWPro@aw.com

Visit us on the Web: http://www.awprofessional.com